AUXILIARY POLICE

AUXILIARY
POLICE The Citizen's
Approach to
Public Safety

MARTIN ALAN GREENBERG
Foreword by M. Marvin Berger

CONTRIBUTIONS IN CRIMINOLOGY AND PENOLOGY,
NUMBER 3

GREENWOOD PRESS
Westport, Connecticut · London, England

Library of Congress Cataloging in Publication Data

Greenberg, Martin Alan.
  Auxiliary police.

  Contributions in criminology and penology, ISSN 0732-
4464 ; no. 3)
  Bibliography: p.
  Includes index.
  1. New York (N.Y.)—Auxiliary police.   2. Crime
prevention—New York (N.Y.)—Citizen participation.
3. Volunteer workers in law enforcement—New York (N.Y.)
I. Title.   II. Series.
HV8148.N5G73   1984   363.2′89′097471   83-22683
ISBN 0-313-23955-X (lib. bdg.)

Library of Congress Catalog Card Number: 83-22683
ISBN: 0-313-23955-X
ISSN: 0732-4464

First published in 1984

Greenwood Press
A division of Congressional Information Service, Inc.
88 Post Road West, Westport, Connecticut 06881

Printed in the United States of America

10 9 8 7 6 5 4 3 2 1

IN MEMORY OF

David Freed

and

Antonio G. Olivieri

• **Contents**

• Illustrations

Foreword

One of the fringe benefits of service as a judge of the Criminal Court of the City of New York is the opportunity of enlarging one's sphere of knowledge. In my years of service on the bench, I have learned a great deal about the organization and workings of the New York City Police Department. But not until I read Martin Greenberg's study on *Auxiliary Police*, did I learn the story of the origin and development of the city's Auxiliary Police Force.

In common with many others concerned with law enforcement, I had formed the erroneous impression that the force was of fairly recent origin. Then, in 1972, I had occasion to research the matter in the course of writing an opinion dismissing charges against a Queens auxiliary policeman, Robert Jackson.[1] At that time, I learned that the current legal status of the auxiliary police was defined in legislation originally enacted in World War II days and revived during the Korean War in 1951.

Had Mr. Greenberg's work been available at that time, I would have discovered that New York's Auxiliary Police originated with the planning of Arthur Woods, who became the city's police commissioner in 1914. In 1915, Commissioner Woods conceived the idea of a "Citizens Home Defense League," which, by 1916, had enlisted 21,000 volunteers in its ranks.

In his fascinating study, Mr. Greenberg, formerly president of the Auxiliary Police Benevolent Association, shows how the city's Auxiliary Police Force has grown stronger or weaker, or, at times, has disappeared entirely from the local scene, depending on the support given to the force by the mayor; how the organization was sometimes tolerated only as a branch of the civil defense program and how today the volunteer police force has come to be regarded as an important factor in crime deterrence.

This is a story that has never before been told with such particularity. It is a tribute to Martin Greenberg's scholarship that the facts have been brought together and presented in such meticulously detailed yet readable form.

It is a melancholy fact that of the several million crimes reported annually, about one in nine results in a conviction. In the most common crime categories, burglary, larceny and auto theft, fewer than one crime in five leads to an arrest and fewer than one out of twelve in conviction.

Every commentator of note, dealing with the problem of crime, has stressed the need for community concern with law enforcement. One of the most noted critics, Ramsey Clark, former U.S. attorney general, wrote in his notable book, *Crime in America*:

In a society where at least thirty-eight persons could watch Kitty Genovese slowly stabbed to death on the streets of New York City and not one of them call the police, local citizen participation in law enforcement policy is the only way . . . for the individual to know he will be safe, that protection is possible, or if not, why not.[2]

And to continue from another part of Mr. Clark's book:

If police helpers are used in sufficient numbers with clear demarcation of their duties, professional skills will be released for use where badly needed and professional competence will not be diluted by boredom, waste and inefficiency.[3]

The problem of crime will not be solved by improved police efficiency alone. It will take an enormous effort, involving every agency concerned with prevention and prosecution of crime and rehabilitation of criminals—police, prosecution, judges and correction departments. And more effective functioning of these interdependent agencies leaves untouched the more fundamental causes of crime—ignorance, poverty, unemployment and disease.

But the support and confidence of the people in their police is an important element in improving law enforcement. An informed and concerned citizenry, participating in police activity as helpers can do much to create and nourish such support.

Martin Greenberg's valuable work shows the how and why of such participation.

M. Marvin Berger
Past President of
the Association of
Criminal Court Judges
of the City of New York

. Acknowledgments

In gathering the material for this study I had the cooperation of many persons.

The late M. Marvin Berger, a highly respected and dedicated Criminal Court Judge in Queens County, New York, contributed the book's foreword. Judge Berger also had a distinguished career as a lawyer, newspaper reporter, labor leader and executive officer of the *New York Law Journal*. He was elected by his colleagues as one of only eighteen judicial voting members of the Judicial Conference of the State of New York and also was a past president of the Association of Criminal Court Judges of the City of New York.

The preparation of this book was also assisted by Mortimer Kashinsky, Graham Schneider, John Hyland and Matthew Evans. They are among the foremost leaders of the Auxiliary Police Program in the city of New York. Without their friendship and support, this book would never have been written.

The support and editorial comments of the editors of Greenwood Press were of great value. They painstakingly and perceptively analyzed the manuscript. Earlier drafts greatly benefited from the editorial work of Linda Kandel Kuehl and Ellen C. Wertlieb. James T. Sabin of Greenwood Press oversaw all stages of the book's production and publication.

Diane and Stephen Baumgarten and Susan and Harold Cohen provided hospitality during key stages of the book's preparation while I was in New York for research purposes.

My personal thanks are due to James E. Eagen and Peter F. Vallone for their numerous and generous legal contributions on behalf of the Auxiliary Police Program.

My efforts to understand the dynamics of police work has benefited from the practical wisdom of John Rubino, Ernest Borrelli, Errol Johnson, Emile Racine, Benjamin Ward and many other police officials with close links to the Auxiliary Police Program.

Benjamin Ward currently serves as police commissioner of the city of New York. He replaced Robert J. McGuire, who was commissioner for nearly six years. Police Commissioner Ward has also served as New York City commissioner of corrections, New York State commissioner of correctional services, chief of the New York City Housing Authority police, and he was a deputy commissioner for trials and a deputy commissioner for community affairs during his twenty-three years' experience on the New York City police force.

Commissioner Ward has encouraged a strong citizen's role in public safety throughout his extraordinary career.

My colleagues at Arkansas State University and the University of Hawaii at Hilo have also contributed to the completion of this book. They are, especially, Rick Castberg, Larry Ball, Dennis Rousey, John W. Murphy, Karen A. Callaghan, Darwin Gamble, Terry Pardeck, Lynn Howerton, David Gordon, Larry Nuttbrock and Reverend William Paul Austin. The librarians and staff at these universities significantly helped to make this book a reality.

For permission to use their materials, I wish to express my deepest appreciation to: Henry J. Stern, the late Antonio G. Olivieri, Donald E. Dow, the New York Conference of Mayors and Municipal Officials, U.S. Department of Justice and the New York City Police Department.

Finally, I wish to express my most heartfelt gratitude for the support of my wife Ellen C. Wertlieb, and to Arlene Belzer and Tony Buono who served, respectively as the book's production and copy editors.

My page of acknowledgments would be incomplete if I failed to state my indebtedness to two distinguished and generous professors in the field of justice. I shall always be grateful to Alexander Smith and Abraham Blumberg. Several years ago, they inspired me to undertake further studies and pursue an academic career.

AUXILIARY POLICE

• Introduction

Throughout the nation there is a crucial need for a good model neighborhood crime prevention program. There also exists a need for well-qualified young men and women to select careers in the various fields of criminal justice. It has been estimated there exist 500,000 law enforcement positions in 40,000 separate police agencies in the public sector.[1] Moreover, while tremendous improvements have been attained in police work since the adoption of the Omnibus Crime Bill of 1968 and the gradual implementation of the International Association of Chiefs of Police *Model Police Standards Council Act*, it is apparent that police work is still not counted among the list of professional occupations.[2]

The desire to foster community safety, recruit better qualified police and promote and encourage professionalism within law enforcement form the thrust of this book. The accomplishment of these goals has been on the agenda of most national crime commissions of the past fifty years and many worthwhile recommendations have been made and followed. Yet it has only been in recent years that the community and its vast resources has been tapped in an effort to form a partnership against crime. However, no consensus on how best to utilize the energies of concerned citizens has emerged.

Nevertheless, there does seem to be a general view that the "vigilante" style of involvement is outmoded and that today any citizen participation program in the area of crime prevention should be controlled or at the very least approved by the concerned local police department. In addition, since it appears that the majority of citizens are unaware or care little about their role in crime prevention activities, the police will need to undertake a substantial effort in order to enlist their support in anticrime programs. Concurrently, police agencies choosing to utilize citizens will need to understand the motivating factors that contribute to the successful organization and operation of a citizen anticrime program.

A single program to accomplish the foregoing goals—and which takes into consideration the nature of the community—is currently available and has been in existence for quite some time. In fact, it may be the oldest neighborhood-based citizen anticrime program in the world. The main difference between the tribal or "kin police" of the early Anglo-Saxon and Danish communities in

England during the fifth century and the deployment of auxiliary or reserve police in the twentieth century was the compulsory nature of the former.[3]

Literally, dozens of police-community relations and public relations programs have been inaugurated in recent years. Some of the more popular efforts have included: the block watcher, the crime stopper and the media campaign entitled "Take a Bite Out of Crime" which features a trench-coated dog who gives crime prevention tips. There exist many varieties of citizen watch programs. "Block watchers" are trained by the police to report any suspicious activities and "mobile citizen patrol" watchers do the same while riding in their cars. A variant of the latter type of watch is the "citizen ride-along program." However, its primary purpose is to assist the "rider" in learning about the problems of police work, rather than reporting crime. Under the "crime stoppers program," which is being used in more than 320 cities in the United States and Canada, police select a weekly crime in which all leads have been exhausted. They provide details of the crime to television stations, which play a reenactment on video tape, along with a phone number for anyone who may have information. If the information provided leads to arrest and conviction, a monetary reward is available for callers who identify themselves.[4]

A private variety of the citizen patrol watch type of crime prevention program is the "Guardian Angels." It began as a volunteer subway patrol force in 1979 for the protection of New York City travelers and has expanded to different cities throughout the nation. A way to augment the strength of public police agencies was proposed by an independent committee in 1982. The idea, called "The New Police Corps" by its originators, is to design a program similar to the military's Reserve Officers Training Corps to increase the number of police officers in New York.[5] Both of these programs will be considered in Part III.

Before focusing our attention exclusively on the auxiliary or reserve types of citizen involvement in police work and community crime prevention, it will be necessary to clarify and distinguish between the different terms used in referring to police-related workers. In addition, the role of police officers will also need to be appreciated in order to understand the domain of police volunteers.

The "auxiliary" police officer is usually an individual who wears a police uniform, but does not possess regular police authority. The "reserve" police officer wears a police uniform and usually does possess regular police officer powers, while in uniform and on duty. Auxiliaries and reserves are required to conform to departmental rules and regulations, to undergo recruit and in-service training and to participate in prescribed activities on a regular basis in order to maintain their positions. In most jurisdictions they are uncompensated except for a clothing allowance and participation in state workmen's compensation programs. Their primary job is to serve as a deterrent to crime. It is generally believed that if a person bent on crime spots a uniformed officer on the street he or she will think twice about committing a crime. If auxiliaries spot something wrong, they are instructed to call the stationhouse or utilize their walkie-talkies to call for immediate help. Of course, differences in duties and membership qualifications vary among police agencies. The granting of regular police authority, commonly known as "peace officer powers," usually carries with it the authority to be armed. Officially, members of the auxiliary police in New York City do not carry firearms and do not possess peace officer status.[6] In 1983, City Council Member Susan D. Alter, who represents the 25th District in Brooklyn, introduced a bill that calls for the establishment of an armed volunteer reserve police force. This bill is being given serious consideration by the other members of the New York City Council and many leading civic and police officials.[7]

The exact number of volunteer police units of either the auxiliary or the reserve police variety is unknown. A survey conducted in 1969 revealed that thirty-four American cities with populations greater than 250,000 maintained such units. The full text of this survey is presented in Appendix A. In 1973, Peter C. Unsinger received information about the activities of 131 units.[8]

Volunteer police units exist throughout the United States. Auxiliary or reserve style police have been established in Baltimore, Dallas, Honolulu, Houston, Kansas City, Little Rock, Los Angeles, Memphis, Miami, Philadelphia, Phoenix, San Diego, St. Louis and Topeka. A detailed study of the New York City Auxiliary Police is the subject of Part II.

Since many people are likely to assume that anyone wearing a police-type uniform is or has the authority of a regular police officer, it is important to identify and describe the duties of private security personnel, "special police" officers, community service officers (CSOs), police cadets, Explorer Post members, youth and tenant patrols and various other citizen-observer patrol organizations.

Most security personnel are employed by contract-guard agencies, who are in turn hired by businesses and public institutions. These "rent-a-cops" may be observed throughout the shopping districts of many of our nation's cities. They deter shoplifting, employee theft and vandalism as well as safeguard the transportation of payrolls and daily receipts. Generally, security workers do not possess police powers unless such authority has been delegated to them through legislative enactments. Some institutions may employ their own "in-house" guards, but their legal status is no greater than that of an ordinary citizen or contract-guard employee.

Various commercial businesses require extra police protection; however, most municipal police departments cannot afford the additional costs. Consequently, many jurisdictions have enacted legislation authorizing the deputization of private citizens. This has been done for the express purpose of granting a limited peace officer power to employees engaged in security work. In general, the statutes invest each employee with the title of "special police officer." The precise scope of the authority conveyed varies from state to state, but the practice has led to the creation of dual roles. Each employee must protect the assets and interests of his employer as well as enforce the penal law. In many jurisdictions, the enabling legislation may or may not have provided for selection qualifications, effective supervision and training. However, with respect to the issuance of badges, the wearing of uniforms and the need to take an oath, there has been a greater pattern of consistency.

In 1967, the President's Commission on Law Enforcement and Administration of Justice visualized the need for creating the position of community service officer. The President's Commission primarily viewed this position as a means of counteracting the isolation of the police from the community and as a way of affording minority group members the opportunity to serve in law enforcement. The duties of the uniformed CSOs would include: the referral of citizen complaints to appropriate agencies; emergency aid for the sick; the investigation of minor property losses; assistance to families encountering domestic problems; and other assignments of a purely service nature.[9]

Closely aligned to the community service officer, but belonging to an earlier origin, is the police cadet system. Typical police cadets are between the ages of seventeen and twenty-one. They are usually recruited for police work upon high school graduation. Selection is usually based upon the regular police screening process and its competitive examinations. The cadets are considered paid civilian employees of the police agency until their twenty-first birthday, whereupon they assume full police officer status and responsibilities. During the interim period, they may be required to attend the agency's training program, perform clerical duties, and/or attend a local college that maintains a program in the administration of justice.[10]

Explorers are young adult members of the Boy Scouts of America. There are approximately 30,000 young men and women participating in 1,300 law enforcement Explorer Posts throughout the nation. Their activities range from supervised traffic control to various kinds of community crime prevention projects.[11]

Tenant, youth and community observer patrol associations emerged in the 1960s and 1970s. The rise of these groups often stemmed from racial fears, a crisis situation or incident and/or a desire to oppose crime in ghetto and other urban neighborhoods. Police support and encouragement for these organizations varies tremendously. Members of such patrols often use citizen band radios and their own vehicles in order to deter crime and summon assistance. Since it is extremely boring to be a watchman and nothing more, many of these groups have a tendency to disband after a year or two of operation.

Auxiliary police volunteers should not be confused with citizen observer programs conducted as a police-community relations exercise by many police departments. These programs require citizens to sign a waiver of liability before being permitted to ride in a police car in order to observe as the officer responds to nondangerous assignments. After completing the tour each observer may be asked to fill in an evaluation sheet. Significantly, these programs are primarily educational and observers do not participate in any police assignments.

In recent years, various communities have utilized the availability of funds

from the Federal Comprehensive Employment Training Act for special programs during the summer months. A Senior Security Patrol was created during
the summer of 1979 in New York City. The unit consisted of two hundred young
members of minority groups who were assigned the task of protecting elderly
persons in high-crime areas by quickly reporting incidents to the police. The
street patrols functioned in the East Bronx, Harlem, Jamaica, Bedford-Stuyves-
ant, Flatbush and Coney Island.[12]

In 1975, a team of researchers from the Rand Corporation identified a total
of 850 active neighborhood patrols in cities throughout the United States. Some
of their findings were: patrols last on the average of 4 to 5.5 years; patrols are
found in neighborhoods of all income levels, both white and racially mixed;
building patrols seem to prevent crime effectively; and patrols are occasionally
susceptible to vigilantism.[13] These groups exist side by side with the units of
the auxiliary or reserve police in some departments. However, they may be easily distinguished because of their lack of a full police uniform. The extent to
which these groups adhere to the policies of the local police agency helps to
eliminate any vestiges of vigilantism. Chapter 3 examines the history of vigilantism and the police.

In 1976, George Washnis presented the findings of a study undertaken by the
Center for Governmental Studies. The study, financed by the National Institute
of Law Enforcement and Criminal Justice, involved thirty-seven different police-
community crime prevention projects in seventeen cities. Washnis concluded:

Police and city planning officials need to assess their own city's total crime prevention
requirements; furthermore, community organizations should be involved in initial and
continual planning stages. . . . It is not enough that police officials alone be involved
in planning; block leaders and other residents should also participate.[14]

In 1983, the National Institute of Justice[15] released a report entitled "Part-
nerships for Neighborhood Crime Prevention." It contains a survey of fifty-
nine different crime prevention programs that have been successfully implemented in local police departments and communities. Every successful program
involved a linkage between the police and the community that consisted of mutual respect and trust. The high level of citizen participation in the San Diego
and Detroit Police departments was given special emphasis.[16]

The phrase "crime prevention" has been used repeatedly in this introduction. It has traditionally been one of the essential functions of the role of the
police officer, but crime prevention cannot succeed unless the community actively participates in the process. The National Crime Prevention Institute defines crime prevention as "the anticipation, recognition and appraisal of a crime
risk and the initiation of some action to remove or reduce it."[17] The National
Crime Prevention Institute was established in 1971 through the efforts of John
C. Klotter. It was originally a joint undertaking by the Law Enforcement Assistance Administration of the U.S. Department of Justice, the Kentucky Crime

Commission and the University of Louisville.[18] By 1983, over 10,000 police and related criminal justice workers had received training at the institute. Police learn how to teach citizens methods to reduce their risk of becoming crime victims and citizens may also attend classes in order to teach such methods to community groups.[19]

Several other organizations sponsor national programs in the area of crime prevention. This list includes: the American Association of Retired Persons/ National Retired Teachers Association; the American Farm Bureau Federation; the American Legion; the "Crime Resistance Program" of the Federal Bureau of Investigation; Kiwanis International; the National Alliance for Safer Cities; the "Take a Bite Out of Crime" media campaign of the Crime Prevention Coalition;[20] the National Council of Senior Citizens; the National Organization of Black Law Enforcement Officials; the National Automobile Theft Bureau; the "National Neighborhood Watch Program" of the National Sheriffs' Association; the "National Cargo Security Program" of the Transportation Association of America; the Texas Crime Prevention Institute at Southwest Texas State University; the United States Jaycees; the Junior Leagues of the United States and Canada; the "Hands Up Program" of the General Federation of Women's Clubs; the International Association of Chiefs of Police; and the National Exchange Club.[21]

The role of the police as teachers of proper security precautions to reduce criminal opportunities and the public's vulnerability to criminal attack is now established. Police also try to prevent crime by being very visible in the community, preserving order and cooperating with other agents of the criminal justice system. Moreover, police assistance in the delivery of social and community services may effectively serve to deter youthful offenders and troubled adults from crime.

In addition to crime prevention, the police are generally called upon to enforce the law, preserve the peace, provide social services and protect civil liberties and rights. Differences of emphasis are placed on these basic police roles or functions in accord with local and regional preferences and these activities frequently overlap one another.

The law enforcement emphasis is exemplified by having the majority of available police officers patrol the streets in cars within instant reach of a dispatcher. Motorized patrol has replaced the neighborhood foot patrol in most communities and rapid response to calls for service has been used to judge effectiveness. The role of law enforcer or "crime fighter" also includes the interrogation of suspects, testifying in court and all the other steps necessary to complete a criminal investigation and assist in the prosecution of offenders. Each of these tasks must be accomplished in a manner consistent with the freedoms secured by the Constitution.

A fundamental role of the police is that of order maintenance or peacekeeping. It is one of the most challenging and time-consuming parts of police work for it involves a continual exercise of discretion about whether to arrest persons and how to intervene to quiet disputes. It has been estimated that police spend 30 percent of their time on the peacekeeping function and between 10 and 20 percent of their time on crime prevention and law enforcement activities. The remaining 40 to 60 percent of their time is allotted to service-related activities.[22]

The personnel of most police agencies are available twenty-four hours a day. Consequently, many people are likely to turn first to the police for help. Police officers must handle all types of emergencies or problems that no other agencies are equipped to handle. Police routinely assist stranded motorists, accident victims, the disabled, the disoriented, and are a calming presence at the scenes of transit and environmental disasters. Furthermore, many police departments provide speakers for groups on such topics as crime prevention, traffic safety, child and drug abuse and the rights of citizens. All police agencies provide traffic and crowd control services and maintain a system for receipt and return of lost or stolen property.

The use of auxiliary or reserve officers as unpaid assistants to the regular police could greatly help any overburdened police department. The many roles of the police permit room for citizen helpers. Although some departments may deem it appropriate to limit the duties of police auxiliaries to specific tasks, others may train newly recruited auxiliary officers to handle all of the basic police functions. However, no matter how they are deployed, their presence should help to foster safer neighborhoods and the advancement of police professionalism. The achievement of the latter objective will certainly depend upon a better understanding of the police role on the part of the public and a deeper appreciation of the auxiliary police role on the part of the police. Conceivably, a much deeper sense of the concepts involved should arise from such police-citizen contacts and this understanding is surely a prerequisite for the establishment of a true profession. Moreover, auxiliary members, who have already become versed in the dynamics of police work, should prove to be an excellent pool from which regular police may be recruited.

The intent of this book is to present an exploratory study of the auxiliary police.[23] Since the author has been unable to locate any other work that describes in detail the use of volunteer police in a particular city, the present work may serve as a foundation for future empirical studies on the subject. The author is firmly convinced that the public's role is vital in the achievement of social control and that the establishment of carefully trained and screened units of the auxiliary police can play a major role in the prevention of crime, the maintenance of order and the delivery of numerous public services.

Another important objective of the present work is to inform the members of the general community and the men and women who comprise the auxiliary police about the potential for citizen participation in public safety as well as to define and clarify the identities and roles associated with the position of auxiliary or reserve police officers. It is hoped that a clearer understanding of such issues will lead to more satisfactory experiences by the volunteer police and foster greater enthusiasm for participation.

PART I

POLICE HISTORY AND THE VOLUNTEER

Law and Justice I established
in the land. I made happy the
human race in those days.

> King Hammurabi's
> Code of Laws, opening
> words

We hear it said that successful police
work depends on the cooperation of the
public and the police. In fact, in a
democracy every citizen has a serious
obligation to do police work, and the
existence of a paid police force does
not alter this duty.

> Louis A. Radelet,
> *The Police and the Community*, p. 4.

1 • The Early History of Law Enforcement

An awareness of the rich heritage of law enforcement and how law and other instruments of social control evolved from ancient to modern times is an important preliminary step for understanding the history and role of the auxiliary police.

The need for order is a social imperative in every community. Historically, the development of unofficial rules of conduct or social expectations for behavior, called "norms," preceded the emergence of law. Norms have been further categorized into concepts associated with their degree of importance to the community. For example, "folkways" or "customs" which are violated bring only mild censure, whereas broken "mores" or "taboos" invoke harsher reactions. These norms were backed by a community arrangement for sanctioning those who disobeyed them.[1] Thus, the first peacekeepers were probably private citizens who participated in the tribal and clan life in the earliest civilizations. Although these ancient peoples have no written records, anthropological studies reveal evidence of the existence of such a normative system. It is likely that tribal members who failed to live up to the expectations of the group were punished by the group or family. If a wrong of a serious nature was committed, the consequences were felt immediately. The lesson must have reduced disobedience to a bare minimum.[2]

The "law" is the more formal and standardized expression of the norms. In every society the law has become the pronouncements of leaders that have been made in the form of legal codes or statutes and in the form of judicial decisions or case law. The law in statutory form usually defines an offense or crime and the types of punishment available. This category of the law is described as the penal code or criminal law. Of course, not all law is criminal law and today the "civil law" refers to official rules that control contracts, estates, personal injury, corporations and the many facets of everyday business and social relationships.[3] However, it is important to emphasize that the law becomes the subject of enforcement efforts only after the unofficial normative system of social control fails to keep the peace. The enforcement of the civil law rests primarily on the courts. The enforcement of the criminal law rests on the police and correctional agencies as well as the courts. Moreover, an individual who is wronged criminally may also seek redress in a civil court. On the other hand, a violator of the civil law cannot be brought to the criminal court unless a specific provision of the penal code was involved. A situation may arise in which a civil matter evolves into a criminal case. For example, landlord-tenant and family disputes have been known to get out of control. If an assault occurs as a consequence of the escalation, police may arrest the wrongdoer and refer the matter to the criminal court.

The normative system of social control and the official statement of the law as recorded in codes are generally supported by a set of ethical values which creates "either a sense of justification or a sense of guilt in the minds of individuals."[4] It is difficult to distinguish basic values from the rules of everyday social life and statutes. Legal scholars have adopted the concept of the "moral law" to refer to the shared ideas about what is right and wrong and desirable or undesirable in a particular society. At times the basic values of people on the moral law may be embodied in norms and laws, but on occasion they may be out of step. For example, many Americans believed that the use of intoxicating liquors was immoral and harmful in the period just before the 1920s. Their concern resulted in the Eighteenth Amendment to the U.S. Constitution which placed severe restrictions on manufacture, sale and consumption of alcoholic beverages. However, a huge market still existed and opportunities for organized crime were created. Nevertheless, the importance of the moral law lies in its ability to control human behavior even in the absence of significant social norms, laws, police, courts or correctional facilities. Without moral or ethical ideas and standards, who would watch the watchman and who would "police the police"?[5]

The normative system of monitoring everyday social behavior is performed by relatives, friends and neighbors. Some writers refer to it as a system of "kin policing" and it was not until the nineteenth century that modern policing was given its own name.[6] However, as ancient villages became ancient kingdoms additional norms were imposed upon the community and these norms were set down in written form. Moreover, the stratification of society into distinctive social, economic and political groups created a class structure demanding special considerations and protections. One of the earliest known codes of written law was inscribed in stone during the reign of a Babylonian king, Hammurabi (fl. 1792–1750 B.C.). A segment of King Hammurabi's code has been translated and it is preserved today in Paris at the Louvre Museum.[7] Robert S. Clark has described how the relations between the king's messengers, his judges and the people were governed by Hammurabi's code:

Judges' decisions not only set forth the rights of the parties, but also directed enforcement. Judges also had power to send other agents, if necessary, to report to them, or to inquire and observe on their own account.[8]

Records of other elaborate and extensive codes of justice exist for ancient monarchies and empires. By 1500 B.C., a sovereign of Egypt instituted compulsory military service with an active and a reserve component. While at home, the reserve force could be used to enforce locally the king's laws. Clark indicates that the long line of Egyptian kings who ruled with little interruption may have been due to the existence of this early system of citizen police.[9]

The Hammurabi code served as a model for later civilizations and its "eye-for-an-eye" approach, while often brutal, centralized the authority of the king and his officials. In many ways such laws helped to remove the principle of *lex talionis* (the law of retaliation or vengeance) from the hands of the family and victim into the purview of the state. However, the ancient Greeks maintained an effective system of "kin policing" or private retribution until Athens became the center of a vast empire. Foreign travelers and merchants poured into Greek cities and in 594 B.C. Solon revolutionized the laws of his day. The punishments were eased, the procedures became more democratic and the provisions of the law were clarified. However, class interests and the acts of powerful citizens eventually led to the establishment of a dictatorship.[10]

The Law of Twelve Tables (451 B.C.) was developed by the ancient Romans after studying the work of Solon and other Greek laws. These tables defined the rights of the upper class (right over property, etc.) and the procedures for seeking the help of the courts.[11] Life in Roman times was comparable to life in the Greek empire and the disorder in cities stemming from class struggles for dominance and survival created a need for an efficient system of law enforcement. Augustus (63 B.C.–A.D. 14), the first Roman emperor, organized the citizens of Rome into a semimilitary force known as the "Vigiles." Their responsibilities included fire protection and street patrol. However, their main purpose was apparently to protect the ruling class from the threat of rebellion. The "Praetorian Guard" and the "Urban Cohorts" were also used to maintain law and order in Rome.[12] These forces were unique to Rome and inability to stem disorder and corruption among government agents throughout the Empire contributed to its eventual decline. In the period of the Emperor Justinian (A.D. 529), a major revision of the Roman law was attempted. The new Justinian code brought together in one source the many laws of the Empire.[13] It became a model for the new and independent nations of Europe that were to emerge after the Dark Ages and after the struggle for domination between church and state had been resolved.

The central issue of the conflict between church and state was which authority should "supplement the moral law by providing physical punishment for wrongful acts"?[14] The question was resolved by deciding that secular (non-church) laws would regulate only overt acts and no punishment would be prescribed for thoughts. However, the ethical and moral teachings of both the Old Testament (1300–150 B.C.) and the New Testament (A.D. 50–150), also known as the Judeo-Christian tradition, have continued to serve as an inspiration and guide for modern courts and legislatures.[15] Nevertheless, the resolution of the struggle spanned most of the Dark and Middle Ages and has had a profound impact upon the establishment of the legal systems of England, Europe and ultimately the United States.

The English "common law" developed from the decisions and rules announced by individual English judges during the Middle Ages. In many instances, the judges relied on the general customs, usages and moral concepts of the people within their court's jurisdiction. There were differences in the laws applicable to peasants of local villages or manors, manor lords or nobles, the merchant class and the people living in larger communities. However, in time, many judges sought to base their decisions on what they believed were in the best interests of the people as a nation. In this way, the "various sets of customs yielded broad principles which the judges felt would be applicable everywhere in the kingdom and these were called 'common' law."[16] Eventually the decisions of the judges were regarded as authoritative precedents to be followed in future cases and this practice of resorting to the common law is still applied in England and in the United States. The common law involves both civil and criminal cases. However, most states in the United States have abolished common law crimes and all state legislative bodies have enacted comprehensive penal codes. Thus, it is very unusual for a person to be charged with a common law crime in the United States.[17] Nevertheless, the common law has been and wherever applicable continues to be a major source of the law together with the proclamations of kings and the enactments of legislatures.

Some of the earliest English courts exhibited criminal justice procedures which have been described as "accusatory" in form. There was a great dependence upon the taking of oaths, but the concept of trial by jury as a right of the average man was not consistently granted until the era of the Stuart kings in the 1600s.[18] One party simply accused another before a community meeting. The sitting judge did not determine a person's guilt or innocence after hearing preliminary statements, but rendered a judgment about how the matter was to be finally decided and who would be put to a special test. Only one side was tested or tried. There were three methods for learning the truth: compurgation, ordeal and battle.

Compurgation involved making a sworn statement as to the truth of one's own claim which had to be supported by a stated number of "compurgators" who swore that they believed the accused. The correct statement of the oath and the required number of compurgators meant that justice had prevailed. An inability to gather sufficient compurgators or an inaccurate oath was proof of guilt. Significantly, the test of compurgation was similar to the modern use of character witnesses, in that the compurgators did not testify to the facts of the case but only attested to the defendant's reputation for truthfulness.

The test or trial by ordeal involved a physical event. One type of ordeal involved having to place one's hand in boiling water. A clean wound after three days signified innocence. In trial by cold water, the accused was securely tied and lowered into very cold water. Persons who stayed afloat were considered guilty. Generally, accused persons were forced to submit to a test of ordeal only if they were strangers in the community or lacked a sufficient number of friends who would be willing to serve as compurgators.

The settlement of disputes through battle was introduced into England by William the Conqueror. It was believed that God would strengthen the person who was in the right. The term "champions" was later used to describe professional fighters who could be hired in all civil cases determined by battle. In 1072, King William created the position of "vicecomes." The vicecomes were traveling judges and the forerunners of today's circuit court judges. The vicecomes replaced the "shire reeves" who had been the chief judicial and law enforcement officers in the shires (counties). However, the shire reeves were allowed to retain their law enforcement functions. In the United States, the modern position of sheriff can be traced to this early division of court and police responsibilities.[19]

In the twelfth century, the "inquest" also known as the *recognitio* was developed as a procedural means for obtaining the ends of justice. It marked a significant turning point for the accusatorial system of justice, especially as it became associated with the attempt to suppress heresy. In English history the inquest evolved into the modern jury system. In Europe, the initiation of the Inquisition by the Catholic Church contributed to the development of a different system of criminal justice. The Inquisition did not succeed in reversing England's move to the accusatorial system, but it did exist side by side with the accusatorial model for a period of time.

The inquest in England first involved the meeting of townfolk who were required to answer any question of interest to the Crown under oath. King Henry II (1154–1189) molded these procedures into a jury of accusation, the earliest forerunner of the modern grand jury system. During this period the tests of ordeal and compurgation were abolished and in 1215 King John was forced to sign the *Magna Carta* (Great Charter). The immediate effect of the document was the provision of jury trials for the landowning barons. The Statute of Westminster (1275) "extended jury trial rights to all common men and formalized the English court system and procedure."[20]

An early requirement of the English jury system was that each juror should have personal knowledge of the facts of the case. However, as the size and complexity of society grew, personal knowledge became a difficult standard to maintain and it eventually became a disqualification for membership on a jury. It was not until the eighteenth century that defendants were permitted to call witnesses in their own behalf.

The inquest procedure became a nightmare at the close of the twelfth century owing to the decrees of Pope Innocent III. Church judges were empowered to conduct prosecutions and trials and to render judgment. One of the Pope's orders called for a new oath that was highly self-incriminatory in nature. The oath (also known as the oath *ex officio*) only required a person to swear to answer truthfully, but in a short time the mere refusal to swear to the oath became an immediate ground for a heresy conviction. In addition, persons who did take the oath took a great risk of committing perjury because they were not informed beforehand about the nature of the complaint or any other relevant evidence.

The Church's desire to suppress heresy was the cause that inspired the oath and began that awful period in history called the Inquisition. The Inquisition was at first concerned only with overt acts of religious dissent; however, it later became concerned with a person's privately held thoughts and beliefs. All known methods of torture were used in an effort to discover a person's true mental state. The oath was used later in secular courts. Many of the practices associated with the oath *ex officio* survived until the reign of Charles II (1660–1685). Its demise was assisted through the courage of citizens like John Lilburne, who repeatedly refused to submit to the oath even after weeks of torture. The Council of Rome formally abolished the oath in 1725.[21]

One of the most important legal documents in the history of England was the Petition of Right (1628). Among the many rights contained in this law, two have been enlarged and incorporated within the Constitution of the United States: freedom of speech and the right to a writ of *habeas corpus*.[22] The writ enables persons restrained of their liberty to have an immediate hearing regarding the legality of the detention.

Habeas corpus, though not a part of the Bill of Rights, is the critical safeguard without which all other constitutional protections would remain unenforceable, since its suspension would deny the courts the power to release persons [held] in violation of other protections.[23]

By the eighteenth century, English judges began to assume the role of an "umpire" to insure that fair trials would take place. However, prior to that time, the Court of the Star Chamber (composed of royal ministers) and the Court of High Commission (composed of church leaders) practiced the often painful art of interrogation on the basis of mere suspicion and without any specific accusation of crime. Significantly, the maintenance of the English judge's passive role, the development of the grand jury system, the provision for public jury trials, the separation of English law schools (known as the Inns of Court) from the universities, where Roman law was emphasized, and the growth of common law helped to preserve the accusatorial system of justice in England. In Europe, the inquisitorial system came to dominance owing to Roman law and the methods of the Inquisition. The Roman law was spread throughout the continent by students trained at Italian universities. Scholars in the Roman law enjoyed great prestige. The Roman or inquisitorial system emphasizes the role of the court in ascertaining the final verdict. The judge is given primary responsibility for obtaining the evidence, conducting the examinations of witnesses and parties, and assumes the role of an active fact-finder. The basic philosophy of this system involves a trust in the abilities of judicial officers to administer justice based on the inherent soundness of the laws recorded during the period of the Roman Empire.[24]

The law, pretrial and court procedures help to define the style of a society's legal system, but the police aided by the prosecution determine who will be introduced into the justice system. The police possess an extraordinary amount of discretion in deciding which cases should be channeled into the courts. Their law enforcement functions are exemplified by the techniques of criminal investigation, arrest and readiness to testify against the accused. In addition, the police maintain order and prevent crime through their presence on patrol and their response to citizen complaints. They may also safeguard the civil and criminal rights of defendants, victims and witnesses and perform a myriad of social service duties. However, these major goals or roles of policing have been recognized only in recent times. Inasmuch as the United States has borrowed from the law enforcement model in England, at least in its initial history, the remainder of this chapter will focus on the origins of the police in England.

The disintegration of the Roman Empire made the continent of Europe and England the site of constant warfare and invasions. The closest equivalent to the modern police officer that emerged at the time of Alfred the Great (870–901) and whose origins can be "found in the tribal laws and customs of the Danish and Anglo-Saxon invaders" was the "Saxon tythingman."[25] Every male person over the age of twelve was required to participate in a "mutual pledge" system, also known as the tything system. A tything was a group of ten families, headed by a "tythingman" responsible for the acts of the persons who were in his group. It was each tythingman's duty to raise the "hue and cry" when a crime was committed, to collect his neighbors and to pursue a criminal who fled from the district.[26] If such a group failed to apprehend a lawbreaker, the tything could be required to pay a fine or to make some form of restitution. In this way, it was clear that the citizenry would be obligated to insure its own security. After the Normans invaded England in 1066, they tightened this system of community policing by instituting the "frankpledge." The frankpledge was a deposit of something of value with the local shire reeve in order to serve as a guarantee that any accused person would appear at one of the twice annually held court sessions. The deposit had to come from the tything as a whole and this new system was often used by Norman shire reeves for the purposes of extortion.[27] In some respects the use of the frankpledge resembles the modern system of requiring a cash bail or the posting of a bond in order to gain release from custody pending the outcome of a criminal trial.

The first shire reeves were appointed by the king, barons, or other members of the nobility. The shire reeve also could raise a "hue and cry," but instead of merely requiring the members of a tything to come together and apprehend an accused, he was able to summon the *posse comitatus* which consisted of the tythingmen and tything members of several hundred tythings. T. A. Critchley has described how the position of shire reeve became necessary:

Groups of tythings were formed into a hundred, the head man of which was known as a hundred man or royal reeve, who exercised administrative and judicial powers through a hundred court; and overall, the shire reeve, or sheriff, had a general responsibility under the King for the conservancy of the peace of the shire.[28]

By the end of the thirteenth century the position of constable had emerged. The constable assisted the shire reeve and he brought accusations against persons before local manorial courts.[29] Constables were initially appointed by local noblemen and were placed in charge of the weapons and equipment of each hundred.[30] In time, the role of constable as the principal peacekeeping agent of the Crown replaced that of the ancient tythingman in the English manors or villages of the Middle Ages. In the United States, the title of constable is still used to designate a rural police chief, especially when the entire police force consists of only one full-time person. In England, the parish constable and night watchman were to be replaced by "a single body of constables embodied into a police *force*, the governing principles of which were unity of command and professional excellence."[31]

In 1285, the Statute of Winchester formalized many of the features of the "mutual-pledge" system for the more urban areas of England. The law provided for a system of night and day patrols in each of the large towns of England. Men between the ages of fifteen and sixty were required to perform watch service on a rotating basis between sunset and sunrise.[32] They were responsible for protecting property against fire, guarding the town gates and apprehending anyone who committed a crime. The "hue and cry" could be commenced by any watchman and the entire community of able-bodied males was required to join in the pursuit of any wrongdoer. A failure to participate in the watch or to aid in the pursuit of fugitives would result in punishment. The constable kept the records of who performed the night watch service, kept the peace during the daytime and took charge of any prisoners and cases for court presentation. The position of "justice of the peace" was created by formal statute in 1361. The town constable then took on the added responsibilities of criminal investigation, serving summonses and arrest warrants. In this way, the constable became clearly subordinate to the judge as had the office of sheriff in an earlier period.[33] However, while the sheriffs were men of considerable wealth and power, the constables were unpaid except for some usual fees and expenses and the office was filled in the more urban towns at the parish level on a rotating basis:

by house-row among all parishioners qualified according to local traditional requirements or customs, or sometimes, in rural areas, according to the tenure of ancient farms; and refusal to accept office was punishable by fine.[34]

The development of policing in England continued to follow this style, known as the "watch and ward" system of law enforcement, for nearly five hundred years. The "watch" referred to the evening patrols and the "ward" concerned the activities of daytime security. In addition, at the same time that the Statute of Winchester was issued, a local law for the city of London provided: "There shall be established bailiffs and these bailiffs shall make an inquiry of all persons and lodgers and shall observe them at night."[35] The "bailiff" was required to conduct this search at least twice each month. He was entitled to employ aides to carry out these duties called "sergeants."[36] In the United States, the term "bailiff" is now used to refer to any uniformed law enforcement officer assigned to maintain order in a court. The "sergeant" of police is now usually the immediate supervisor of a section, squad or platoon of patrol officers.

However, as time passed the voluntary observance of the "watch and ward" system of policing weakened and it became the common practice to pay others to do the required service.[37] Generally, the substitutes employed were too old to be of any value. Rising crime rates caused wealthier merchants to hire their own private watchmen to guard themselves and their businesses and to recover stolen property. However, it was not until the eighteenth century that local city governments began to levy taxes in order to pay for a nighttime watch.

The advent of the Industrial Revolution at the end of the eighteenth century was accompanied by a vast migration to urban areas and the need for a regular system of policing became greater than ever before. In addition, the invention of gin by a Dutch chemist in the seventeenth century, provided an inexpensive liquor for the masses. "Gin democratized drunkenness and brought new terrors to London and then to all cities."[38] Laws to license the manufacturers and distributors of gin succeeded only in furthering corruption among the London watchmen responsible for their enforcement.

The need for better law enforcement spurred the creation of a number of fragmented civic associations, such as the Bow Street Horse and Foot Patrol. Sir Henry Fielding, a distinguished magistrate of his day, and his brother, John Fielding, organized this "police system" in order to protect the streets and highways leading in and out of London. Included among its units were the famous "Bow Street Runners," who earned their title out of the need to run quickly to the scene of a crime. However, its members "eventually became little more than bounty hunters, interested primarily in collecting rewards for their captives and confiscating their booty."[39] The Bow Street station functioned from 1754 to 1780.[40]

The first regular professional police force in the city of London was established in 1800 when the English Parliament adopted the Thames River Police Act. In 1797, Patrick Colquhoun published a popular treatise on police work and it has become a landmark document in the history of police science. The book called for the creation of a special police unit for the areas adjacent to the Port of London. The shipping merchants and insurance companies helped pay for a force of sixty full-time police officers in 1798 and their success led to its new status as a publicly funded police force in 1800. However, in London "the main burden of maintaining law and order still rested on the elderly, ailing, or indifferent shoulders of isolated pockets of parish constables and watchmen."[41]

Colquhoun's Thames River Police served as the model for the development of the first London-wide police force which was subsequently adopted throughout England.[42]

The principal spokesman and founder of England's highly organized and centralized police system was Sir Robert Peel (1788–1850). The Metropolitan Police of London was established through Peel's efforts in 1829. London's new constables were assigned to specific districts and foot patrol posts. Numbered police badges were issued to identify each of the newly appointed law enforcement officers. They wore uniforms, worked day and night shifts, and were structured along military lines. The headquarters of the Metropolitan Police was called "Scotland Yard," in honor of the Kings of Scotland who years before were believed to have resided at the headquarters' site.[43] Moreover, Peel's "bobbies," as they later became known, have served as a model for subsequent police organizations in the British Empire, in Paris (1854) and in New York City (1836).[44]

In 1856, the English Parliament mandated similar police forces for the cities and towns outside of central London. Generally, the English police system has remained practically unchanged since that time.[45]

The English law, court and police systems served as models for the early settlers of America. However, these systems were adapted and molded to fit the circumstances of the New World. For example, ward politics played a major role in the development of many American police departments and the protections set forth in the U.S. Constitution and the Bill of Rights came in reaction to such infamous institutions as the Star Chamber in England and dissatisfaction with English rule in the American colonies.

English common law prohibited search warrants and arrest warrants that did not describe in detail the places to be searched and the things or persons to be seized. However, the American colonists were subjected to "writs of assistance," which gave local English officials almost unrestricted authority to enter homes of private citizens and to seize their belongings. The Founding Fathers had first-hand knowledge of these arbitrary procedures and adopted the Fourth Amendment to protect personal liberty and privacy. The language of the Fourth Amendment was mainly derived from a similar provision in the Massachusetts Constitution of 1780. The Fourth Amendment provides:

The right of the people to be secure in their persons, houses, papers, and effects, against unreasonable searches and seizures, shall not be violated, and no Warrants shall issue, but upon probable cause, supported by Oath or affirmation and particularly describing the place to be searched, and the persons or things to be seized.

The early history of law enforcement has plainly revealed that a fragmented, uncoordinated and voluntary system of policing will fail because of the tensions generated by the growth of population and the rise of cities with conspicuous class divisions. The absence of an effective and publicly supported police system places the burden of peacekeeping entirely upon the people and their unofficial methods of social control. However, many personal methods of self-protection can be extremely dangerous. Moreover, a lawless community will arise if the safety of society depends solely on the people's ability to defend themselves.[46]

An essential purpose of the framers of the U.S. Constitution was to establish a government that was strong enough to enforce the law, yet not so strong as to threaten individual liberty. This objective pervades the Constitution. Today, the guarantees and rights enumerated in the Constitution, which involve the apprehension, prosecution and conviction of defendants as interpreted by the Supreme Court, comprise the fundamental features of the accusatory system of justice in the United States.

2 • The Early History of New York City's Police

The early history of New York City's police system featured turmoil, confusion and partisan politics. However, the role of the early police, while seldom carefully stated, was generally known and accepted. In colonial times (1625–1783)

there was great similarity between the functions and responsibilities of the Dutch *schout-fiscal* and, his counterpart, the English constable. Both were charged with keeping the peace; suppressing excessive drinking, gambling, and prostitution; and preventing disturbances when church services were in progress.[1]

The first permanent settlement in colonial New York City took place in 1625 and the Dutch named their community New Amsterdam. They appointed an official in accordance with their heritage called a *schout-fiscal* to serve as "a combination sheriff and prosecuting attorney" as well as a supervisor for the West India Company.[2] In 1634, the first full-time sheriff's office was established in colonial Virginia. The southern colonies were settled by the English and they invested the office of county sheriff with many of the same responsibilities of English sheriffs.[3] In 1664, the English gained control of New Amsterdam. They renamed the Dutch seaport New York and instituted a military guard; and in 1700, a high constable and twelve subconstables were appointed by the local mayor.[4]

However, it was the institution of citizens' night watches that provided the most common form of order maintenance in colonial America. A night watch composed of all adult males, serving on a rotating basis, was established in Boston in 1636.[5] In 1651, citizens were armed and given a hand rattle to announce their presence or to signal for help during nightly patrols. Some of these community members were hired to protect the commercial districts in New Amsterdam in 1658. Appropriately, these early patrol units, paid or unpaid, were known as the "Rattle Watch."[6] The English experience with the use of a night watch was duplicated in the newly emerging communities of New England. When the wealthier citizens began to pay for substitutes on a regular basis, it became the accepted practice to offer a small sum for such work.[7] After the American Revolutionary War, a Watch Department was established on a permanent basis in New York City. At first, the watchmen were paid in shillings, but by 1803 "the pay scale provided that the captains would receive $1.50 and the watchmen $.70 for each night of actual service."[8] There were 33,000 New Yorkers in 1790 and when an offender was pursued, all citizens within hearing of the watchmen's outcry were obliged to join in the pursuit.

The creation of the United States in 1776 severed all political ties to England and provided opportunities to develop very unique and distinctive legal and law enforcement systems. The framers of the U.S. Constitution produced a document which separated the powers of government and provided for a system of checks and balances in order to reduce the concentration of powers in a single branch or official of government.[9] The idea that policing should be primarily a local matter was determined at that time. The power to organize police agencies within the states and their subdivisions was not granted to the federal government by the Constitution, but was reserved for the states through the Tenth Amendment in 1791. In addition, the Constitution did not specify that it was a federal responsibility to ensure the health, morals, welfare and general well-being of citizens within the separate states. However, over the years these vital obligations have come to be recognized as the responsibility of all levels of government. The term "police powers" is the accepted legal phrase which refers to all of these important goals.[10]

Article IV, Section 4 of the Constitution provides: "The United States shall guarantee to every State in this Union a Republican Form of Government." When the framers of the Constitution gathered in Philadelphia in 1787, they probably had in mind a form of government that "rests on the consent of the people and operates through representative institutions," in contrast to a monarchy or direct democracy.[11] Each state in the United States is free to establish its own form of government so long as the form adopted does not violate this constitutional requirement nor is inconsistent with any other limitation. A state constitution may impose additional restrictions on its own state and local governments in order to provide greater safeguards for individual rights and liberties. The U.S. Supreme Court helps to interpret what is a proper exercise of federal or state powers.

The estimated 40,000 separate federal, state and local law enforcement agencies in the United States have derived their existence and authority from the U.S. Constitution, all of the state constitutions, federal and state laws and federal and state court decisions. In addition, local law enforcement agencies have to abide by the ordinances, charters and administrative rules adopted at municipal or county levels of government. The authority of all state and local police departments can be traced back to a specific act of a state legislature. In the nineteenth century many state legislatures sought to maintain direct control over local law enforcement. However, by the end of the century this practice had been generally discontinued. Most of the police agencies in the United States are dispersed throughout the many counties, cities, towns and villages that form America's unique system of local government. In many communities, the voters have a direct influence in the selection of sheriffs, prosecuting attorneys and judges or they elect other officials who may appoint law enforcement personnel. Moreover, a police officer's responsibility for enforcing law is usually confined to his or her particular jurisdiction and this authority may never extend beyond state lines except in an emergency or by previous agreement.[12]

The hopes and interests of the American people expressed on election day have created a distinctly democratic form of policing in the United States as compared to the more centralized police systems of England and Europe. The United States has established through congressional legislation various federal law enforcement agencies such as the U.S. Marshals Office, the Secret Service, the Federal Bureau of Investigation, and the Immigration and Naturalization Service, but each agency was created as an arm of a specific department of the Executive Branch of the federal government. Their responsibilities are limited to the fulfillment of their respective department's mission. However, the duties of the early U.S. federal marshals did involve a very broad set of duties in the western territories. The federal marshals were the first official law enforcement officers in the federal system. They derived their authority from the Judiciary Act of 1789 and were empowered to employ deputies and to summon the *posse comitatus* (all able-bodied citizens aged sixteen to sixty-five). In 1792, the Congress declared that all marshals would have the same powers as sheriffs in executing federal laws.[13] In 1789, Congress also established the Revenue Cutter Service to help prevent smuggling and in 1836 special agents were employed to investigate violations of the postal laws and regulations. In this way, the role of the federal government in law enforcement developed in a sporadic and highly specialized manner through a series of congressional statutes over the next two hundred years.[14]

In 1800, the public safety of the residents of New York City rested in the hands of the mayor, a high constable, sixteen regular constables who were elected annually, forty marshals appointed by the mayor, two special police justices, the night watch and the local city legislature, the Common Council. The Common Council determined the salaries and fees of all of these officials, helped to clarify their responsibilities and established minimum qualifications. By 1803, all members of the Watch Department could be selected and dismissed by a majority vote of the Common Council. The special justices directed the activities of the marshals and constables and every morning they oversaw the dismissal of the night watch. All watchmen were under the direct supervision of the Common Council and the special police justices. The Council members were the mayor, the recorder and the aldermen elected from the city's wards.[15]

Marshals and constables received set fees for their services. Their duties consisted of serving court papers, escorting prisoners, detecting and arresting lawbreakers, quelling riots and performing other functions related to the maintenance of peace during the day. An individual who was elected to serve as a constable but refused to undertake the office could be fined. These early law enforcement officials possessed neither badges nor uniforms in order to identify themselves.[16]

The office of the high constable was filled by Jacob Hays for the entire first half of the nineteenth century. He was the chief assistant to the mayor on law enforcement matters and regularly participated in the investigation and apprehension of serious offenders. He was empowered to enforce all state and local laws and his exploits earned him an enviable reputation. The office was abolished in 1844, but Hays, who was an early political ally of Aaron Burr, "was allowed to keep the title and emoluments of High Constable" until 1850.[17]

The members of the night watch wore leather hats and were nicknamed "leatherheads" by members of the community. The hats were numbered and if a watchmen lost his hat more than once he might be dismissed. In addition to his other duties, Jacob Hays became a captain of the watch. Occasionally, a constable would also supervise members of the watch. However, the professional development of New York City's early police system was greatly impeded by the lack of coordination between the marshals, constables and watch members. Fortunately, the rate of crime was relatively stable between 1800 and 1830, even though the city's size and population vastly increased.[18]

By 1830, the population of New York City had swelled to nearly a quarter million, chiefly as a result of immigration. The old police system lost its ability to cope with the problem of disorder owing to an upsurge of crime, vice and corruption. Severe epidemics took the lives of hundreds of slum dwellers. A major cause of these conditions was overcrowding, as landlords packed more and more newcomers into unsanitary and poorly ventilated tenements. Conceivably, many of the inhabitants of these dwellings sought to escape from their environment by any means possible, legal or illegal. In 1833 a delegation of city officials visited the new Metropolitan Police of London in order to determine if such a system could be adapted to the needs of New York City.[19] However, the efforts of these early police reformers were buried in the web of partisan politics until the middle of the following decade. It was a common practice for local politicians to appeal to the sympathies and prejudices of the voters and such practices greatly added to the social turmoil of the day. The passions of the people were especially aroused during election periods. The polls were open for three straight days during the city elections of 1834 and a riot ensued throughout the entire three-day period. The use of a company of armed militia was necessary to quell the disturbances.

The reliance upon military forces to control civil disorder was an act of desperation and their continued use demonstrated the need for a unified system of police. The deployment of troops for the purpose of domestic security can seriously threaten the existence of civil rights and liberties within any community.[20] However, a civil police must not only be unified to function effectively, but be well versed in the techniques for handling unruly groups. The Astor Theater

Riot in 1849 and the New York City Draft Riots in 1863 took place after the unification of the day and night segments of New York's early police system. The use of the militia in these instances resulted in a tragic loss of life. The police had to call upon military troops because of their inability to cope with the rioting crowds. Moreover, even with modern training and equipment, present-day police departments have had to resort to units of the National Guard when confronted by a large-scale civil disorder.[21]

The issue of police unification was resolved in the mid–1840s after all debate and discussion had been exhausted. In 1837, an economic slump eliminated many of the gains which the working class had been able to achieve. The Whig party had succeeded the Federalists (the party of the old New York aristocracy) and through its control of the press advocated strong feelings against crime, vagrants and the continuation of unlimited immigration policies. However, the Democratic party and its many officials at the ward level feared the loss of its local patronage authority should the police be unified in accordance with Whig proposals. Moreover, the city's marshals and constables were generally opposed to the idea of unification for purely financial reasons. They viewed such a plan as a scheme to deprive them of their earnings from the various fees and rewards they collected.[22]

Nevertheless, on the eve of reconciling their differences, the Democrats and Whigs were faced with a third contender for political power. In 1843 the American Republican party was formed to represent the interests of native Americans. The "nativists" opposed aid for Catholic schools and public jobs for persons of foreign birth.[23] Moreover, they won the city elections of 1844 and the new mayor, James Harper, was given the authority to choose with the consent of the Common Council a police force consisting of two hundred men. Significantly, the new police force did not displace any of the other law enforcement personnel of that era, but since its members were required to work day and night shifts new ground was broken. The force was given a regular salary scale, the military ranks of captain and sergeant were used for supervisory positions and collar insignia and uniforms were prescribed.[24]

In 1845, the Democrats regained control of the city's government and adopted a bill that had been endorsed by the state legislature and governor in 1844 but never implemented. The new measure replaced Mayor Harper's police force as well as most of the existing offices having anything to do with police, such as the Watch Department and the marshals.[25] Under this measure eight hundred policemen were appointed by the mayor upon the recommendation of Common Council aldermen and two tax assessors from every ward. The office of police chief was created, but was not empowered to make assignments or appoint and dismiss police officers. These important administrative powers were shared by the mayor and the Common Council. Day and night shifts were scheduled and an emblem in the form of a star-shaped badge was adopted for purposes of identification. Military ranks were used and a maximum salary scale was adopted for every rank. Appointments to the force were made only for one year at a time. This period of appointment was changed by law to two years in 1846 and to four years in 1849. However, police appointments, promotions and dismissals were still controlled by local politicians. Moreover, the influence of partisan politics was assured by having each election ward's boundaries also serve as police patrol districts. Police in each of the districts were commanded by a captain and housed in a station, presently known as "the precinct station house." Ostensibly, the system of fees and rewards was eliminated.[26] Thus, the first unified police department was established in New York City, but its use for patronage purposes was not substantially modified until the close of the nineteenth century.

The first police chief of New York City's new municipal police force was George W. Matsell (1806–1877), who had been serving as a police justice since 1840 and had earned a reputation as a dedicated official. He was appointed by the mayor in 1845 and occupied the position for twelve years.

He set himself to re-organize the old sleepy Leatherheads . . . and with a squad of men at his command, he was in the habit of going about the city a great deal at night, breaking up many places of evil resort through his personal exertions.[27]

Matsell is credited with having originated the slogan: "The finest police force in the world."[28]

The New York State Legislature adopted new charter provisions for the city in 1853 and the reforms included a board of police commissioners with the power to appoint and discipline all police officers. The first commissioners were the city mayor, city recorder and city judge. The reforms also included the adoption of an unlimited or "good behavior tenure" system, the adoption of an official police baton for use only in self-defense, drill training and a new official uniform.[29] Mayor Harper in 1844 had attempted to adopt a standard uniform, but most police and citizens seemed to feel it was a symbol of servitude.[30] A coercive tactic was employed to crush this opposition in 1853:

Officials in New York took advantage of the fact that their police served four year terms of appointment. When those terms expired in 1853, the city's police commissioners announced that they would not rehire any man who refused to wear a uniform.[31]

Mayor Fernando Wood dominated New York's political scene in the latter half of the 1850s and he took a serious interest in police activities. In order to instill a sense of pride and to boost morale, Wood ordered a public parade of the police and presented medals of merit which he paid for out of his own funds. He appointed police surgeons to aid injured or ill officers and to screen applicants for police work.[32] However, he used off-duty police for electioneering and those on duty during the 1856 election did nothing to "interfere with the 500 repeaters who roamed the city casting numerous ballots for Wood."[33] Wood and his Democratic machine won the city elections, but the new Republican party candidates did well in the state races. Political reformers succeeded in breaking Wood's control of local politics and the police through the adoption of the Metropolitan Police Act of 1857. The new state law created a police system which extended beyond the traditional city boundaries. The counties of New York, Kings, Westchester and Richmond were included in the plan. In 1860, the towns of Newtown, Flushing and Jamaica in the county of Queens were added. The new system was administered by a board of commissioners appointed by the governor.[34]

Mayor Wood lost all control over the new police system when Governor King appointed five commissioners, none of whom was a Democrat. The commissioners appointed a new police chief to take charge of the daily operations of the force who had the title of "General Superintendent of Police" and they were also empowered to "appoint special policemen at the request and expense of any individual or group."[35] Wood attempted to keep control over his municipal police force as long as he could. The matter was resolved only after the advent of a police riot, various court decisions and strict obedience to the cause of partisan politics.[36] The last word came from the New York Court of Appeals on July 2, 1857, which upheld the constitutionality of the consolidation act on the grounds that the state had the right to maintain order throughout its jurisdiction and that nothing in the state constitution restricted the use of a special district plan. Wood disbanded the Municipal Police a few days later.[37]

The carrying of pistols by members of the police began in the Metropolitan Police era and by the late 1860s it was a regular part of the police uniform and equipment. However, the board of police commissioners did not officially sanction the practice when it was originally established by individual police captains. The captains felt that this innovation was necessary for the protection of their police officers on routine patrol.[38] The type and make of the revolver was not standardized for New York City's police until the mid–1890's. The first official police pistol was the .32 caliber Colt.[39] It was not until 1877 that the ordinary citizen was required by law to obtain a pistol permit. The maximum fine was ten dollars for failing to obtain one and the local ordinance was rarely enforced by the police. In those days, virtually anyone who asked for the permit could obtain one.[40] The arming of the police and the disarming of the average citizen was a crucial break with past practices. Up until this time, the police "continued to rely on active citizen participation—to the point that the policeman sometimes seemed the auxiliary in the battle, and the 'man in the street' the principal."[41]

However, the tradition of an armed citizenry was maintained in the western half of the United States in the nineteenth and twentieth centuries. The lack of effective police agencies in western communities necessitated the use of citizen deputies and firearms to enforce the law. Many western towns relied solely on a single sheriff or marshal for the maintenance of public safety and the use of ordinary citizens to supplement this official in times of trouble was a practical and common event.

An almost family-like cooperation existed between law enforcement and the community. . . . Citizen involvement with the police, as much as any other factor, eventually fused the scattered early settlements and mining camps into homogeneous communities.[42]

Generally, the New York experiences were duplicated in other cities with expanding population and social problems. Each city closely examined the policies of its neighbor city and unified police departments emerged in New Orleans, Chicago, Cincinnati, Baltimore, Newark, Philadelphia and Boston during the 1850s.[43] In 1861, President Abraham Lincoln personally requested Zenas C. Robbins, a member of the newly created board of commissioners for the Metropolitan Police in the District of Columbia, "to take the first railroad train to New York and, upon arrival, to thoroughly familiarize himself with the features of the New York Police System and the experiences of its leadership."[44] Robbins' report was used to determine the organization and administration of the first regular police force in the nation's capital.[45]

By the end of the nineteenth century almost every major city had completed the unification of its police force by establishing centrally administered, full-time, uniformed and armed law enforcement agencies. The development of these modern police institutions has given rise to speculation about their true origin. Some authors have not been content to see the police as merely a natural response to overcrowding and the need to regulate social disorder. One view emphasizes that the organization of political parties through the efforts of business and civic leaders prompted the rise of the modern police system. This occurred when the new urban middle class became interested in the political system and its power over the police because of their desire to stay ahead of lower-class groups. They formed coalitions with the ruling elite class and their common concerns gave rise to a strengthened police system.[46] It has been noted that the members of the working class were often brutally suppressed when they sought to organize in order to reduce their exploitation, and yet "it was primarily the low wages paid to immigrant workers that created slums, not to mention forced segregation and other forms of discrimination."[47] The Tompkins Square Riot in 1874 involved an instance in which New York police "viciously attacked workingmen who had gathered to demand relief for the unemployed during the depression."[48]

Eric Monkkonen concludes that the modern police idea was spread in the United States as a result of a cultural phenomenon involving the growth of urban service bureaucracies. He maintains that once the unified system of police proved successful and was adopted in a few major cities, it "spread from larger to smaller cities, spurred not by precipitating events any longer, but by the newly developing service orientations of city governments."[49] Thus, crime rates and riots did not contribute to the development of the police in many communities; rather "city governments seized the innovative scheme of uniformed police as a convenient and fashionable means of social control without regard for specifically threatening situations."[50] Significantly, Monkkonen's research indicates that New York City was the first to uniform its police and thus served as the cultural innovator for the rest of the nation.[51]

In 1863, the New York Metropolitan Police comprised more than 2,000 members. A life insurance fund was established in 1864 and half-pay retirement pensions were achieved in 1868.[52] The Metropolitan Board of Health was established in 1866. It was modeled on the organization of the Metropolitan Police. Police brutality increased in the 1860s and it was often very difficult to find qualified jurors. Voting frauds were common during this era. In 1868, the board of commissioners was unable to appoint citizen election inspectors because of partisan politics. In 1870, a new city charter revision returned the control of the police to the mayor. The mayor was the tool of a political machine headed by the infamous William M. Tweed.[53] From 1872 to 1881, the city's police were required to supervise the personnel employed to clean the streets. Women were hired for service as jail matrons in 1888.[54]

The Reverend Charles H. Packhurst began a crusade against police corruption in 1892 and his sermons on the subject coincided with the interests of the Republican party. The Republicans, led by Thomas Platt, controlled the New York State Legislature and were able to establish a special investigation committee to look into the administrative practices and daily operations of the city's police force in 1894. Supporters of Reverend Packhurst, such as the New York Chamber of Commerce, provided expense money. Hundreds of witnesses from all walks of life offered testimony concerning bribery, election fraud and other corrupt practices. Some witnesses presented detailed explanations about detectives who shared the illegal gains of petty thieves and one witness listed the cash payment that was demanded for an appointment to each police rank. The payoff for the position of patrolman was $300, for sergeant $1,600 and from $12,000 to $15,000 for captain.[55]

The special committee was chaired by Senator Clarence Lexow. The current practice of utilizing a legislative subcommittee for purposes of investigation was first instituted with the assembly of the Lexow Committee. Moreover, since New York corruption was not a unique phenomenon, the device was quickly adopted for purposes of investigating police departments in Atlanta, Philadelphia, Kansas City, Baltimore, Chicago, Los Angeles and San Francisco.[56]

The publicity engendered by the findings of the Lexow Committee led to the election of a fusion party candidate for mayor at the next election. The new mayor, William L. Strong, supported a bipartisan police commission plan for the city and in 1895 such a measure was adopted by the New York State Legislature. It was a compromise measure that meant that two Democrats and two Republicans would always be on the board of police commissioners which consisted of only four members. One of the two Republican commissioners appointed to the board was Theodore Roosevelt.[57]

One of the most important events in early police history was the use of station houses for emergency lodging of destitute individuals. The feeding and lodging of thousands of homeless persons by New York City's police force constituted a major expense item during the latter half of the nineteenth century, especially during times of economic depression. Jacob Riis, a newspaper police reporter and close friend of Theodore Roosevelt, was a consistent critic of this system from 1883 until its demise in 1896. He advocated the creation of a separate system of lodging for such persons and he shared this view and other opinions about policing with his friend, Theodore Roosevelt. Roosevelt became the president of the board of police commissioners. He often acted as if he was the only police commissioner. In addition to ending the lodging practice, Roosevelt argued for stricter recruitment standards and the use of telephone call boxes on city streets.[58]

Roosevelt's tenure as head of the board of police commissioners lasted until 1897 when he resigned to become the assistant secretary of the navy. Some writers have postulated that his resignation was connected with his quest for higher office, since the Spanish American War was imminent, but others contend that he left mainly out of frustration when he was stymied in his efforts to achieve needed police reforms. Indeed, few reforms of a long-lasting nature were achieved, because the bipartisan board was equally divided on key issues and the real control of the police remained at the local ward level.[59] Later, Roosevelt's criticism of this problem did lead to abandonment of the board of police commissioners in favor of a single police commissioner policy in 1901, but the greater problem of internal corruption was not brought under control. In 1897, the Greater New York Charter was ratified, merging all the separate police units within the five boroughs into the New York City Police Department. By the time of the appointment of the first commissioner in 1901, there were 6,400 uniformed police officers on the force.[60] Meanwhile, the career of Theodore Roosevelt led to the presidency of the United States. He made a lasting contribution to police professionalism when he directed his attorney general, Charles J. Bonaparte, to establish a small investigative unit within the Justice Department, now known as the Federal Bureau of Investigation. The FBI celebrated its seventy-fifth anniversary on July 26, 1983.[61]

In 1908, President Theodore Roosevelt became an active supporter of the National Rifle Association (NRA) when it moved its national headquarters to Washington, D.C.[62] Today the NRA is the chief advocate against the gun control lobbyists in the United States. In 1905, concern about guns in New York City raised the maximum fine from $10 to $250 and established a maximum prison term of six months for failing to comply with the provisions of the pistol permit law. In 1910, the number of homicides with firearms increased by almost 50 percent. In that year the well-known novelist David Graham Phillips was shot to death on a New York City sidewalk and the city's mayor, William J. Gaynor, was seriously wounded. The city's newspapers devoted many articles to the long and painful recovery of Mayor Gaynor. The New York State Legislature adopted the strictest gun control measure in the nation by making the unlicensed carrying of a concealable firearm a felony. Its chief and most powerful sponsor was Senator Timothy D. "Big Tim" Sullivan. The "Sullivan Law" became effective on September 1, 1911, and the city's criminal justice system responded with a vengeance.[63] "The first man convicted under the new law, an Italian immigrant arrested with a pistol in his pocket, was arraigned, indicted, convicted, and sent on his way to a year's stay in Sing Sing within thirty days."[64]

Today the "Sullivan Law" remains on the books, having survived numerous attempts of repeal. However, the opportunity to purchase weapons in other states and the declarations in the Fourth Amendment prohibiting unreasonable searches and seizures have greatly complicated the enforcement of this law in New York.[65] George Beto, professor of criminal justice at Sam Houston State University and a former director of the Texas Department of Corrections, believes that gun control measures are impossible to enforce:

We have had 200 years of gun culture, and people aren't about to give that up. People don't want good law enforcement and they aren't going to cooperate with it. If we wanted good law enforcement, we'd quit wasting all our energies fighting between law enforcement agencies and develop a system that would be good. We could do it, but the people don't want it. They want to be free and independent, and they don't want the law to apply to them, only to those who would threaten them.[66]

The momentum for and against gun control rose and fell in the 1920s and 1930s. In 1922, the American Bar Association passed a resolution to totally eliminate the availability of handguns for private citizens.[67] However, after the much compromised National Firearms Act was adopted in 1934, "public opinion, especially among police chiefs and in the legal profession, had swung against gun control."[68]

In the 1920s the use of the police patrol car became widespread and by the early 1930s, the availability of the two-way radio and private telephone service completely transformed the nature of the daily operations of the New York City Police Department and the expectations of the public. Significantly, the radio patrol car replaced most foot patrol posts and the public learned to use the telephone to call the police, rather than looking for them on a street corner or having to run to the nearest call box or police station. A flashlight call system was used to help citizens and police supervisors contact foot patrol officers for several years during the first quarter of the twentieth century in the more busy precincts. The telephone call box was effective so long as an officer was in hearing distance of the bell on the box, but this entailed a fixed post system which greatly reduced the mobility and patrol range of the police. In order to remedy this problem a lamp was designed of sufficient brilliancy to attract attention, even on a bright day, at a distance of about 700 to 1,000 feet. The lamp was fixed to the top end of the control post which contained the telephone call box. The light was turned on by the precinct desk officer. The first precinct to have this installed was the Twenty-third in 1915.[69] This system was supplemented by the "reserve platoon" which was established in the latter half of the nineteenth century in order to ensure that a sufficient emergency standby force was available in case of a riot or similar crisis.

The "reserve platoon" involved an arrangement which required police officers to spend extra hours in the station. They were housed within dormitories attached to local police stations. This practice, also known as the "two-platoon system," was used extensively in the United States. Generally, such a system put 25 percent of the police on patrol during the day, 50 percent on patrol at night and 25 percent on reserve duty in the station house. The system allowed for very little time off. An alternative was the three-platoon system. Patrols lasted for only eight hours, but time off was reduced to broken time periods and rest was difficult. Moreover, the reserve force was reduced by more than one-half under the three-platoon system. Theodore A. Bingham, a retired brigadier general in the U.S. Army, who served as the city's police commissioner from 1906 to 1909, introduced a "five-platoon" system which reduced the number of consecutive patrol hours to six, put twice as many officers on nights than days and permitted one day off for every five days worked.[70] The invention and utilization of radios, automobiles and telephones permitted the quick recall of officers from their homes and beats so that the reserve platoon and the flashlight, bell and other early call back systems could be eliminated. However, some call boxes which are directly connected with the local precinct are still being used, especially by auxiliary police assigned to foot patrol posts during the evening hours.

The use of modern communications equipment has permitted citizens to call upon the police for a wide range of services. It is generally understood that contemporary patrol officers spend as much as 80 percent of their time in the delivery of a host of miscellaneous services that are considered to be of a noncriminal nature. The public can now expect police to respond to calls about noisy neighbors, domestic fights, disorderly teenagers, missing children, traffic accidents, utility troubles and disabled and elderly persons.[71] Moreover, just the sight of a radio patrol car is considered to be an important fear reducer for the people in many communities. Patrick Murphy, the president of the Police Foundation and the former head of four major police departments including New York City, has commented: "The main point of aimless police patrol seems to be to reassure the citizen that the police department, like the city zoo, exists."[72]

However, many big cities are finding it increasingly difficult to respond to these nonemergency calls because of a lack of personnel. Ironically, the public's expectation for such assistance took years to build, but today economic constraints have limited the ability to comply with the demands for service. The tremendous strides to reduce political interference, to improve working conditions, to sensitize the police to the needs of minorities, to strengthen police supervision and to select and train qualified men and women for careers in law enforcement are currently being threatened because of lack of sufficient personnel. Significantly, the police wish to devote as much time as they can to each call for help or service, but personnel resources are inadequate in many police agencies. In addition, society has become more mobile and heterogeneous. Some of the burdens placed on big-city police officers have now been recognized in the form of stress management workshops and by the employment of staff psychologists and other counseling professionals to assist the police and their families.

The reform efforts to limit the power of ward politicians and to have law enforcement officers adhere to high standards of ethical behavior have met with general success. Nevertheless, the growth of huge complex organizations, such as the New York City Police Department, and the advent of strong police unions, such as the Patrolmen's Benevolent Association (PBA), also represent a threat to the important gains made in the professionalization of the police in America. The increase in power and remoteness of administrative decision making tends to reduce citizen participation in the police process. Certainly, the social problem of crime has not diminished, but rather than relying more on neighborhood alertness and cooperation, the public safety of the community has been entrusted to a highly centralized and bureaucratic organization. Moreover, recent efforts by citizen groups and even citizens who have been recruited by police authorities, such as auxiliary police, to upgrade their training and availability for assisting in the police function, have frequently been opposed by PBA leaders and a few police administrators. In many respects, citizens who currently wish to become more actively involved in the police function have been frustrated by the claim that they are only amateurs and therefore incompetent to render professional police services. Nevertheless, it was estimated that in 1983 there were five million citizens in twenty thousand different communities throughout the United States engaged in "Crime Watch" or other types of community crime prevention programs.[73]

Parts II and III of this book will explore the efforts of ordinary citizens to become reinvolved in the police function. However, before turning to the history, practices and problems of reestablishing a citizen's role in law enforcement in association with regular police, the following and last chapter in Part I will consider how Americans have reacted in the absence of regular police or any other type of consistent pattern of social control.

3 • Vigilantism and the Police

Vigilantes do not build respect for
the law—they destroy it. There are
a great many responsible roles for
citizens to play today in the support
of law enforcement and criminal justice.
Crime can be reduced only if the criminal
justice system is strong and effective.
It cannot be strong if every group tries
to take the law into its own hands.[1]

Edward H. Levi
Former U.S. Attorney General

The Spanish language provides us with the word "vigilante." It means watchman or guardian. Through the years the term has taken on a new definition in the United States and in many other countries.[2] The new and more familiar meaning of vigilantism has been described by the historian Richard Maxwell Brown. Brown's research has documented 326 large scale or historically important vigilante movements in America during the period from 1767 to 1904.[3] He learned that most of the vigilante movements were led by members of the upper class and took place in newly settled areas. These movements are distinguished from the activities of mere lynch mobs who are estimated to have killed 4,730 persons between 1882 and 1951.[4] The phenomenon of vigilantism as described by Brown involves: 1. an extralegal organization, 2. which exists for a specific period of time, 3. in an area with inadequate or absent law enforcement, 4. for the purpose of establishing law and order.[5] Brown comments:

Often a vigilante movement could achieve its aims by taking only one or a few lives. . . . The fearful example of one or two hangings (frequently in conjunction with the expulsion of lesser culprits) was on many occasions enough to bring about the vigilante goals of community reconstruction and stability.[6]

H. Jon Rosenbaum and Peter C. Sederberg define vigilantes as consisting of individuals or groups who identify with the established order, but who seek to defend it "by resorting to means that violate . . . formal boundaries."[7] This definition is in conformity with Brown's in that it indicates behavior that goes beyond the notion of summary "justice" or "taking the law into one's own hands." Thus, the idea of vigilantism is more complex than that given by former U.S. Attorney General Edward H. Levi at the beginning of this chapter. Brown concludes that American public opinion has generally supported vigilantism and it was often the shortcomings of law enforcement agencies that led to the formation of such groups.[8] He points out that vigilantism has a philosophical basis in the democratic tradition of "popular sovereignty" and that the doctrine of "vigilance" included an economic rationale. He notes that the forerunner of today's Better Business Bureau was organized in 1845 and was known as the Merchant's Vigilance Association of New York City. Moreover, the cities of Philadelphia and New York had committees as early as 1838 to help slaves who had escaped from the plantations of the South.[9]

The first vigilante movement took place in colonial South Carolina during the period from 1767 to 1769. The effort was designed to eliminate outlaws from the area's Back Country and the vigilantes of that era were called "Regulators." The group was active until a system of courts and sheriffs was introduced. However, the method for dealing with frontier disorders practiced by the South Carolina Regulators was to be duplicated again and again as settlers followed the trails to the western region of America. Texas experienced the greatest number of vigilante movements and Montana helped to popularize the term "vigilante" because of the significant number of events and people involved.[10] At one point in time, the "Vigilantes of Montana" included "as many as twenty-five hundred responsible men from every economic and social class."[11] The discovery of rich gold deposits in 1863 and in 1864 created a wave of gold seekers and the founding of such cities as Virginia City and Helena. The citizens of that era became outraged when they learned that their own local sheriff was the leader of a well organized band of outlaws and they banded together to eliminate the problem.

Some noteworthy vigilante movements also took place in urban environments. In the early 1840s, the Irish Catholic immigrant population in Philadelphia constituted a noticeable foreign minority. Hostility toward this group involved an ancient conflict with Protestants, the lack of available work and the existence of adequate living space. Friction between the earlier and late arrivals boiled over in May and July of 1844 and many persons were killed and injured.[12] Historically, this period is known as that of the "Native American Riots." It demonstrated the problems associated with a lack of a professionalized police force. In those days, the City of Philadelphia was policed by a small group of politically controlled constables and a nighttime watch. A county sheriff had the only authority to summon volunteer police to cross the city's district lines. If the sheriff felt he had insufficient volunteers, he could contact the commanding officer of the local state militia for the mobilization of his unit. Usually, the citizen volunteers were unarmed and they seldom suffered any serious injuries. However, it often took many hours to organize the necessary forces and sometimes the system failed to protect the rights of the minorities who needed protection. At such times, the loss of life and the destruction of property were the end results.[13]

The conditions in Philadelphia gradually improved when its institutions of government became more solidified and the economy took an upturn. Moreover, the growing acceptance of the abolition movement and the war with Mexico in 1846 also helped to deter additional riots. The war attracted many of the young men who had engaged in the street violence.[14]

If you look at the reverse side of a U.S. dollar bill you will discover the watchful or vigilante eye. This symbol is the same one that was used by the San Francisco Vigilance Committee to adorn its stationery. The formation of this group in 1856 is described by Brown as a pivotal point in the history of American vigilantism. He considers this movement as a part of the transition from a frontier and rural concern for stamping out horse thieves and outlaws to an urban concern for political dominance. He describes the San Francisco episode as an example of "neovigilantism" that served "to wrest control of the government from the dominant faction of Irish-Catholic Democrats."[15]

At its peak the Vigilance Committee of San Francisco was composed of 6,000 to 8,000 members and operated out of a headquarters called Fort Gunnybags. They were organized "into pistol and rifle companies, artillery and cavalry units, sharpshooting squads, and even a medical contingent."[16] This impressive array of public effort was spearheaded by the city's business leaders who sought to remove the incumbent political organization from power. The murder of a newspaper editor and a U.S. marshal by supporters of the incumbent leader, David Broderick, furthered the cause of the Vigilance group and led to the hanging of four men and the exile of twenty-eight others as well as Broderick from the city.[17]

The Vigilance Committee helped elect its members to the positions of sheriff and chief of police at the next regularly scheduled election. Clearly, political reform and not concern for general peacekeeping was the real reason for the new vigilantism. The quasi-military organization of the committee was necessary to effectively gain control from the Broderick machine which had "simply stuffed the ballot boxes and counted out the opposition"[18] in the past.

In the 1830s the use of barbed wire became widespread in Texas. When this invention was used to limit the grazing lands for cattle and sheep owners, the result was a constant range war through the late nineteenth and early twentieth centuries. The various factions engaged in fence cutting, shooting, stampeding and poisoning. Deaths occurred on both sides. Eventually, "the era of the open range was closed, making possible the settling of the Western plains."[19]

Economic factors were also implicated in the New York City Draft Riots of 1863. In this episode of violence and killing, the police and local militia were overwhelmed by rioters fearful of black labor competition and the inability of many persons to pay for a draft exemption as provided by law. The situation was fueled by hatred toward those who could pay for the exemptions and by the knowledge that black workers were exempted under the law. Various sources have claimed that the death toll of whites and blacks numbered in the hundreds before regular army troops were able to restore order on the fourth day of the riot.[20]

An episode more in keeping with Brown's definition of vigilantism was the advent of the anti-horse thief society. In 1851, the legislature of the state of New Jersey officially approved such a group and later granted them the power of arrest. A similar movement flourished in the states of the upper Mississippi River region from the 1840s to the 1890s. It became known as the Anti-Horse Thief Association "with thousands of local chapters and over a hundred thousand members in Kansas, Oklahoma, Missouri, and Arkansas."[21] The invention of the automobile and its replacement of the horse and buggy during the first quarter of the twentieth century rendered these groups unnecessary.[22]

The use of private police forces to control labor camps and the activities of unions is a tragic episode in police history. A unique system of cooperation existed in Pennsylvania between employers and the police. From 1865 until 1931 a state law authorized railroad, iron and coal industries to hire persons with the authority to act as police officers throughout the state. These companies were able to utilize the police to control any labor dispute in the state and there was no provision to hold these forces accountable to anyone except their employers. In other states, employers had to arrange for the appointment of private police with local sheriffs and other officials for strike duty. However, under the two systems the company paid for the services of the special police, guards and special deputies. From time to time, units of the National Guard were used to patrol communities experiencing labor strife. The combined forces of the state were usually successful in defeating a strike or limiting the opportunities for a union to organize.[23] This episode of violence and labor abuse persisted until public opinion in favor of the workers and a liberal governor, Gifford Pinchot, combined their efforts. In 1931, Governor Pinchot revoked the police commissions of all the special police under the old Coal and Iron Police Act and he directed his staff to prepare a full investigation. On the federal level, the U.S. Senate Committee on Education and Labor under the leadership of Senator Robert La Follette, exposed similar abuses. "The new political power of organized labor itself also helped to put new constraints on official law enforcement agencies."[24]

During World War I, a group later criticized by Senator Robert La Follette as thugs used to terrorize the public was assembled by Albert M. Briggs, an outdoor advertising executive. Briggs' persistence with the head of the U.S. Department of Justice's office in Chicago led to the establishment of the American Protective League. Briggs offered a volunteer solution for the need to investigate suspected German agents with existing funds and departmental equipment. He promised men and automobiles which could be used by the Justice Department at the discretion of the Chief of the Bureau of Investigation. President Wilson had desperately tried to avoid going to war with Germany and now the nation needed all the help it could attract. Early recruitment of volunteers for the American Protective League (APL) was fostered by rumors of sabotage and the threat of invasion. Moreover, many conservative businessmen grasped at the opportunity to support a secret network of informants in order to learn about union activities. The APL was officially requested to protect property, investigate violations of the Espionage Act, locate draft evaders, arrest deserters, report "disloyal" and "suspicious" activities, and even perform the "unlikely task of enforcing vice and liquor regulations in areas around army camps and naval bases."[25]

The tactics used by APL members to stifle dissent and their participation in various raids to find draft evaders earned them periodic criticism from liberal leaders, but in the main their practices led to little public outcry. The Justice Department decided to disband the league at the end of the war and members were given honorable discharge papers and gold badges as symbols of their dedicated service. However, some peacetime vigilante groups were composed of former APL veterans. This occurred in Minneapolis, Cincinnati, Seattle and Chicago. These groups continued to agitate for the recall of the APL and their members volunteered their services against *Bolsheviks* and other radicals who they believed were seeking to destroy American society. The infamous "Red Raids" were endorsed by federal and local officials and former APL chiefs and members were recruited to participate. In the forefront of this activity was U.S. Attorney General A. Mitchell Palmer who fancied that he might become the next president. Palmer lost the Democratic nomination for president in 1920 and left his office in 1921. The new Republican administration had no interest in pursuing the Palmer policies and by 1925 even the American Civil Liberties Union supported the Bureau of Investigation.[26] This bureau was renamed the Federal Bureau of Investigation in 1935. When APL veterans were ready to assist the federal government during World War II, J. Edgar Hoover rejected the offers and insisted that counterespionage work should be undertaken only by highly trained and carefully screened personnel.[27] The membership of the league ranged in the hundreds of thousands and at that time they were the largest body of secret agents ever recruited by any nation.

Between 1920 and 1924, the Ku Klux Klan (KKK) movement experienced a resurgence and some former APL members became active in local Klans throughout the South and the Southwest.[28] The KKK arose just after the end of the Civil War. Members of the Klan wanted the political and economic institutions to be controlled by whites and any means to achieve these purposes, including murder, was condoned. By the mid–1890s, the U.S. Supreme Court declared segregation to be legal and the tactics used by Klan groups effectively eliminated blacks from having any significant role in the criminal justice system.[29]

The Ku Klux Klan was a major weapon for reestablishing white supremacy during the Reconstruction period. Samuel Walker has identified how the criminal justice system functioned during the late nineteenth century and during the first half of the twentieth century:

Crimes by blacks against blacks were treated with indifference and inaction, while crimes by whites against blacks were hardly crimes at all. Crimes by whites against whites were "normal" crimes, while crimes by blacks against whites could provoke the most vicious retribution.[30]

The activities of the American Protective League were supposed to be kept in secret and the KKK, also known as the "invisible Empire," conducted its affairs with careful attention to the need for secrecy.[31] In 1957, The Tuskegee Institute reported that the United States had suffered a total of 4,733 lynchings during the previous seventy-five years of its existence. The vast majority of the persons hanged were blacks.[32]

Although the Klan's beginnings were Southern, supporters were drawn from most states, including New York and California. In all fairness, many persons were attracted to the group solely because of the "Americanism" which was stressed in their literature and the intrinsic appeal of participating in a secret fraternal group. In the mid-twenties, the Klan claimed to have over 3 million members. An estimated 40,000 white-sheeted Klansmen paraded in the nation's capital in 1925. However, its anti-Catholic, anti-Jewish, and anti-black themes and hypocritical tactics caused many members to drop out and the Klan became fragmented and its power weakened. Some vestiges of the Klan still exist in sections of the United States.[33]

A common thread runs through all of these "vigilante" episodes—namely, the inability of regular law enforcement agencies to cope in times of crisis and the availability of individuals to assume control or to express their hostility toward minority groups. At these times, there was a blurring of the official and unofficial roles of the community members. Brown has sought to reconcile the collaboration of legitimate and illegitimate power by drawing upon two models of the criminal justice system: the "Due Process Model" and the "Crime Control Model." In the former model, emphasis is placed upon safeguarding the rights of individuals who find themselves in the grip of the criminal process, while the latter model's concern is with the quick restoration of social order and the punishment of the accused. Brown sees vigilantism as belonging to the "Crime Control" pattern and as involving the application of extralegal action. The activities of lynch mobs, the KKK and other vigilantes would fall into this category. The anti-horse thief society, coal and iron police, APL organization and many associated police agencies could be said to fit into the "Crime Control" scheme but with emphasis given to legal action. "The key point is that both extralegal vigilantism and legal crime control share the same overriding value emphasis: the repression of criminal conduct."[34] Furthermore, during the nineteenth century and on into the twentieth Americans supported a dual system of legal and extralegal justice by adherence to the primary value of repression to crime with little regard for procedural safeguards. Thus, Americans . . . saw vigilante participation as an act of public spirit as important in its own way as the election of upright officials.[35]

Undesirable behavior on the part of police officers has taken many forms. Their administration of "curbside justice" or summary punishment, harassment, corruption and participation in other abuses of the legal process have been well documented. Some authors have referred to these activities as an illustration of the adoption by police of a vigilante role.[36] Many arrests made by police are for drunkenness and disorderly conduct and on many occasions some use of force must be made in order to gain control of the accused and to transport the suspect to the station house. Before the advent of the call box and patrol wagon, the obligation of providing such services fell totally on the shoulders of the arresting police officer. A well-placed blow to the suspect could mean an easier trip. Thus, perhaps, the practice of police brutality was created as a simple solution for a complex problem of social and economic origins. Unfortunately, many police agencies in the United States have utilized the police in a manner reminiscent of the past. Harlem, Watts, Newark and Detroit were occasions in the 1960s when the arrests of blacks by white police officers led to major episodes of violence.[37] All too often the police have seen themselves and have been seen by others as representatives of the establishment with a special mandate to keep minorities "in their place."[38]

It has been estimated that the number of U.S. citizens participating in "crime watch" or other community based crime prevention efforts reached five million by 1983. Significant citizen anti-crime efforts were underway in 20,000 different U.S. communities and cities.[39] In New York City, 150,000 community residents were engaged in crime prevention activities and some 9,000 of them were serving as auxiliary police.[40] In San Francisco and in Oakland, over 35,000 citizens had volunteered their time to assist in police sponsored crime prevention programs.[41]

Currently, it is rare to learn about citizen groups or police who mete out their own brand of justice. The overwhelming majority of the anti-crime programs involving citizens are completely unlike the vigilante movements of the past. Moreover, the police have advanced their abilities to cope with changing social conditions and they are giving greater emphasis to the task of improving police-community relations. However, all of these advances require a resolve and commitment to maintain and foster human rights.

It is crucial to indicate that auxiliary or reserve police do not fit or conform to the classic definition of vigilantism described by Brown at the beginning of this chapter. The auxiliary and reserve units are in existence because of specific statutory authority. They will be in existence as long as such statutory authority remains. The specific statutes for the authorization of the New York City Auxiliary Police are presented in Part II of this book. The police agencies and other segments of the criminal justice system perform adequately in those cities in which auxiliaries function. Auxiliaries do not themselves seek to establish law and order, but rather serve only to assist regular police. Moreover, in many communities their training is similar to that given to regular police and special emphasis is placed on the task of protecting civil liberties and rights.

The citizen role in the prevention of crime is intimately connected with the concept of respect for human worth and dignity. Neither the recruitment of thousands of auxiliary police officers nor highly professional and aggressive patrol and detective work can bring about neighborhood peace. It must be understood that

the public peace—the sidewalk and street peace—of cities is not kept primarily by the police, necessary as police are. It is kept primarily by an intricate, almost unconscious, network of voluntary controls and standards among the people themselves. In some city areas—older public housing projects and streets with very high population turnover are often conspicuous examples—the keeping of public sidewalk law and order is left almost entirely to the police and special guards. Such places are jungles. No amount of police can enforce civilization where the normal, casual law enforcement of it has broken down.[42]

PART II

HISTORY OF NEW YORK'S VOLUNTEER POLICE

Citizen backing for law enforcement
is a necessity in a democratic society.
With it, the police can act as the
community's right arm in fighting the
city's evils. Without it, the police
tend to become an alien force imposing
its power on a resentful population.

Judge George Edwards,
The Police on the Urban Frontier, p. 77.

4 • The Citizens Home Defense League

Nearly everyone has heard of the "Vigilantes" of our historic Old West, citizen volunteers who combated the lawlessness of the Gold Rush pioneers in the early 1850s, but why should there be a voluntary auxiliary police force today? The answer to this question begins with this chapter.

The goal which permeated every aspect of modern day police organization (whose establishment has been sketched in Part I) was the desire to have a professional force, functioning twenty-four hours a day. Today most large urban police departments require huge budgets, the latest scientific aids and the most up to date administrative techniques for the supervision of thousands of employees. The New York City Police Department is the biggest in the world and the recruitment of its first civilian support group resulted in an equally large organization.

In the fall of 1914, Arthur Woods,[1] the city's newly named police commissioner began to ponder the following problem: In the case of a great emergency such as a flood, earthquake, tidal wave, conflagration, or possible invasion, what would become of the city's five million inhabitants? The solution he developed, with the aid of his staff, gave rise to the creation of the city's first auxiliary police force.

Unlike many of his predecessors, who were handicapped by a lack of experience, Commissioner Woods had been a serious student of police work as a newspaper reporter and since 1897 as the secretary of the Citizens Committee on Police in New York. From 1907 to 1909, he served as a deputy police commissioner in the city. In preparation for this position, Woods went to Europe and studied the methods of Scotland Yard. Upon his return, he reorganized the Detective Bureau; instituted a three-month training course for new recruits, the forerunner of the present Police Academy; and at the same time directed the Department's Bureau of Repairs and Supplies. He performed all these tasks while serving as a fourth deputy commissioner.[2]

Soon after Woods became police commissioner, "district leaders, aldermen and some persons of supposed influence around City Hall complained bitterly about losing their 'in' at Police Headquarters."[3] However, the writer William Hard has perhaps best expressed the contribution made by Woods:

He strove to make police work positive instead of merely wholly negative. He also strove
. . . to hurl the negative and arresting impact of police work not upon the trivialities of
personal moral error but upon actual violences against life and against property. That
distinction, since there are only twenty-four hours in a day, is fundamental to making
police work really effective.[4]

One of the first steps Commissioner Woods adopted in order to assure New
York's preparedness in the event of a crisis was to prepare the city's regular
uniformed force for any eventuality. Significantly, he set up courses in every
precinct for training "in the theory and practice of self-maintenance and relief
work."[5]

By the close of 1915, the war in Europe was threatening to spread throughout the world, and it was thought that the New York Police Force would have
to participate with the regular army in the protection of our borders. Consequently, Woods developed a plan to enlist a "Citizens Home Defense League,"
which could release the police for such service. In general, the "League members would do routine police work, such as patrolling, while the regular force,
experienced in heavier police duty, would be gathered in the trouble zones or
guarding bridges, reservoirs, watersheds, powerhouses, arsenals, or transportation lines."[6]

As originally envisioned, the plans for the league differed from other contemporary citizens groups recruited in Chicago and Berkeley, California. In New
York City, the volunteers were to be called upon for emergency work only,
without the aid of arms, badges, or uniforms. Only when needed, would they
be sworn in as special patrolmen. In Chicago, however, the members were given
badges and were authorized to make observations of every day violations and
to call them to the attention of the police.[7] And in the city of Berkeley, which
lies across a bay from San Francisco, all unpaid members were immediately
sworn in as special policemen with power to make arrests should the necessity
arise. However, no arms were permitted to be carried, all applicants were carefully screened, the force was small and its only responsibility was to enforce
the state and city traffic laws in the hometown of the University of California.[8]
Thus, New York's volunteers were to be used strictly as an emergency force
rather than as an ever-present anticrime or traffic safety organization.

However, realizing the importance of having this emergency force readily
available, Commissioner Woods encouraged citizens to join by instituting the
widest possible enrollment standards. For example, no restrictions in the way
of height, weight, or age were established; only the need for good health and
character were required.[9]

By May of 1916, 8,000 citizens had been enrolled, and by July, there were
21,000 members. They were organized by precincts and after a time revolver
practice was made available. Twice a month, drills and lectures were held in
local armories, public schools and halls. A button was awarded for attendance
at six successive meetings upon the certification of the regular precinct captain.[10]

Members were drawn from every walk of life and in the language of that day, the police commissioner's personal secretary reported:

Among them are men who have had experience on the plains or as woodsmen, railway men, baseball and football men, and men who have had active military service both here and abroad. There are day laborers and men of means, business and professional men, actors and writers, mechanics earning $4 a day and men whose income is big enough to support both town and country homes. Some of the members go to and from their daily labor in trolley cars; others are driven by hired chaffeurs. There are members who own strings of big automobiles, men who are expert as racing drivers. There are owners of high-powered motor boats, yachtsmen, men who can build anything from a pump to an airplane, men who are paying weekly installments on a $2,000 home and men who own sky-scrapers and apartment-houses. There is a good representative class of citizens in this Home Defense League.[11]

In addition, members came from the city's colleges. At Columbia University, a group of the school's top athletes and more than two hundred students volunteered. They promised to serve until they were more urgently needed as soldiers or National Guardsmen.[12]

Three notable league achievements during its brief existence included: the recruiting of a large number of aides for the Red Cross; the use of volunteers in the city's efforts to reduce street accidents; and their dramatic assistance during the polio epidemic in the summer of 1916, when members volunteered to help in the sanitary patrol of the city, block by block.[13]

By July 9, 1916, 205 deaths had been reported in the city resulting from an outbreak of polio. The emergency was considered great enough to justify the first call for the services of the league. Members were assigned to accompany regular police patrols in order to assist in cleaning up the city. Each man was instructed to make a report in writing of the condition he found.

In many districts of the city prominent men and men of affairs were among the volunteer vigilance forces. At the West 177th Street Station, for example, residents of Washington Heights came out in Palm Beach suits, white flannel trousers and other summer garb that distinguished them. But they all seemed eager to work, and went at their task with intelligence.[14]

Several months before the league responded to its first call, the *New York Times* published the following editorial about the significance of league participation:

Perhaps the chief significance to be found in the Citizens' Home Defense League which Commissioner Woods is organizing, or encouraging to organize, as an auxiliary police force, lies in the speed and ease with which an enrollment of 8,000 members has been obtained. . . . Every man who joins the Home Defense League is very evidently a believer in that best form of preparedness—the preparing of himself to play a more or less effective role when the call for his services comes. Herein may lie an incidental benefit from circumstances properly held lamentable. It evidences a needed change from the habit of entrusting all dangerous tasks to small classes highly paid for assuming risks to life—policemen, firemen, professional soldiers. That is the tendency in every high civilization, but it is one that has its perils, as many a once great nation has demonstrated. It is not well that the one thought of too many citizens, on seeing ''trouble'' of any sort, is to back away from it and to think full duty done when a man in uniform has been called to settle it.[15]

We have seen that auxiliary police are not unchecked vigilantes, but serious-minded men and women who have taken the opportunity offered to render service to their city. We may never have a great fire, and we may be outside the earthquake zone, but such citizen participation is surely a value too precious for any democratic society to lose.

5 • The New York Police Reserves

The fears of 1915 and 1916 became the realities of 1917 and 1918 as the United States sent more and more troops overseas. On April 4, 1917, the Senate voted for war against Germany. On May 25, 1917, the Legislature of the State of New York formally authorized the city's police commissioner to appoint citizens to perform duty in the Police Department "during the continuance of the state of war now existing."[1] Under the Selective Service Act of May 18, 1917, the new American army was created and the first American troops arrived in France in June 1917. The ranks of the Police Department were drained of men and by the war's end, the United States was to have dispatched more than 2 million soldiers to the battlefields of Europe.

Contemporary newspaper reports suggested that New York City might be bombed because of Germany's desperation at our entry into the war. One report asserted that a U-boat could launch an attack against our coastal cities, because the latest type of German submarine was capable of carrying six seaplanes which could drop bombs.[2] Statements such as these aroused the people to strengthen their home defenses.

These national events also coincided with a change of guard at City Hall. A new police commissioner, Richard E. Enright,[3] was installed, and one of his first official acts was to order the rechristening of the Home Defense League to "Police Reserves of the City of New York." This announcement came soon after a meeting of six hundred commissioned officers of the league had voted for the change.[4] Undoubtedly, this name change, and other modifications which were to follow, had been at least partly generated by the new state law that had conferred peace officer powers on all persons appointed under its provisions.

A journalist of this period compared the new reserves to the old "rattle-watch," which existed under the Dutch in the 1650s:

In organizing these police reservists we are reviving the plan of the old "Rattle Watch," . . . when the watchmen were admonished to be on duty before bell-ringing under penalty. . . . At this time when the national German bandits and murderers are at large in the world our precautions for guarding the city cannot be too numerous or too painstaking.[5]

Exhibit 1
Chapter 651
Laws of New York, 1917

AN ACT to authorize the police commissioner of the city of New York to appoint citizens to perform duty in the police department of said city during the continuance of the state of war now existing. (Became a law May 25, 1917.)

The People of the State of New York, represented in Senate and Assembly, do enact as follows:

Section 1. During the continuance of the state of war now existing, the police commissioner of the city of New York is hereby authorized and empowered, in his discretion, to select and appoint for service in the police department of the said city and at pleasure remove so many persons, from among citizens, as he may deem necessary, under such titles as he may designate, and define the duties to be performed by such persons, and may delegate to them any of his powers, except the power of making appointments, removals and transfers. Such persons so appointed, pursuant to the provisions of this act, shall serve without pay, until the board of aldermen of the city of New York, upon the recommendation of the board of estimate and apportionment of said city, shall determine that such persons be paid compensation and shall fix the amounts of such compensation. The persons appointed pursuant to the provisions of this act shall be and have all the powers of a peace officer. Nothing in this act shall be construed to constitute any of the persons appointed hereunder members of the police force, or to entitle them to the privileges of the regular members of the police force or to share in the police pension fund. Persons appointed under the provisions of this act shall be exempt from civil service examinations, and the civil service law, rules and regulations and the provisions of any other law or any city ordinance relating to the qualifications, promotion, removal or reinstatement of city employees shall not apply to such persons.

Section 2. This act shall take effect immediately.

Perhaps an even closer comparison can be drawn by recalling the period of the early 1700s when unpaid citizens' watches patrolled the colonial settlement of New York. One author has observed that this system "placed a heavy burden on the poor, who either lost time they could ill afford or had to pay precious cash for substitutes."[6] Of course, membership in the reserves was not compulsory, for the volunteers only provided support for an existing police force, and as later developed, the reserves involved citizens of relative wealth.

The leading proponent behind the Police Reserves was Lewis Rodman Wanamaker (1863–1928), merchant, patron of the arts, aviation enthusiast and supporter and head of the Wanamaker department stores. In February 1918, he was appointed a special deputy police commissioner in charge of the reserves, a nonpaying position. His responsibility involved the task of reshaping the old Home Defense League into a disciplined organization. Wanamaker instituted a formal interview process for the city's newest auxiliary police force, rather than admitting all comers as had the previous body. In addition, a complete set of rules and regulations were drawn; uniforms, badges, service awards and revolver training were planned from the beginning; and air, harbor and mounted squads were recruited. Furthermore, plans were made to recruit a unit of 1,000 men between the ages of nineteen and twenty-eight who would take all emergency and special patrol work assignments. It was intended that after approximately three years of such training the members of this unit would become eligible for direct entry into the ranks of the regular police service. Formal evening classes would cover the same material as that provided for regular police candidates.[7]

The new auxiliary force, forward looking in its approach, also included the first women's division of the Police Reserves. There were nineteen members in the very first unit formed, all of whom happened to be the wives or sisters of regular policemen.[8] In less than a month, nearly 3,000 women had been recruited and were assigned to police stations throughout the five boroughs. Police Inspector John F. Dwyer was given overall authority for the daily conduct and operations of the new reserve force.[9] However, skepticism concerning the value of the women's division was voiced by at least one local newspaper of that prewoman's liberation era:

The natural consequence of giving votes to women is the haste of politicians to confer office upon women and to create position for them as a lure for women voters. . . . But of all the propositions of this kind so far advanced none seems to us so little justified or to hold so little promise as the Police Reserve of Women to be organized by Commissioner Enright. It is to be a volunteer body, organized by inspection districts, and to reach into every block in the city through one resident woman who shall be responsible to the Police Department for the morals of her block. . . . The danger which the plan holds of converting unfounded gossip, or even malice, into official police reports is at least considerable.[10]

Nevertheless, the duties of the Women Reserves as outlined in a general order by Special Deputy Commissioner Wanamaker appeared less suspicious and characteristic of the First World War period:

The duties of the Women's Police Reserve will be to carry on the Auxiliary Red Cross work now being done by the auxiliaries attached to the different precincts; to be vigilant and alert in their respective localities, to discover irregular and unlawful conditions and to report the same to the department; to teach patriotism and civic duty and aid in the Americanization of the alien elements of the population; to detect and report cases of disloyalty and sedition, relieve cases of distress and destitution, comfort the unfortunate, advise and direct the weak, foolish and idle, and set an example of unselfishness and patriotic devotion. Members of the Women's Reserve can be very useful also in looking after boys and girls who may be prone to be delinquent, keeping bad company or pursuing such a course that would lead to crime.[11]

These duties outlined were obviously time-consuming enough to prevent women from having the time to engage in the "unfounded gossip" or "malice" which had been feared.

During the Police Reserve's first summer, a series of field day exercises were held to demonstrate the effectiveness of the men's training and to raise money for the purchase of uniforms and equipment. Among the events on official programs were air shows consisting of planes and crewmen from the First Provisional Wing of the U.S. Army, and concerts performed by noted singing greats, often led by Enrico Caruso, the famous operatic tenor.[12] In the months to come, benefits were held by Caruso which led to his appointment as an honorary captain in the reserves.[13] However, he was not the only celebrity to be given membership. In 1925, Babe Ruth was recruited.[14]

At the height of the reserves activities, there were 14,000 members. Old photographs depict units wearing olive drab uniforms and campaign hats in the style of the soldiers of that day. One unit, numbering four hundred men, was equipped with eight Colt automatic machine guns and three hundred rifles. It was aptly called the "Machine Gun Battalion," and it enjoyed an enviable reputation in Police Reserve circles for "being the only machine gun unit attached to a regular police department in the world."[15]

Meanwhile, the fighting in Europe continued to influence the growth of the auxiliary units. Finally, on November 11, 1918, the struggle on the Western Front ceased when Germany agreed to an armistice. However, the war effort was not over until the Treaty of Versailles when final peace terms were reached with Germany. Furthermore, because of the objections voiced by some senators to a provision of the treaty which called for the establishment of a League of Nations, the war with Germany "did not officially end for the United States until July 2, 1921, when Congress passed a joint resolution declaring that hostilities were over and reserving a victor's rights and privileges."[16] Throughout this extended period, the New York Police Reserve was actively supporting the Police Department in its efforts to keep the nation's largest city safe.

In the spring of 1920, Governor Alfred E. Smith signed a new state law which provided for a permanent force of police reserves as an adjunct to the regular force in the city of New York.[17] This bill was introduced in the legislature by State Senator Charles C. Lockwood of Kings County, who foresaw the necessity of maintaining an emergency pool of trained, disciplined and equipped citizens. The law provided that the new Reserve Police Force could not exceed 5,000 in number, that members would serve without pay and that when ordered to active duty they would have all the powers of a police officer.[18]

Under the mandate of the Lockwood Bill, Commissioner Enright picked the most active members from the old reserves and recruited others. All were to have the same authority as the regular police when assigned to duty and be subject to the rules and regulations of the police department. The city was to provide a regular police uniform for each member. In addition, new orders were established for the mobilization of reservists for extended periods of service.

Exhibit 2
Chapter 711
Laws of New York, 1920

AN ACT to amend the Greater New York charter, in relation to the establishment of a police reserve. (Became a law May 11, 1920.)

The People of the State of New York, represented in Senate and Assembly, do enact as follows:

Section 1. The Greater New York charter, as re-enacted by chapter four hundred and sixty-six of the laws of nineteen hundred and one, is hereby amended by inserting therein a new section, to be section three hundred and eight-b thereof, to read as follows:

Section 308-b. The police reserve of the city heretofore organized under chapter six hundred and fifty-one of the laws of nineteen hundred and seventeen, entitled "An act to authorize the police commissioner of the city of New York to appoint citizens to perform duty in the police department of said city during the continuance of the state of war now existing," shall be continued as the police reserve under the control and jurisidiction of the police commissioner. The police commissioner shall appoint a special deputy, who shall serve without compensation, to command the police reserve, and may detail from time to time such members of the regular force as he may deem necessary to assist in the instruction, drill and administration of its affairs.

Section 2. Such police reserve is to provide a trained, disciplined and equipped force of male citizens, whose services may be called upon by the police commissioner in the event of conditions arising requiring the services of a larger number of men than that constituting the regular force.

Section 3. Enlistment in the police reserve may be obtained under rules to be promulgated by the police commissioner and shall be for a period of two years unless sooner relieved from service in the discretion of such commissioner. No person shall be enlisted as a member of such police reserve unless he be a citizen of the United States, at least five feet five inches in height, able to read, write and speak the English language distinctly, exempt from federal draft, and in good physical condition as evidenced by the certificate of a physician or surgeon.

Section 4. Such police reserve shall not exceed five thousand in number, and may be divided into regiments, battalions or independent units, in the discretion of the police commissioner.

Section 5. The members of the police reserve shall serve without pay. Whenever ordered on active duty by the police commissioner they shall have all the powers of a police officer and be subject to the rules and regulations of the police department.

Section 6. This act shall take effect immediately.

The immediate impact of this command was to deplete the force of many working men, who could not afford to lose their wages because of the new requirement that they could be called upon to devote eight straight hours at a time to a volunteer activity.[19]

Nevertheless, this special branch of the city's police performed increased tours of duty on a number of assignments. A few of these functions included assisting the police in the Brooklyn Rapid Transit strike in 1920;[20] the use of police women reserves for traffic duty, during a milk truck drivers' strike in 1921;[21] and a massive drive to put an end to a rising crime wave in 1922.[22]

The reserves' mobilization in 1922 to aid the police in their efforts to cope with violent criminal acts demonstrated the mutual dependence between the city's police force and its unpaid police auxiliary. Reservists who owned fast-running automobiles were asked to devote them to their crime prevention assignments, and a similar request was made to members owning horses. Soon members were working both evening and daytime patrols, some in uniform and others in plainclothes.[23] Every member was urged to carry his revolver at all times, even when out of uniform,[24] and the reserves continued to carry arms while in civilian clothes until 1926, when a new order was issued barring this practice.[25]

In time, as the roaring twenties unfolded, the Police Reserve program gradually ebbed. A number of causes contributed to its decline. Although a reserve member when called to duty shared all of the hazards of police work, he received few of the privileges accorded the regular officer. For example, he had to pay for his own carfare, his own pistol, and all his incidental expenses. Over a period of nine years, more than 10,500 recruits paid for their own instruction and practice in marksmanship at a private training school. It was reported that the attempt to qualify for the expert's gold badge, which is the highest award presented for revolver qualification, gave rise to the phrase: "Ten dollars for the medal and a thousand dollars worth of ammunition."[26]

A second reason for the curtailment of reserve activities was the weakness in the administration of city government under Mayor Jimmy Walker, whose tenure lasted from 1926 until 1932. Beginning in 1926, New York had three new police commissioners in three years. Significantly, the purposeful utilization of the reserves required the commissioner's initiative and resourcefulness; however, Walker's appointees lacked both qualities and the reserves were disregarded.

By 1928, many reservists were given discharge notices. Some members demanded that a thorough investigation be made into the management of the Police Reserves for the previous two years, but their public appeals failed to prevent their final release.[27]

These events were in stark contrast to the reviews, drills and thrilling air shows held only a decade before when encouragement was given by such officials as Mayor Hylan:

In training and being prepared for any emergency the officers and men enrolled in your ranks are a mighty factor in the cause of law and order, which this Administration is confident can be relied on whenever needed. . . . You set a fine example of patriotic and high public spirit. You sacrifice your time, comfort and convenience by drilling and training so that you may fit yourself to be able to efficiently perform police duty in time of need, without compensation of any kind or hope of reward. In doing this you are rendering real service. And, besides training, you have responded promptly whenever called upon for duty. . . . Your faithful service to the city in the past and your desire for further service are appreciated and will be rewarded as far as is legally possible. Let me assure you I am with you to the end.[28]

A third factor also influenced the deactivation of the Police Reserves. In 1928, Rodman Wanamaker died. His donations of funds and personal attention to all reserve activities were important, but in the long run his preoccupation with the commercial world and aviation interrupted his devotion to the Police Reserves. Lindbergh's achievement in 1927 preceeded by only one month the success of Wanamaker's trimotored airplane in crossing the Atlantic.[29] Thus, it was probable that the reserve was made to take a back seat, while the aviation industry was born.

Perhaps if the Police Reserves had been allowed more representation from the middle class and immigrant populations of the city, the elected officials of that day would have been more responsive to the cause of "good government" through the medium of civic accountability. The active presence of such community groups, participating in their own policing, would have provided a direct channel for a local electorate to have learned about the functioning of many public agencies and to have voiced their findings on Election Day.[30]

The final blow to the reserves was the Depression of 1929. Not only were no new calls issued for their services, but few persons could have afforded to miss the opportunity for any available employment. In 1934, the Police Reserves of the City of New York was abolished by Police Commissioner O'Ryan. Its official elimination was simply a matter of formality inasmuch as the organization had ceased functioning in 1928.[31]

6 • The New York City Patrol Corps

By 1933, the nation was in the hands of Franklin D. Roosevelt, the thirty-second president of the United States, whose New Deal programs were to help rescue the economy, and New York City was under the stewardship of Mayor Fiorello La Guardia, who in 1921, as president of the Board of Aldermen, received a special medal from Deputy Commissioner Wanamaker along with four hundred members of the Police Reserves.[1]

In the same year too, Prohibition was repealed and the sale of liquor could no longer serve as the main source of gangland income. In 1934, Mayor La Guardia appointed Lewis J. Valentine as police commissioner, a career officer, who was "tough, loyal to the Department, and above all honest, the very characteristic that the mayor himself brought to his post."[2] For the next eleven years each of these men would continue in office, leaving the future use of auxiliary forces entirely within their control.

In 1936 both world and local problems created crises for city officials. A new militant Germany came into being and Italy had invaded peaceful Ethiopia. Once again wartime anxieties were aroused. In addition, local power shortages, reminiscent of today's brownouts threw part of the city into darkness. A reliable source of manpower was urgently needed in order to handle serious emergencies, be they temporary internal dilemmas or major threats to national security.

At the behest of the mayor, the heads of the city's major agencies and departments conferred and a plan was developed to survey various civil service groups for available manpower. First, they attempted to learn how many of the city's retired policemen were physically able to respond in the event of an emergency call. Next, they planned to examine all persons who were on the eligibility list for patrolmen.[3] Finally, a survey was to be made of the availability of all the duly licensed special officers who worked in the city although not connected with the Police Department. The men in this category mainly included guards who worked in banks, subways and hospitals.[4] Apparently the surveys yielded unsatisfactory results since no new reserve or auxiliary police force was established until the outbreak of World War II.

On December 7, 1941, the Japanese attacked Pearl Harbor, and the people of the United States were called upon to mobilize themselves for civil defense. Initially, Mayor La Guardia planned to organize a home militia, to be known as the New York City Guard, but he withdrew this proposal when the adjutant general of the New York State Guard, Ames T. Brown,[5] informed him that the state military law prohibited any municipality from organizing a "private army"[6]:

You are quoted in todays press as having made a statement in your radio address yesterday that you intend to organize a military body consisting of a regiment of volunteers to be known as the City Guard. Attorney General Bennett has advised me that under the Military Law of the State, municipalities may not organize military forces or use the word "Guard." Obviously, if the municipalities of the State were given such authority it would result in the setting up throughout the State of hundreds of little armies. If in your opinion additional police protection is needed you already have full authority to recruit additional forces of the regular police or to appoint special patrolmen without pay under Chapter 18 of the N.Y.C. Administrative Code. Moreover you also have the power to organize an auxiliary police force as recommended by the U.S. Director of Civilian Defense. I regret that you did not consult with military authorities of the State prior to making your announcement.[7]

The next day, the mayor presented a modified plan in which he emphasized that he was only contemplating the formation of an auxiliary police organization under the provisions of the applicable laws. On the following day, General Brown replied that he would be glad to cooperate with the mayor's plans for the establishment of auxiliary police forces as recommended by the U.S. Office of Civilian Defense.[8] In this manner, the program was found acceptable to the powers in Albany and Washington, and the incident was closed.

The new organization was called the "City Patrol Corps," and it was to rely heavily upon the veterans' organizations for its first members. In essence, the new body consisted of auxiliary policemen who would patrol the streets between the hours of 4:00 P.M. and midnight, and be assigned to guard bridges, tunnels, acqueducts, airfields and defense factories, thereby relieving regular policemen and army troops for other duty.[9]

Mayor La Guardia named a retired major general of the U.S. Army, Robert M. Danford, to serve as commandant. Danford had been the chief of the army's field artillery, and from 1919 to 1923 was commandant of cadets at the United States Military Academy at West Point.[10] In his foreword to the City Patrol Corps manual of instructions, General Danford wrote:

The New York City Patrol Corps is a Home Front organization, the members of which are proudly volunteering their time and services as a substantial contribution to the National all-out effort to win the war.

The mission of the Corps is to give the Police Department effective assistance, particularly with reference to guarding the greatly increased number of critical points and areas, which, if left unprotected, might tempt the saboteur.

Men from the factory, shop and office are called upon to develop quickly, a high degree of efficiency in this voluntary service. Appropriate study and instruction are required.[11]

The corps was to be distinctly separate from the Police Department. Mayor La Guardia was able to establish this autonomous force because the New York State War Emergency Act[12] granted broad authority to local governments within the state to direct all activities relating to the protection of their civilian populations, expressly authorizing the establishment of volunteer agencies, such as an auxiliary police. Significantly, because this statute did not specify how such agencies were to be structured, Mayor La Guardia was free to organize an auxiliary police force of his own design.

The mayor had originally hoped that 3,500 men and 500 women could be recruited, and as corps membership mounted to nearly 8,000 in less than six months, his modest estimate was more than doubled. From the beginning, physical examinations and fingerprint checks were conducted by the Police Department, and applicants were required to enlist for a period of at least one year. Membership was open to all citizens over nineteen years of age, with no maximum age limitation. Recruiters encouraged men to enroll who were exempt from military duty because of age or slight physical defect. A course of instruction was provided for a period of eight nightly sessions with many subject areas covered such as first aid, basic military drill, local laws and procedures relating to police work, guard duty and revolver practice.

The first members of the corps were easily recognized. They wore khaki coats and woolen pants and were able to purchase additional khaki pants, shirts and black silk ties.[13] A distinguishing emblem was adopted in the form of a cloth shield to be worn on the cap and left shoulder. The design consisted of a blue windmill figure, with the white letters "N.Y.C." above, and the letters "P.C." below it. As soon as availability permitted, members who qualified were equipped with pistols, as well as white steel helmets and nightsticks. Because of wartime shortages—the mayor announced at a press conference—the supply of nightsticks issued to the Patrol Corps would be made from the hardwood legs of confiscated pinball machines.[14] Furthermore, many .38 caliber revolvers which had been seized by the police and thereafter tested for accuracy were turned over to the corps. These weapons became available because the law which had previously required their destruction had been repealed. All male recruits were required to score four out of five hits on a moving target at fifteen yards before being issued a firearm.[15]

The City Patrol Corps was structured along military lines. Colonels, captains, lieutenants, sergeants, privates and other military ranks were utilized. Members had the power to arrest, since all were sworn as special patrolmen; however, they were instructed only to exercise such authority in the defense of their posts and not to arrest for routine infractions of the law.[16]

The City Patrol Corps was organized into five divisions, one to each borough. General headquarters was located at 300 Mulberry Street. Each borough was subdivided into divisions, sections and companies. Aside from the responsibility of providing guards in each police precinct for certain key points,[17] corps detachments were later assigned to nightly street patrols, to assist the regular police. For special emergencies, such as important public meetings, large gatherings, accidents or fires, the City Patrol supplied the extra guards needed. Daily, each precinct reported to corps headquarters its requirements for needed services and personnel. For unforeseen emergencies the corps maintained special reserves on call. Generally, the hours for duty were divided into two shifts, the first from 4:00 P.M. to 8:00 P.M., the second from 8:00 P.M. to midnight. Members could expect to be called for duty about three times every two weeks, unless an emergency arose; minimum service of at least one night a week was usual.[18]

Although by the summer of 1942, membership in the corps had already surpassed 3,500 and there was a waiting list in Brooklyn, Mayor La Guardia, with the cooperation of the City's Director of Selective Service, prepared the following message for all Class 3-A deferment holders:

You have been temporarily deferred from duty with the armed forces by your local draft board, and placed in deferred classification 3-A. This temporary deferment does not entirely relieve you of your civilian responsibilities and patriotic duties to your country.

The City Patrol Corps of the City of New York is now engaged in enrolling men in the duty of guarding places vital to the war effort, which are considered sensitive and vulnerable to sabotage. New York City needs able-bodied men for this service.

You owe it to yourself, your family, and your neighbors to come forward and assist the local authorities protecting your city.

If you fail to apply for enrollment with the City Patrol Corps, your defense status with the protective forces of the city will be reported to the local draft board.

It is suggested that you report within five days from receipt of this notice to the registration office, indicated herein, nearest your home, and present this letter to the City Patrol Corps recruiting officer.[19]

A Class 3-A deferment meant that because of dependents or occupation, a man was not to be in the prime category for the draft. Nevertheless, letters written on the mayor's office stationery such as the one printed above, and signed by him, were mailed out to many registrants by local draft boards. A small controversy errupted when the Selective Service director stated that when he consented to help, he was unaware that the letters would contain any threatening statements. Furthermore, he made it known that no recriminatory action was authorized under existing law against any registrants in a deferred status who refused to join in any civilian defense activities. In reply, Mayor La Guardia asserted: "Anyone who objects to the letters or to the government frank [free mailing privilege employed by the local boards] is a contemptible Fifth Columnist."[20]

Meanwhile, a women's division of the City Patrol Corps was organized. Their assignments were to include clerical work at headquarters and division offices, driving male volunteers to their guard posts, assisting regular policewomen at parks, beaches and other public places and operating canteen facilities. A special concession was extended to those women who volunteered only for clerical duties in that they were not required to be in uniform, drill or take a physical examination. However, the fingerprint check was not waived.[21]

In January 1943, a new kind of corps member was seen on patrol. Company H of the corps included a mounted unit. Each volunteer paid for the use and care of his mount. The horses were rented from a local riding academy. The company's first duties involved safeguarding the areas around Kings County Hospital.[22] Many of the city's streets were dimmed because of the wartime need to conserve power and to prevent enemy submarines from spotting U.S. and Allied ships along the coast. Other corps members on foot patrol were detailed to escort USO volunteers and other persons who feared to go out alone in the darkened city.

As the war years dragged on, the ranks of the police force were thinned by the draft, and civic groups throughout the city brought their complaints of inadequate police protection to the steps of City Hall. When a delegation of clergymen went to see the mayor after a young boy had been beaten, robbed and left in serious condition on one of the city's unlit streets, the mayor responded:

I'll tell you how you can do something about it. Organize, from the membership of your churches, a company to join the City Patrol Corps. You can make your streets and your homes safe.[23]

When further protests concerning the presence of muggers, prowlers and burglars in residential communities were voiced, the mayor publicly stated:

It wasn't so long ago that a gentleman wrote me a letter and sent the letter to the newspapers and got his name in the papers proclaiming that there wasn't sufficient police protection and stating they were going to organize vigilantes. I called the gentleman down and said, "You don't have to organize vigilantes. You can do it in a neighborly, orderly American manner." I told him that they could recruit from their own neighborhood and provide the protection for their families and their homes, but at the meeting that was arranged—the gentleman did not show up. That is what I call a loud-mouth. Now, we are not going to win this war by talking.[24]

In the months that followed, continuous recruitment campaigns were carried on by the corps commanders in each borough. New units were established such as the rowboat and motorcycle patrols in Central Park. In the expectation of attracting new members, judo and jujitsu instruction was made available. In addition, the hours of service were readily adjusted to suit new members. For example, a few Broadway actors were assigned duty in the afternoon, except on Wednesdays and Saturdays when their theatre performances were scheduled.

Meanwhile, women volunteers were offered pistol practice, and some were assigned to Grand Central Terminal in a special Women's Police Aid detail.

Like members of the New York Reserve and Home Defense League of the past, corps members were drawn from all walks of life. When the restriction which limited participation to citizens was lifted, a "United Nations Company" was formed. Many European and Asian refugees, who had recently escaped from their occupied lands, became members, anxious to help in protecting the liberties and freedoms found in this country.

Significantly, the creation of the corps was a departure from national practice, which had the auxiliary police as a branch of the air warden service. Here, the mayor decided to have a separate unit, distinctively uniformed. Indeed, the city did recruit thousands of air wardens, auxiliary firemen, nurses' aides and other defense forces which fell into about twenty different groups. However, membership in the City Patrol Corps was exclusive; applicants could not be affiliated with any of the other agencies of civil defense.[25]

A long-prayed-for day was May 7, 1945, the day that General Jodl, Chief of Staff of the German Army, signed an unconditional surrender; and on September 2, 1945, General MacArthur accepted the formal surrender of Japan, aboard the battleship "Missouri" in Tokyo Bay. America's civil defense emergency was over and the provisions of the War Emergency Act expired upon the announcement of peace in Europe by President Truman. Consequently, from that moment until the corps' last patrol on August 30, 1945, all members who continued to serve did so with the knowledge that their governmental protection against financial loss resulting from injury had ceased, and September 30, 1945, was the corps' official demobilization date.[26]

However, soon after the corps' demobilization, a rapid rise in crime brought to light the corps' valuable contribution. John J. Kenny, the volunteer commander of the city's largest Patrol Corps division, declared:

I believe that the legal protection offered by the War Emergency Act could easily be provided by the City of New York and that it is within the civic powers of the city to act swiftly in the face of a crime situation that could get worse before it gets any better.[27]

In addition, an editorial in support of the reinstitution of the City Patrol Corps appeared:

Vigilantes have been suggested as a remedy. If what is meant by this is something patterned after the loosely organized bands of citizens who took the law in their own hands in . . . pioneering days, we are, naturally dead against it. Such a suggestion has possibilities of much greater evil than the one we are now facing.

But there is one avenue of relief of which we have heard nothing said to date. The Police Department is admittedly undermanned. Under present regulations it will be months before additional police can be enrolled in numbers sufficient to be of any service. They must be trained, must pass rigid civil service tests, must serve probationary periods as rookies. During all of that time the condition for which they are needed gets worse. Why not remobilize the City Patrol Corps?[28]

The editorial went on to state that "they performed many useful services, making arrests, preventing crimes and their presence on the streets must have deterred many a criminal."[29] Nevertheless, Mayor La Guardia turned down the proposal for reassembling the Patrol Corps, and by the time Mayor O'Dwyer took office, the cause had lost its initial momentum.

Every member of the corps was discharged at one rank higher than the one he held. General Danford reported that corps members had served more than 4.3 million patrol hours. At the final ceremonies held in honor of the disbanded companies of the Patrol Corps, Mayor La Guardia expressed the hope that the people of New York would some day truly come to appreciate their service, and added:

Your services were essential, useful and necessary. You walked the beat day and night, in all kinds of weather; you took the rap now and then, but you stuck to your post. . . .

Let some of the barflies and night club bums come out and do a little work.[30]

This final note of bitterness in Mayor La Guardia's remarks may provide a clue as to why he decided to dissolve the City Patrol Corps. It was a well-known fact that throughout La Guardia's third term, he actively sought a presidential appointment that would free him from his toils at City Hall. However, his wartime service was limited to civilian defense and propaganda broadcasts to Italy. One author has particularized La Guardia's frustrations in this way:

La Guardia's aspiration to become a general did not do him or his city any good. Some of his friends concede that it diverted his attention from municipal affairs. . . . His frustrations with respect to the overseas job when added to his disappointment with OCD,[31] the difficulty of running the city during the war and perhaps his own failing health, filled his last years with bitterness.[32]

Furthermore, La Guardia's loss of enthusiasm and popularity, culminating in his decision not to seek a fourth term certainly contributed to his decision to retire the City Patrol Corps, which was after all his own singular creation.[33]

Although the corps was not originally formed to patrol the streets as a deterrent to crime, local needs and the shortage of regular police combined to bring this about. In addition, when the danger of attack by enemy raiding and sabotage squads became slight, more and more members were reassigned to crime prevention work. In this way, the City Patrol Corps unquestionably strengthened the forces against civil disorder and helped to preserve our democratic system in a period of world upheaval.

7 • The Civil Defense Auxiliary Police

During World War II, Mayor William O'Dwyer (1946–1950) was a brigadier general in the army, and in the years when the Police Reserve rendered service, he was a policeman who spent his off duty hours attending law school. The years of his administration coincided with a great city apartment shortage, labor strikes and a police scandal involving protection payments of over one million dollars a year.[1] Such problems must have preoccupied the city's new chief executive and contributed to the brief hiatus in the history of the auxiliary police which took place during the last years of the forties. The serious state of world conditions, however, was soon to dictate the need for its continued service.

On June 25, 1950, the North Korean Army crossed the 38th parallel into South Korea. The Security Council of the United Nations held North Korea accountable for the invasion. On the next day, President Truman ordered American military forces to help the South Koreans.

Meanwhile, Mayor O'Dwyer named Arthur Wallander, his former police commissioner, to be the director of the city's new civil defense effort.[2] Wallander immediately tackled the numerous tasks necessary to protect the city such as forming plans for air-raid drills, evacuation, fire-fighting, clearance of debris and damaged structures, air-raid shelters, decontamination, emergency medical and welfare aid and the registration of necessary volunteers. His plans also called for the organization of an auxiliary police corps. A total of 40,000 men and women would be sought to more than double the strength of the regular uniformed police. The volunteer force was to be patterned after the regular police system, but members would have military titles.[3] In effect, the Civil Defense Auxiliary Police was to be a revival of the organizations which had preceded it.

On December 16, 1950, President Truman declared a state of national emergency because a few weeks before Red China had sent in her own forces and had retaken Seoul for the North Koreans.[4] New York City's civil defense network, which had been in the planning stages for almost six months, was now put into effect. In the final organization chart, the city's defenses were divided into five divisions: Police Emergency, Fire, Public Works, Health and Emergency Welfare. The auxiliary police and rescue service came under the Police Emergency Division. (Charts 1, 2 and 3 set forth relationships among the city's civil defense network and particularize the hierarchy of the auxiliary police.) All the facilities of the mass media were called upon to aid in the recruitment of volunteers. The *New York Times* carried the following announcement:

Auxiliary Police Corps—Requirements: Physically strong men and women, responsive to discipline, ''capable of commanding respect.'' Duties: General police work supplementing the regular force; anti-looting, anti-sabotage guard; assistance to other services in air raids.[5]

The complete list of official requirements for enrollment, included the following qualifications: 1. at least twenty-one years of age; 2. U.S. citizenship or declared intention of becoming a citizen; 3. city residence; 4. no prior felony conviction or serious misdemeanor; 5. sufficient fluency in English to carry out assignments; 6. excellent character and good reputation; 7. sufficient intelligence, good judgment, tact and initiative; 8. no serious physical or mental condition.[6]

By the end of January 1951, more than 6,000 men and women had joined the auxiliary police. A cadre of auxiliary police superior officers were recruited for each borough by civil defense headquarters in consultation with the commanding officers of police precincts. In many instances, former police officers, military officers and officers of the City Patrol Corps were chosen for executive posts. A special training class was established for them so that they could return to their local police precincts and instruct the new recruits. This course known as the Instructors Command and Leadership School covered such subjects as police authority, the penal law, rules of evidence, techniques of modern warfare, sabotage, espionage, and in turn all recruits had to pass a primary course in these same subject areas.[7]

In later months, the Civil Defense Bureau of the Police Department established a regular program for auxiliary police training. It consisted of required intermediate and advanced courses for those members who aspired to higher ranks of service. (In general, these courses are still in effect today and usually involve nine sessions of three hours each. In addition, in-service lectures are provided by police experts throughout the year, with teaching and supervision carried out by members of the police department.)

To a large degree, the first year of the city's new auxiliary police corps involved planning, organizing and training. However, by March 1952, the volunteers were participating in full-scale civil defense training. For example, the men and women were called upon to respond to simulated bombing incidents of various degrees of severity by being stationed at emergency call boxes to facilitate communications, and by being available to direct responding emergency vehicles and to guide evacuees to shelter. Often as a final touch of realism, young volunteers, presumed lost, were assisted by auxiliary policewomen, and looters would be arrested in the ruins of a simulated disaster scene. While this show was taking place, other volunteers sought prospective recruits from among the spectators.[8]

In order to be prepared for any major disaster that might befall the city, the auxiliaries treated the air-raid drills as if each alarm was the real thing. The volunteers were presented with theoretical problems involving air, ground, and underwater atom bomb bursts, chemical and bacteriological warfare, high explosive and fire bomb damage. On numerous occasions, practice air-raid drills required auxiliaries to evacuate tenants, aid the injured, help survey the scene to determine whether there was any contamination and protect homes and property.

Similar exercises continued throughout the duration of the Korean War and into the midfifties. The city's "CD Police," as they were then called, never failed in their enthusiasm for the program.[9] Of course, there were at times complaints from the auxiliaries: some volunteers felt they were given too few assignments, and in nearby Yonkers, some auxiliary police in civil defense resigned because their proposed uniforms had been described as "costumes fit for circus clowns, storm troopers and space patrolmen."[10]

The officially approved uniform for the city's auxiliary police included a regulation blue shirt, with grey piping on the shoulder strap, dark blue trousers, square top overseas cap with grey piping and a grey tie and belt. In addition, a gray cloth shield was worn over the shirt pocket on the left side by patrolmen, and a gold embroidered shield was worn by officers. The "CD" emblem adopted by the state of New York was prominent in the design and similar cloth arm patches in a triangular shape were also used so that the volunteers could be easily identified by the many city-dwellers whom they were to assist.

On July 27, 1953, the Korean armistice was signed at Panmunjom, but the Cold War and the threat of nuclear attack made necessary the continuance of our defense measures since it was assumed that any attack would be against our major centers of population and industry. Unquestionably, the most critical target area facing attack was the city of New York.

The advent of the hydrogen bomb redirected civil defense planning in that a greater emphasis was placed on fallout shelter preparation than on the mobilization of the city's volunteers. Consequently, although 20,000 auxiliaries had been recruited during the Korean War, that number gradually declined. However, before the latter half of the 1950s, the Civil Defense Auxiliary Police began to concentrate on a different problem. Significantly, on the evening of December 4, 1953, with only twenty-four hours notice, approximately 4,000 auxiliaries reported as directed for active duty between the hours of eight and midnight.[11] This marked the beginning of the nightly patrols which are still in progress in each of the police precincts within the city.

The new duties of the volunteer police involved more than the limited training for such natural disasters as fires, floods and hurricanes. Paralleling the earlier City Patrol Corps, the auxiliaries were soon engaged in the prevention of

Chart 1
Auxiliary Police Organization Chart, 1950

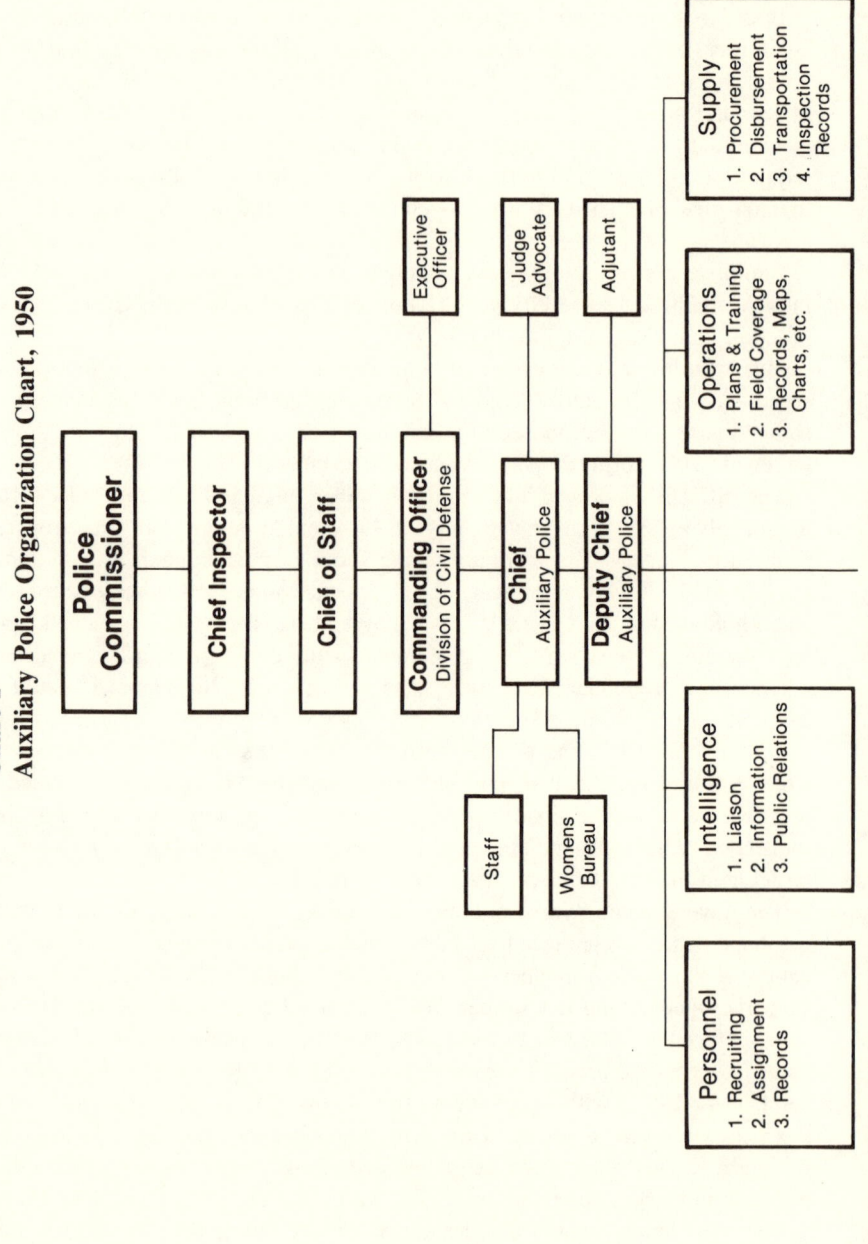

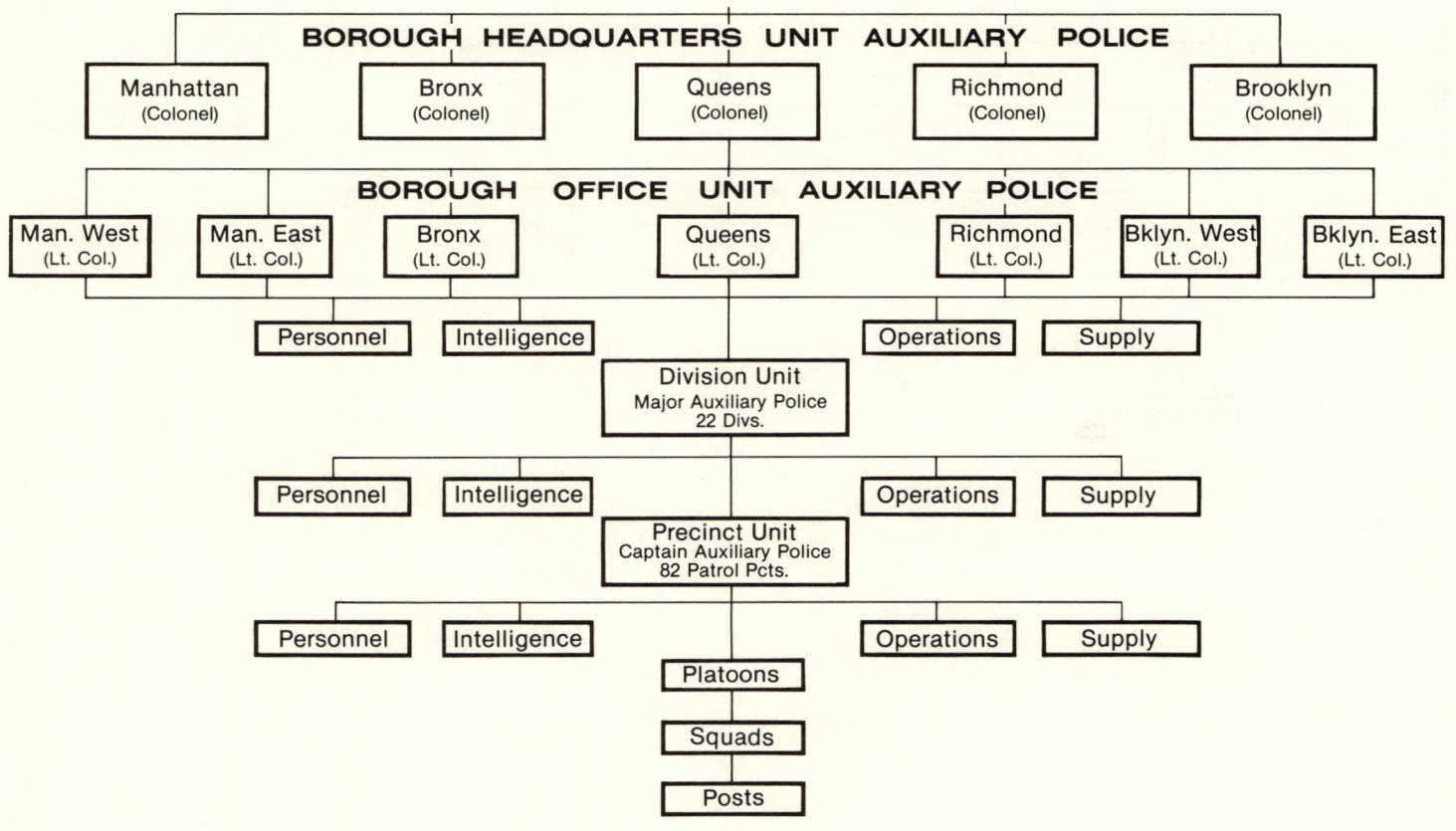

BOROUGH HEADQUARTERS UNIT AUXILIARY POLICE

| Manhattan (Colonel) | Bronx (Colonel) | Queens (Colonel) | Richmond (Colonel) | Brooklyn (Colonel) |

BOROUGH OFFICE UNIT AUXILIARY POLICE

| Man. West (Lt. Col.) | Man. East (Lt. Col.) | Bronx (Lt. Col.) | Queens (Lt. Col.) | Richmond (Lt. Col.) | Bklyn. West (Lt. Col.) | Bklyn. East (Lt. Col.) |

Personnel | Intelligence | Operations | Supply

Division Unit
Major Auxiliary Police
22 Divs.

Personnel | Intelligence | Operations | Supply

Precinct Unit
Captain Auxiliary Police
82 Patrol Pcts.

Personnel | Intelligence | Operations | Supply

Platoons

Squads

Posts

Chart 2
Office of Civil Defense City of New York, 1951

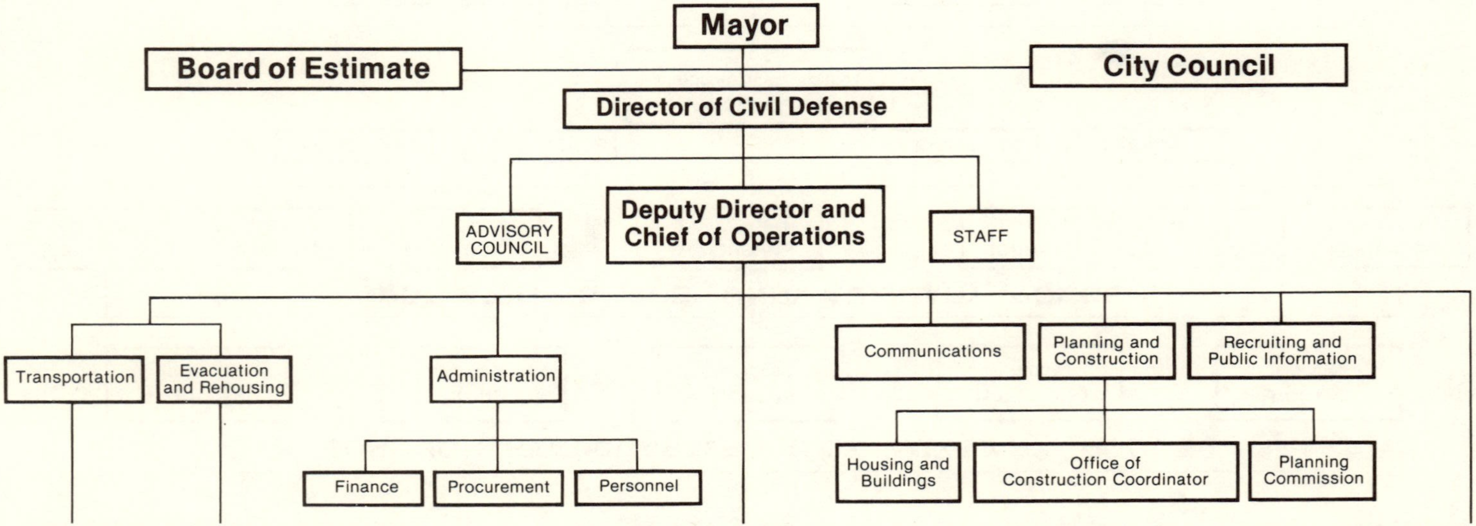

Organization chart — emergency services.

Transportation	Evacuation and Rehousing	Police Emergency	Fire Emergency	Public Works Emergency	Medical Emergency	Welfare Emergency	Public Health	Control and Report Centers
Board of Transportation	Board of Education	Uniformed Police Force	Uniformed Fire Force	Dept. of Public Works	Dept. of Hospitals	Dept. of Welfare	Dept. of Health	City Central Control
Dept. of Marine and Aviation	Dept. of Welfare	Auxiliary Police Corps	Auxiliary Fire Corps	Borough Works (5)	Chief Medical Examiner	Dept. of Markets	Dept. of Sanitation	Borough Control Centers
Railroads	Police Dept.	Air Warden Service	Auxiliary Communication Corps	Dept. of Sanitation	American Red Cross	American Red Cross	Volunteer Teams	Precinct Report Centers
Bus Lines	Dept. of Hospitals	Emergency Taxi Corps		Dept. of Housing and Buildings	American Women's Voluntary Services	Salvation Army		
Trucks	Dept. of Health			Dept. of Water Supply, Gas and Electricity	Private and Voluntary Hospitals	American Womens Voluntary Services		
Steamship Lines	Private and Parochial Schools			Dept. of Parks	Auxiliary Medical and Nursing Corps	Private Welfare Agencies		
Air Lines	Dept. of Traffic			Dept. of Marine and Aviation	Auxiliary Ambulance Corps			
Liaison with Port of New York Authority	Liaison with Federal Agencies			Public Utilities	Coordinating Committee of Hospital Services			
Triborough Bridge and Tunnel Authority	New York State and County Agencies			Private Contractors	Coordinating Committee of Medical Services			
				NYC Housing Authority				
				Board of Transportation				
				Port of NY Authority				
				Tri-Boro Br. & Tun. Auth.				
				Board of Water Supply				
FUNCTIONS	**FUNCTIONS**	**FUNCTIONS**	**FUNCTIONS**	**FUNCTIONS**	**FUNCTIONS**	**FUNCTIONS**	**FUNCTIONS**	**FUNCTIONS**
Develop Transport Schedules for Evacuation	Evacuation Planning	Patrol	Fire Preventing	Demolition and Clearance	Collection and Treatment of Casualties by Hospitals	Emergency Welfare Centers	Sanitation and Hygiene	Communications and Operating Centers for Dispatching Services
Provide Transport Facilities for Movement of Personnel and Supplies	Selection and Assembly of Evacuees	Traffic	Fire Fighting	Road and Sewer Repairs	Casualty Stations	Emergency Rest Centers	Radioactive, Chemical and Bacteriological Detection	
	Designation of Assembly Points for Transportation	Bomb Reconnaissance Wardens		Utility Repairs	Emergency Medical Field Units	Central Registration Bureau	Decontamination	
	Evacuee Destination	Fire Watchers		Heavy Rescue Squads	Medical and Stretcher Teams (First Aid Posts)	Mass Feeding Stations		
	Rehousing of Evacuees	Light Rescue Squads		Illumination Control	Mortuary Service	Congregate Shelters		
		Messenger Service						
		Building Control						
		Report Center Management						
		Air Raid Warning Transmission						

Liaison boxes:

- Liaison with US Government, NY State Counties, Other States and the Armed Forces
- Liaison with City Departments and Agencies
- Liaison with Public Utilities
- Liaison with Veterans Organizations and other Private Cooperating Agencies

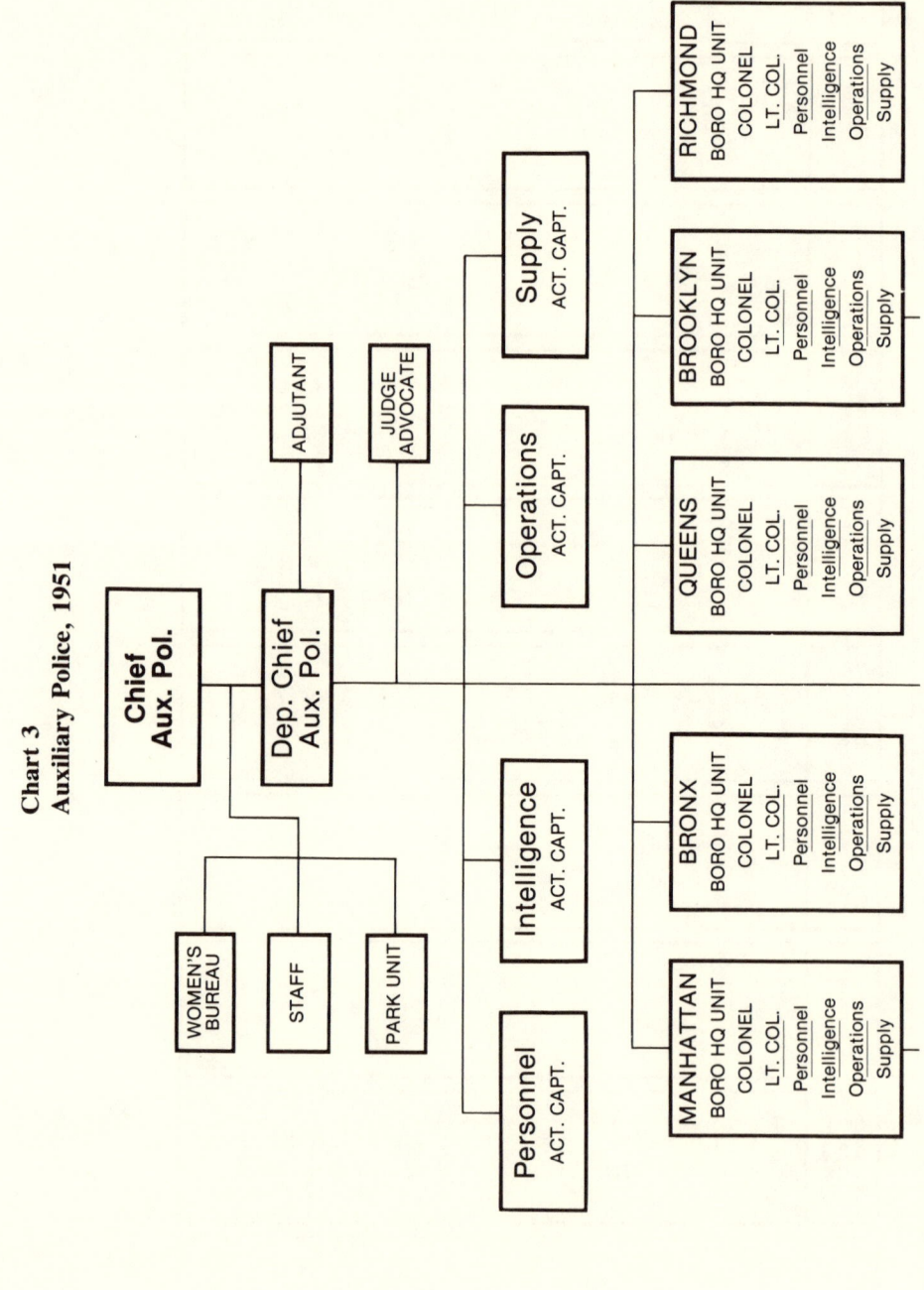

Chart 3
Auxiliary Police, 1951

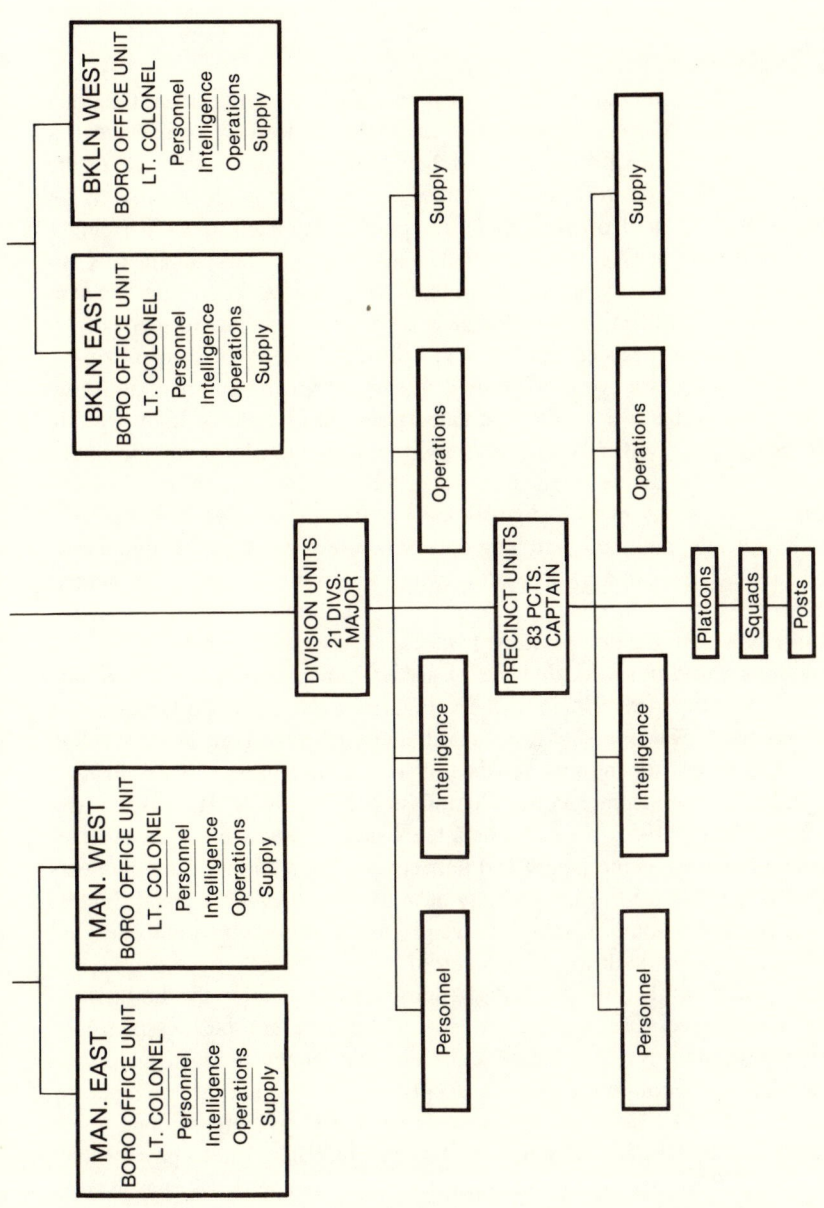

street crime. Special patrols of CD auxiliary police undertook evening patrol work. The neighborhood civic associations now sought the help of the auxiliary police in the same way they had relied on the Patrol Corps members in the World War II period. Frequently, local community groups merely contacted their police precinct if they felt trouble brewing, and auxiliaries were assigned to special neighborhood posts.

This pattern of assigning the volunteer police was a departure from the practices of the past. Anticrime assignments for the Police Reserve of the twenties were made only by direct order of the police commissioner. In the case of the City Patrol Corps of the forties, such duties generally came about through the initiative of the mayor. However, under the plans formulated by Civil Defense and police officials in December of 1953, each local precinct captain was authorized to assign auxiliary policemen in pairs for patrol work. Needless to say, from that time the utilization of volunteers varied from precinct to precinct.

By the time Russia placed Sputnik I in orbit in October 1957, members of the city's auxiliary force were being used in ever increasing numbers on traffic posts, in parks, at parades and public gatherings and in areas of high juvenile crime. During this period and on into the sixties, a visitor to a local precinct house after work would be likely to encounter a small assembly of uniformed auxiliaries carefully picking up their nightsticks, looping the rawhide carrying strap around their hands, and then marching outside, more often than not, into a cold or rainy night. They came to do a little extra to help protect their community; yet they received no remuneration, no uniforms, and no reimbursement for travel. In fact, the only item the city provided free of charge was an identification card.

Many units raised funds for their necessary equipment by holding dances and other functions. In many instances, the volunteers contributed the largest sums at these events. It was apparent to all that the city of New York was providing little encouragement for the maintenance of its volunteer police. This situation was highlighted when former Police Commissioner Francis W. H. Adams, who served from 1953 to 1955, appeared on a television interview program and criticized the auxiliaries as inefficient and unnecessary. In addition, the volunteers were threatened with a $100 fine or sixty days in jail if they wore metal shields. The crisis prompted some members to resign; others said they would quit, and in a few instances work slowdowns occurred.[12]

Colonel Mortimer Kashinsky, the auxiliary commander for the borough of Queens, commented that "most auxiliary policemen are businessmen and homeowners putting in a lot of time and their own money trying to help their country, city, and community and are deeply hurt by the allegations made by Adams."[13] Robert E. Condon, the city's director of Civil Defense, said he favored the metal badges and regretted the fact that members had to pay for their own uniforms.[14] At that time Police Commissioner Michael J. Murphy had rejected the repeated requests of the auxiliaries for metal shields on the grounds that they were not peace officers and that too many agencies outside the Police Department had shields.[15]

As a direct consequence of the concern felt by many members over these issues, a number of volunteers organized the Auxiliary Police Benevolent Association. They believed that only by the formation of an interest group could the auxiliary police be maintained and a way be found to cope with the city's indifference. Since its inception in 1964, under the leadership of Graham Mark Schneider[16] and John Hyland who has held the presidency since 1974, the association has been the voice of the auxiliaries in their struggle for recognition and fair treatment.

Because of the lack of support for and knowledge of the Auxiliary Police, various communities organized substitutes. Often labeled as "vigilante organizations" by the press, they were generally short-lived. Most were undisciplined, ill-equipped, provided no character investigation of their members, offered no training and in the event of accident offered no compensation.[17]

One notable exception to the general rule was the volunteer civilian patrol in the Crown Heights section of Brooklyn, known as the "Maccabees." The group, which was founded and directed by Rabbi Samuel Schrage from 1964 until it disbanded in 1971, claimed to have a peak membership of five hundred men. They patrolled unarmed in cars equipped with two-way radios and large flashlights. No doubt, prevailing local needs, capable leadership and religious ties were responsible for their endurance. Eventually, many former Maccabees joined the auxiliary police unit in that community.[18]

A disastrous plane crash in 1960, the visits of world leaders to the United Nations, the Cuban missile crisis, the great electrical power failure in 1965 and the visit of Pope Paul VI were but a few of the occasions during the sixties when the auxiliary police and its emergency service units turned out in force to give unselfishly of their time to aid the Police Department.

Less momentous perhaps, but nevertheless significant, was their dedication during a period of civil disorders and rising crime. They rendered service at church crossings, beaches, parades, concerts, dances and all other large public gatherings. They patrolled unprotected areas in the late hours of the evening, such as hospitals, bus and subway stops. They reported criminal activity, obtained witnesses and rendered first aid. Above all else, their uniformed presence while they diligently walked their beats served to deter crime.

8 • The Auxiliary Patrol Force

By the midsixties there were approximately 3,000 auxiliary police volunteers in the city. However, less than half of that number were actively engaged in patrol work on a regular basis. The majority held reserve status for use only in an emergency. For more than a decade, official orders for the auxiliaries had been channeled to the local volunteer units from the city's Civil Defense Headquarters, under the leadership of a salaried Chief of Auxiliary Police. However, by 1966, the auxiliary chief only supervised the Shelter Management Section, whereas the day-to-day operations of auxiliary police supervision were administered by the Civil Defense Bureau within the Police Department. This unit, composed of a handful of regular police officers, also had the responsibility for recruiting and training auxiliary personnel. In the same year, Mayor Lindsay received a report from his staff recommending that the Police Department have complete charge of the auxiliary and rescue service.[1]

Timothy J. Cooney, the man chosen by the mayor to serve as an interim director of Civil Defense, pointed out that at the scene of any disaster the police are always in charge. Confusion was encountered when "some CD official would come around and flash his badge and start ordering the CD auxiliary police to do this while the police wanted them to do that."[2] In order to correct the problem, so that there would be no doubt in anyone's mind as to who would be in charge during an actual emergency, Cooney urged that the auxiliary police should be placed directly under the control of the police. His report also included tables and charts showing the economic advantages to be derived to the city by switching the various sections of civil defense to other existing agencies. Consequently, in September 1967, Mayor Lindsay formally abolished the positions of Chief of Auxiliary Police and Commandant of Civil Defense Wardens, closed down the building serving as Civil Defense headquarters in Manhattan and placed fire and police auxiliary forces under the command of their respective city departments. Altogether, 125 jobs were eliminated. In the event of any disaster, the mayor's Emergency Control Board was to assume the coordination and direction of planning.[3]

However, these actions were only the beginning of many changes to be initiated under the Lindsay administration. The auxiliary police really took on a new image when Police Commissioner Howard Leary announced that for the first time in their sixteen year history, a metal shield would be authorized. It was to replace the old-style cloth patch which had been the object of much bitterness in the past. Previously, the use of their grey-colored accessories, such as ties, belts and uniform piping, had been abandoned by the members themselves. Police officials chose a seven-pointed design for the new badge, a symbol of law enforcement more commonly used in the West than in New York.[3]

In succeeding weeks, Commissioner Leary announced the start of a major effort to recruit new members. Diversified new duties were promised, such as permitting patrol with members of the regular force and rendering clerical assistance to local detective squads.[4] For the most part however, these assignments did not materialize. Perhaps the reasons for this had to do with the hiring of new civilian administrative aides, as well as the pressures exerted by the powerful Patrolmen's Benevolent Association which had always resisted any form of civilian participation because that would deter the hiring of more police.[5]

Nevertheless, a dramatic increase in auxiliary enrollment was achieved. Many events contributed to this success. For example, the Central Park Auxiliary Police Unit placed continuous ads in the local press, noting the issuance of metal shields in order to attract members.[6] The Police Department printed thousands of recruitment posters which were circulated in every neighborhood so that local merchants could display them in their store windows. Additional help came from feature stories published in the city's major newspapers. When the *Daily News* carried a full page photo story about the auxiliary police who patrolled Brooklyn's Prospect Park on horseback, fifty new members were recruited.[7] A tremendous boost for the auxiliaries came when Mayor Lindsay appeared with Commissioner Leary on the mayor's weekly television show. Mayor Lindsay urged New Yorker's to join the auxiliary police in the community in which they lived or where they worked. In subsequent years, the mayor continued to use this medium to promote leadership. Historically, his initial appeal was the first to have occurred since the time of Mayor La Guardia's call for City Patrol Corps recruits.[8]

Meanwhile, through the chain of command headed by Chief Inspector Sanford Garelick, police commanders on the borough level openly appealed for volunteer police. In Queens, Assistant Chief Inspector Alexander Kahn remarked:

We welcome this kind of civilian participation because it brings another segment of the public in close contact with the police.

We also feel with their intimate knowledge of persons and places in their own community, the police would be more able to work more effectively in coping with many of the problems. . . . They would be the eyes and ears of the community and in this way help stamp out the trouble makers and create better conditions for the children and adults.[9]

By these means of official sanction, the old civil defense corps was being replaced by a new community self-defense organization. At the same time, our military involvement in Southeast Asia seemed to have furthered interest in auxiliary police work at home.

In 1968, some members of the city's legislature proposed the establishment of a paid auxiliary police force. The first movement in that direction was made by John J. Santucci who introduced a bill for an experimentally paid group to work in his election district. When Councilman Santucci became a state senator, a second bill was introduced by Councilman Lawrence Bernstein, which provided for a paid corps of auxiliary police throughout the entire city. Neither bill has ever been enacted.[10] When one newspaper reporter of that period interviewed the members of a local volunteer unit on the subject of salaries, he learned, interestingly enough, that they would have preferred the city to contribute to the cost of their uniforms and transportation expenses.[11]

For a very brief time in the spring of 1968, one experimental and unarmed paid civilian patrol corps actually saw service in the Harlem community. The project was sponsored by the Vera Institute of Justice and the mayor's Criminal Justice Coordinating Council. About 42 corpsmen, all between the ages of eighteen and thirty, were provided with distinctive tan jackets with suede collars and walkie-talkie radios. They were briefed on crime reporting and self-defense tactics by police instructors. Their purpose was to prevent crime, provide community services, bridge the gap between the community and the police and provide employment opportunities for the young men involved. In general, the corps was designed to operate independently of the area's police.[12] From time to time, during the ensuing years, similar community service groups have been organized depending upon the availability of federal funding. Some were sponsored by various Model Cities Programs and their recruits were called community service officers.[13]

At first glance it might appear that these groups duplicate the work of the unpaid auxiliaries; but it is much too soon to draw any conclusions about such small units which usually operate only during the daytime. Nevertheless, many police volunteers who serve in those sections of the city where such patrols work, might find it difficult to understand why these programs disregard them. For example, when walkie-talkie equipment was provided to the Harlem corps, the auxiliary police had none. Not until a year later did the use of extra precinct mobile radios become authorized.[14]

Throughout most of the decade of the sixties, Captain Emile E. Racine served as the commanding officer of the Civil Defense Bureau. He assisted in the transition which made the auxiliary police an active patrol organization. Under his tenure the Police Department assumed full responsibility for the selection, assignment and training of the auxiliary police. In 1967 he coordinated the redrafting of the regulations of auxiliary conduct to conform with regular police procedures. Racine gave every volunteer a feeling of special pride and satisfaction by his enthusiastic participation at semiannual graduation and award ceremonies. On such occasions, auxiliary members and their families were invited to the Police Academy. There they were honored by the highest ranking police and public officials. Racine served as master of ceremonies and supervised the entire evening's program. He achieved public attention as the commanding officer of the 77th Precinct. It happened that his service at the Brooklyn precinct coincided with those of Dave Greenberg and Bob Hantz. As plainclothes officers, they earned the nicknames "Batman and Robin" because of their courageous police work. Racine received other demanding assignments and earned additional promotions until his retirement in 1975.

The auxiliary police made the transition from the decade of the 1960s to the 1970s by welcoming a new police commissioner, Patrick Murphy. "In my 23 years as a lawyer," said Eugene Gold, the Brooklyn District Attorney, "there was no Commissioner who compared with him as a leader and as an innovator." [15] On the other hand, Robert M. McKiernan, president of the Patrolmen's Benevolent Association said, "He should have been a commissioner of social service and not a commissioner of police." [16] If, on the eve of the commissioner's retirement, reporters would have questioned members of the auxiliary police, they would have been told how this one man with the aid of an equally competent staff totally revitalized the auxiliary program.

Until November 1971, the Civil Defense Section of the Police Department supervised the auxiliary program. In that month, by order of Commissioner Murphy, it was redesignated the Auxiliary Forces Section within the Office of the Deputy Commissioner of Community Affairs. [17] Furthermore, the auxiliary police and rescue service became, respectively, the Auxiliary Patrol Force and the Auxiliary Emergency Service Force. At the same time, the morale of the volunteers was considerably raised by the change from old military titles used since 1951 to ranks employed within the Police Department. For example, colonels and majors became, respectively, auxiliary inspectors and deputy inspectors. [18] By the following year, a new shoulder patch and hat insignia bearing the member's shield number were added. The shoulder patch replaced a triangular "CD" patch, a relic from the early fifties. The new shoulder emblem was an exact duplicate of those newly designed for the members of the regular police, except that the word "AUXILIARY" was included at the top of the emblem. In addition, for the first time, auxiliary policewomen were permitted to join their male counterparts on foot patrol.

Another major step taken by the Police Department during this period of revitalization was to inform the members of the regular police about the nature and function of the auxiliary force. This aim was accomplished through the use of the department's in-service training programs, as well as by the appearance of special articles within the pages of department publications and bulletins. Unquestionably, it was Commissioner Murphy's goal to bring about a more complete unity or meshing of the auxiliaries into the overall structure of the police system.

In succeeding months, a massive recruiting campaign was mounted. Within two years, the number of active auxiliary members doubled, even though more than a thousand inactive personnel were discharged. Barry Farber, a leading radio personality in New York, devoted large segments of his broadcasts for the purpose of publicizing the need for more auxiliary police. His guests included Benjamin Ward, the deputy commissioner of Community Affairs, and Deputy Inspector Robert Luhrs, the commanding officer of the Auxiliary Forces Section. Later on, Barry Gray, another leading nighttime radio personality, actually joined one of the auxiliary police mounted troops located in Manhattan.

It is noteworthy that Inspector Luhrs instituted continuous primary training courses, so that a minimum amount of time would elapse between a newcomer's initial application and training. Furthermore, he circulated a newsletter to keep all members informed of current activities and achievements. Inspector Luhrs revealed his concern for a successful program in this way:

I've been a policeman for 30 years and I've worked in some awful places. . . . And I know that in awful places there are a hell of a lot of good people—a hell of a lot. My hopes for the auxiliary police is that anyone who is of that mind will do something, whether it is auxiliary or whatever. . . . If people can get to the point where they realize that there is some good in this community, and this city has some value, and we can save this city, and we want to do this thing, then I think we have a real good hope for the future.[19]

Of course, all of these measures were undertaken in recognition of the need to cut crime by having sufficient volunteers to patrol on as many evenings as possible. In 1972 alone, the members of the Auxiliary Patrol and Emergency Forces were awarded approximately 600 citations for services rendered beyond the call of duty. Their performances included the capture of arsonists; the rescue of outnumbered policemen; the subduing of armed robbers and muggers; the rendering of life-saving first aid to drowning, accident and heart attack victims; the evacuation of burning buildings; and long arduous details at scenes of disaster.

Naturally, not all auxiliary patrols are especially dramatic; however, many members have been cited for bravery. For example:

Auxiliary Patrolman Robert Goldberg saw three men, one armed with a revolver, sticking up a gas station. When the suspects saw Patrolman Goldberg they fled. He put the victim in a cab and pursued the man with the gun. At the same time he reported the incident via his two-way radio. When the gunman ran into an apartment house, Patrolman Goldberg remained outside, blocking his escape, until the regular police came and made an arrest. It was later learned that the holdup men were about to shoot their victim when Patrolman Goldberg arrived.[20]

Another incident involved off-duty Auxiliary Patrolman Nestor Henriquez as he was walking past a bar and grill in Brooklyn at 7:30 one night.

Looking through a window, he saw two men robbing a patron. He waited by the door. One of the robbers came out and Patrolman Henriquez slipped handcuffs on him. At that moment, the second robber came out, saw what was happening and started firing a revolver. The patrolman took cover, and the handcuffed man got away. The armed robber also fled, but Patrolman Henriquez ran after him and quickly caught him.[21]

However, the objective of the auxiliary police is not to perform heroics since the mere appearance of uniformed auxiliary personnel in an area has resulted in the prevention of crime. Moreover, in the event of a false arrest or any other type of civil lawsuit, the Corporation Counsel of the City of New York will provide legal representation only in cases where they determine that the facts warrant it. In addition, in the event of a judgment against an individual auxiliary police officer, the city will not pay such judgment.[22]

In February 1973, Commissioner Murphy ordered a halt to all auxiliary patrols after several attacks had occurred on regular uniformed police. He feared that the auxiliaries, whose uniforms were almost identical to those of the regular police, might also become the victims of ambush. After a week passed, members were given special instructions on how to patrol in civilian clothes; and many were equipped with two-way police radios to carry beneath their winter overcoats. Thereafter, on a local level, each regular precinct commander was authorized to decide whether the traditional uniform patrols could be resumed. In a short time, all units were functioning again with the volunteers willing to risk the hazards of the street.[23]

The early 1970s involved a period of vast growth for the city's auxiliary police force. However, not every plan for the utilization of the auxiliaries was carried out. Robert Daley, a former deputy police commissioner for Public Information, has disclosed details about one of them.

There were meetings between Deputy Commissioner Ward and myself during which we made grandiose plans for the auxiliary police. . . . Ward and I saw the chance in the model precinct to recruit young businessmen as auxiliary police, particularly men who spoke Spanish. We could begin to integrate bilingual young men into normal patrol operations. We could start with one such auxiliary riding in the back of a radio car. Whenever the car responded to the call of a Spanish-speaking citizen, the auxiliary cop could stand as surrogate for the real cops. Carefully supervised, such a squad of auxiliary cops could earn the respect of patrolmen. Eventually, hopefully, we would wind up with one cop and one auxiliary in many cars, as was currently done in Washington.[24]

In the spring of 1974, another plan was developed by the Police Department. The idea was to enlist additional women members into the auxiliary police for daytime patrols in small neighborhood parks. The plan never achieved fruition or further publicity. Housewives with young children wouldn't enroll, nor were the thousands of working wives about to give up their daytime employment for a police uniform and no pay. Furthermore, many women already held part-time jobs in their local neighborhoods as school aides and crossing guards. Had the plan succeeded, it would have marked the first occasion that women members were permitted to patrol by themselves.[25]

Perhaps the most apt description of the mood during this period was captured by Catherine Calvert, an editor for a popular women's magazine. In 1973 she joined the 17th Precinct unit in order to write an insider's story about the auxiliary program. Her feature article concluded:

As a reporter inside the auxiliary police, I learned a lot during those weeks besides fingerprint types and degrees of arson. A lot about the police, a world in some ways hermetically sealed and bulked with self-defensive pride, but coping in situations that left me rattling. . . . And about the auxiliaries, some drawn to the force by the glitter of the badge and the instant swagger of the nightstick; a great many more, honestly concerned about the situation in the streets, donating thousands of hours of what is often basically boring work. It isn't something I'd want to do permanently—I don't enjoy the discipline or the militarism—but the more APs, the fewer Kitty Genovese stories, and I'm glad there're people willing to come out of their high-rise cocoons and walk a beat with the auxiliary police.[26]

9 . City in Crisis

The Auxiliary Police Force does yeoman work supplementing the efforts of the Police Department in keeping law and order in the massive city that is New York.

The auxiliaries are all volunteers who give their time and effort to protect our citizens against robberies, assault, drug abuses and juvenile crime. Indeed, it would be difficult to imagine this city functioning without the aid of the auxiliary police.

> Abraham D. Beame
> Mayor of the City of New York
> October 19, 1974

The problems which faced many New Yorkers during the latter half of the 1970s were magnified many times in the hearts and minds of the auxiliary police. This chapter considers some of the extraordinary events which took place at the time of the city's worst fiscal crisis since the days of the Great Depression.

In January 1974, Abraham Beame succeeded John Lindsay and became the 104th Mayor in the city's history. Beame selected Michael J. Codd, a former chief inspector, to be his new police commissioner.

In the autumn of 1974 New York City discovered that, after all the years of taking in all people from every corner of the world, it was on the verge of default. No one has been able to predict what would happen if New York City, the financial capital of the United States, were to default.

The last time that the banking institutions had cracked down and virtually ruled over the operation of the city occurred in September 1933. The mayor was not Abraham D. Beame, but John P. O'Brien of Tammany Hall fame, a man who, when asked who his new police commissioner would be, gave the candid answer: "I don't know, they haven't told me yet."

New York City has what is known as a consolidated budget which includes funds for schools, hospitals, welfare, parks, police, firemen, sanitation and many other vital municipal functions. The city was forced to cut expenses for these services in order to balance its budget. In this way, it was hoped that investor confidence in the city's notes and bonds could be restored.[1] The restrictions which followed included laying off 25,000 employees, ending the City University's open admissions and free tuition policies, raising transit fares and bridge tolls, reducing garbage collections, freezing and reducing wages for city workers, closing various schools, hospitals and libraries and suspending the construction of dozens of public buildings. The city also economized by discharging all school crossing guards, reducing office and street lighting and eliminating more than 900 police call boxes. Furthermore, as an added revenue measure, Mayor Beame signed a bill authorizing the use of pinball machines. In 1942, Mayor La Guardia had succeeded in banning the machines on the grounds that they corrupted the morals of youth and fed the pockets of organized crime.[2]

The necessity for increased vigilance by the members of the auxiliary police was apparent. In addition, several major catastrophes increased the demands made upon the volunteer police during 1975.

In February 1975 a major communications disaster occurred on the lower East Side when a blaze knocked out more than 170,000 phone lines at a telephone switching building. The police emergency number 911 was put out of service for a time and dozens of auxiliaries with walkie-talkies were assigned to blanket the area. They patrolled the streets to prevent an upsurge in crime and many performed extra tours during the weeks that followed.[3]

In June several hundred auxiliary police and other emergency workers responded to the scene of the worst air disaster since 1960. An Eastern Airlines jet had crashed at Kennedy Airport during a landing approach. The final toll was 113 dead. A sudden thunderstorm soaked many of the workers. The volunteers rerouted traffic, helped maintain order, prevented looting and assisted in the removal of victims from the wreckage.[4] Auxiliary police units from the 113th Precinct and the 106th Emergency Service Force were cited for their assistance.

A special act of heroism took place on December 3, 1976. It was publicized throughout the Police Department in Police Commissioner Codd's own publication. The commissioner wrote:

PO Richard P. Gorellick of Midtown South Precinct was about to refuel a department van when he was suddenly hit on the head from behind by a man with a hammer. The blows fractured the officer's skull.

Auxiliary Police Officer Chris McKinstry, who was inside the station house preparing to go on duty, heard the sounds of scuffling and calls for help. He immediately rushed out to assist and succeeded in subduing and handcuffing the assailant. Officer Gorellick, who was removed to the hospital in serious condition, later said that McKinstry's quick response and actions saved his life.[5]

On December 29, 1975, a bomb exploded at La Guardia Airport. The explosive force was equal to twenty-five sticks of dynamite. It shredded the baggage claim area of Trans World Airlines, killing eleven people and injuring seventy-five. The nation's airlines offered a $50,000 reward for information leading to the conviction of those responsible for the blast.[6] More than a hundred auxiliaries from Queens precincts assisted with traffic congestion, rescue and crowd control.

It almost appeared for a time that New Yorkers would never survive to see the Bicentennial Year. However, by July of 1976, New York had made itself headquarters for the biggest celebration in the nation's history. New York hosted the spectacular "Operation Sail," a grand parade of 275 naval and international sailing ships. The event was highlighted by the largest gathering of square-rigged sailing ships in 150 years and the most widely viewed fireworks display. Later that month, the city welcomed the Democratic National Convention. The auxiliary police were kept busy at these events and at local festivals throughout the five boroughs. For example, Auxiliary Police Harbor Units conducted patrols, both day and night. They received no reimbursement for gas expenditure or for the use of their privately owned boats. The harbor auxiliary was founded in 1971 through the efforts of Sergeant Howard C. Smith, a regular member of the police department.[7] New recruits are required to attend a twenty-one week primary training course conducted at their Bronx headquarters. The Harbor Units maintain launch bases at locations on the Harlem River, City Island, College Point, Jamaica Bay and Staten Island.[8]

On January 24, 1974, Commissioner Michael Codd directed the issuance of a decentralization order concerning the city's auxiliary police organization. For the first time, important and essential details were available on the topic of supervision and the individualized roles to be performed by various members of the Police Department hierarchy.

The text of the order is set forth below in its entirety.[9]

INTERIM ORDER NO. 9

POLICE DEPARTMENT
CITY OF NEW YORK

January 24, 1974

TO ALL COMMANDS

Subject: DECENTRALIZATION OF THE AUXILIARY POLICE PROGRAM

1.   The Auxiliary Forces (Police) program is being decentralized to improve the program's internal management, provide precinct commanders with additional resources, and promote mutual understanding, respect and cooperation between the police officer and the volunteer Auxiliary Police member. In addition, it is the Department's goal to establish a relationship between the Department and the community at large that will foster a safe urban environment.

2. Membership in the Auxiliary Police affords the citizen an opportunity to understand the objectives and operations of the Department and volunteer his own efforts and talents in achieving these objectives. Furthermore, the program provides a source of community feedback, assists in dispelling harmful rumors and aids in maintaining community tranquility. Auxiliary police participate in Precinct Youth and Crime Prevention Programs and are a trained manpower reserve which can be mobilized rapidly during emergencies and disasters.

3. Precinct commanders are required to maintain and manage the Auxiliary Police program in their commands. They will receive assistance from the area zone inspector who will supervise precinct programs and Field Service Area commanders who are required to provide overall supervision and coordinate the programs within their areas. Staff services and liaison will be provided by the Auxiliary Forces Section.

4. Field Service Area commanders are required to:

   a. Designate a captain to supervise the Auxiliary Police program
   b. Assign a police officer to perform clerical and administrative duties, as prescribed by the Commanding Officer, Auxiliary Forces Section
   c. Insure that recruit and in service training programs are provided
   d. Review the effectiveness of the Auxiliary Police Program
   e. Consolidate precinct monthly "Auxiliary Police Progress Reports", forwarding one copy to Auxiliary Forces Section and one copy to the Chief of Field Services.

5. Field Service Area Zone Inspectors shall, through inspection, determine if precinct commands are maintaining effective Auxiliary Forces programs.

6. Precinct commanders are responsible that an effective Auxiliary Forces program is maintained within their commands and:

   a. Develop effective recruitment programs
   b. Have all applicants investigated
   c. Use auxiliary police to best advantages within the scope of department policy
   d. Foster a close working relationship between police officers and auxiliary police personnel through leadership and example
   e. Encourage members of the service to engage in "rap" sessions with auxiliary police personnel
   f. Have members of the service turn out the auxiliary police platoons and conduct roll call training with auxiliary police superiors
   g. Have superior officers and police officers visit Auxiliary Forces personnel on patrol to assist and guide them, when necessary

    h.   Account for federal Rescue Equipment maintained
        at command

    i.   Rotate assignments of auxiliary police personnel
        and confer with auxiliary police commanding officers
        frequently concerning the performance and conduct
        of personnel

    j.   Submit "Auxiliary Police Progress Report" to area
        commanders each month

    k.   Collect shields, identification cards and uniforms
        of inactive members

    l.   Assign one police officer whose primary duty will
        be to conduct this program as Precinct Auxiliary
        Police Coordinator.

7. The Precinct Auxiliary Police Coordinator shall be
selected for his leadership ability, education and police background. He will be required to personally work with auxiliary
police personnel in developing acceptable ways for auxiliary
forces to participate meaningfully in precinct programs and gain
acceptance and cooperation of members of the service. The
coordinator should actively support the goals of the Auxiliary
Police program and be interested in, and willing to work with,
Auxiliary Forces personnel.

8. Police officers assigned as Auxiliary Police Coordinators will:

    a.   Personally enroll, interview and fingerprint
        applicants for the program

    b.   Examine and verify documentary proof of resi-
        dence, employment, citizenship or alien status,
        and the filed intent to become a citizen

    c.   Perform tours of duty necessary to coordinate
        the precinct program.

9. The Commanding Officer, Auxiliary Forces Section is
required to:

    a.   Maintain staff units and provide staff services
        to field commands

    b.   Maintain city wide records of members of Auxiliary
        Police and Auxiliary Emergency Service Force including:
        (1) Personal folder
        (2) Time records
        (3) Shield identification file
        (4) Rosters and training records required to
            obtain matching fund awards

    c.   Conduct appeal hearings in disciplinary matters

    d.   Prepare and issue training material and bulletins

    e.   Conduct intermediate and advanced training courses

    f.   Account for Civil Defense Rescue trucks and equip-
        ment (in annual inventory)

    g.   Assist precinct commanders in obtaining shields
        and uniforms of auxiliary policemen who are no
        longer active

    h.   Maintain liaison with Mayor's Emergency Control
        Board, per Mayor's Executive Order 51 (1967)

    i.   Formulate and issue Auxiliary Forces Section direc-
        tives to assist and direct precinct programs.

10. In addition to auxiliary police being attached to patrol precincts, the Commanding Officer, Air/Sea Section will maintain and train an Auxiliary Harbor Unit and the Commanding Officer, Emergency Service Section will provide training for members of the Auxiliary Emergency Service Force.

11. Any provision of a department directive in conflict with this order is suspended.

BY DIRECTION OF THE POLICE COMMISSIONER

DISTRIBUTION:
All Commands

There were many other extraordinary events during this period, not the least of which was the enrollment of Percy E. Sutton, the Manhattan borough president. Auxiliary Police Officer Sutton had gained a reputation as one of the nation's outstanding authorities on urban problems. He performed tours of duty at precincts within the Manhattan North Area command.

As we have seen, the chief consequence arising from the city's fiscal crisis was the reduction of manpower in all of the city's uniformed forces, including police, fire and sanitation.

However, the decade of the 1970s was not to close without several other major struggles in the history of New York's volunteer police. One of their number was slain in the line of duty, members stayed off the streets for nearly three months in an effort to legalize the carrying of nightsticks and Council members Henry Stern and Antonio Olivieri issued an independent report outlining the problems of the auxiliary police force. Moreover, the force was to shrink in size to 2,300 members. Each of these events will be considered in future chapters.

10 • Auxiliary Police in Crisis

Novelists have continually depicted New York as a city of dreadful night and one where unspeakable terror lurks around every street corner. These images are a far cry from the relatively uneventful days experienced by most New Yorkers as they live and work throughout the city. However, these same images must have appeared especially real to the men and women of the auxiliary police during the summer of 1975.

The city laid off 3,000 regular policemen on July 1, 1975. During previous months there had been indications about how this change might affect the activities of the auxiliary police program. Significantly, the operation of police scooters by auxiliaries and the scheduling of a special class to train members of the auxiliary emergency service force occurred at a time when regular personnel were being threatened by the fiscal crisis. These events could be construed to mean that the Police Department was preparing to substitute the police volunteers for the regulars. Finally, when the police layoffs occurred, the vast majority of the more than 5,000 volunteer auxiliary policemen halted their nightly foot patrols across the city. This action could be attributed to four main causes: 1. the belief that the regulars were about to strike in which event no auxiliary would patrol; 2. the joint statement by the auxiliary PBA and the regular PBA that there were not enough regular police to back up auxiliaries; 3. the lack of any move by the Police Department to encourage the continuance of patrols; and 4. the existence of an atmosphere containing implied threats and reprisals from regular police.[1]

On July 1, 1975, Captain Robert J. Cornwall, the new commander of the Auxiliary Forces Section, reported that only 81 volunteers had taken their posts.[2] On July 10 Captain Cornwall announced that there were "very few auxiliary police officers patrolling in the entire city."[3] On the evening of July 21, the members of the Central Park Precinct voted to end their month-long suspension of patrols, but decided to resume operations on only two nights instead of their usual five. In a statement to the press, their auxiliary commander remarked:

There's no way to tell when the laid-off men will be brought back. If we don't resume patrols we aren't going to have a unit. . . . We feel we can be of more use to the regular police if we are a functioning unit than if we go out of existence.[4]

On July 28, some of the units in the Manhattan South Area resumed their patrols. A few days before their return, the executive officer of the Manhattan South Area auxiliaries stated: "If we don't get our men back on patrol the organization won't be able to stay together. . . . Some precinct commanders told the auxiliaries to take a month off just to avoid conflict."[5] On August 4, despite rain, over two hundred off-duty auxiliaries and their families demonstrated outside the 69th Precinct in the Canarsie section of Brooklyn in order to show their support for the laid-off police. However, by this time, many of the members of the regular force had begun to feel that the boycott had served its purpose. The administrative officer of the 69th Precinct commented:

They've made their point. We have one of the best auxiliary operations in the city, with close to 100 members. These guys want to get back on the street, and the men of the precinct would be happy to see them back out on the street.[6]

On August 8, Thomas P. Mitchelson, the Chief of Field Services of the New York City Police Department, directed all his ranking officers to make an effort to revitalize the auxiliary police program. Finally, word had come from the highest level in the uniformed force. Captain Cornwall relayed this message to all the members of the auxiliary police on August 14. In part, his communication declared:

During the month of July and extending into August, there has been an extensive decrease in Auxiliary Police patrol throughout the city. The Police Department is concerned about this decreased activity and has directed its personnel to make a determined effort to reverse this unhealthy trend. Auxiliaries should be aware that the policy of the Department is that Auxiliary Patrol is a desirable adjunct to regular patrol.[7]

By late August 1975, many of the auxiliaries had returned to their routine patrol assignments. It had become clear that the city had no immediate plans to rehire the laid-off police and the police volunteers had been encouraged by police officials, their superior officers and their own desire to serve. However, on the evening of August 27, 1975, the public's awareness of the dangers which face all police personnel was suddenly sharpened by the tragic attack upon Auxiliary Police Sergeant David Freed.

David Freed qualified for auxiliary police duty in March 1973. He served for two and a half years in the Central Park Precinct and won numerous "commendations for helping the distressed and assuaging the discontented."[8] On September 12, 1974, he was promoted to the rank of sergeant. On August 27, 1975, he was on duty with his fiancee. They had been assigned together as supervising sergeants and permitted to use a radio motor patrol car.[9] Both auxiliaries were clubbed by a naked man. Four days later, Freed died from the severe wounds he sustained during the attack. It was only a few days before his twenty-first birthday and he had planned to either attend college or obtain employment as a regular police officer.[10]

Freed's assailant was captured on the night of the attack. After a two hour nonjury trial, the defendant was found not guilty of murder "by reason of mental disease or defect" and was committed to the custody of the Department of Mental Hygiene for an indeterminate period.[11]

David Freed had been the first member of the auxiliary police to die in the line of duty in more than twenty-five years.[12] Shortly after the incident, Police Commissioner Codd was said to be in favor of continuing the patrols, despite pressure from the regular PBA to disband the auxiliaries.[13] This influence was felt on August 28, only a day after Freed was fatally attacked. On that occasion a top PBA official sent personal letters to 350 union delegates suggesting they tell auxiliaries that it was unsafe for them to patrol. In a later interview, the official stated that his letter had "mixed results."[14] Evidently, because of the subsequent death of David Freed, the continued repetition of the same theme by PBA leaders had become repugnant to many rank and file members of the city's police force.

As early as 1918, there were complaints of disrespect shown to the Police Reserves, the auxiliary police of that era. On at least one occasion, Rodman Wanamaker, the unsalaried deputy police commissioner who commanded the reserves, wrote to the chief inspector referring to instances in which the police volunteers had been made to feel that they were not wanted.[15] Significantly, the more recent cries of "scabbing" and "they give the public a false security" had become worn by time.[16]

Moreover, as the press reported, the sentiment of most crime-conscious New Yorkers began to weigh heavily in favor of the unarmed auxiliary police. The *New York Post* noted that the mere presence of these uniformed volunteers has been a godsend to the elderly.[17] The *Daily News* reported that many workers had been reassured by the sight of auxiliary patrols as they made their way home along vacant streets from transit stations.[18] In addition, several local newspapers ran editorials commenting approvingly about the work of the auxiliaries. In particular, one such newspaper in an attempt to encourage their use stated:

What is disheartening about the breakdown of the Auxiliary Police force is that it is a citizen participation program where concerned individuals are participating in a program to help the city. This sort of citizen self-reliance is most praiseworthy, and should serve as a model of what the individual citizen can do and should do. It is even more disheartening that the police who demand so much in public support, and deserve public support, should be so responsible for what may turn out to be the doom of the Auxiliary forces.[19]

The death of David Freed stirred new debate concerning the administration of the auxiliary police program. One publication, widely circulated throughout the city's police precincts, asked:

Should entrance requirements for auxiliary volunteers be upgraded? Should they be out there at all, exposing themselves to the hazards of police work? If they do belong on patrol, does their training prepare them adequately for all the dangerous situations which they might encounter?[20]

Some possible remedies to the foregoing questions have been proposed by John Hyland, president of the Auxiliary Police Benevolent Association since 1974, and Graham Schneider, who served as its president until 1972. Hyland has urged that training in the use of nightsticks should be at least equivalent to that given regular police.[21] Schneider has proposed that auxiliaries should be trained in the use of firearms and allowed to carry them only when on patrol. In support of his suggestion, he declared: "As soon as one of our men puts on a uniform, he is taking the same risk that a policeman does, and why shouldn't he have the same protection?"[22]

In October and December of 1975, the Police Department undertook various measures to cope with a few of the problems that had been raised. During the earlier month, a new form was introduced requiring parents of enrollees under eighteen years of age to give written authorization for their child's participation. On the later date, the Police Department instituted self-defense classes at the Police Academy for all new recruits. In addition, each borough command was ordered to set up an annual in-service training program for physical self-defense, baton, frisk and handcuff instruction. Any member who failed to complete a minimum of four hours training was to be assigned only to administrative tasks and no longer permitted to patrol.[23]

More and more New Yorkers were becoming involved in the war on crime. The 5,000 members of the auxiliary police were joined by: 11,000 members of the New York City Housing Authority and Tenant Patrol; more than 8,000 taxi and bus drivers in the Civilian Radio Motor Patrol; several thousand members of Citizen Observer Patrols who keep watch on neighbor's homes by patrolling in private cars equipped with CB radio; thousands of block associations which foster neighborhood security; and the many thousands of individuals who were recruited as block watchers and participants in "Operation Identification."[24] Clearly, such numbers demonstrate that concerned citizens were willing to get involved.

Thus, David Freed's death may not have been in vain. Auxiliary patrols have carried on and their training has improved. The traditional disdain felt by police toward the auxiliaries has lessened. And more citizens have been joining the battle to reduce crime.

11 • The Auxiliary Peacekeeping Force

It is my hope that the current number of volunteers will increase tenfold. . . . The potential for achievement that is inherent in the auxiliary concept is unlimited.[1]

Edward Koch
Mayor, New York City

In January 1978, Edward Koch succeeded Abraham Beame and became the 105th mayor in the history of the city of New York. Koch selected Robert J. McGuire, a lawyer and a former federal prosecutor, to be the city's new police commissioner. McGuire was recommended to Mayor Koch by Manhattan District Attorney Robert Morgenthau. "Morganthau certified McGuire as being of unquestioned integrity, liberal minded and with a special sensitivity to the problems of New York City."[2]

On October 16, 1978, a historic meeting took place at the office of the New York Bar Association in Manhattan. City Councilmen at Large Henry J. Stern and Antonio G. Olivieri conducted the meeting for the purpose of learning about the good and bad within the Auxiliary Police program. Testimony from twenty-eight officials, auxiliary police officers and former volunteers was received. On February 11, 1979, the councilmen issued a twenty-five-page report based on the information gathered during the public hearing and a three-month staff investigation.[3]

The report called for the abolition of higher ranks in the program, assignment of auxiliaries to accompany police serving in "one-man" patrol cars, passage of a state law authorizing nightsticks, granting auxiliaries the power to issue tickets for parking and other violations and a substantial upgrading of their training. Significantly, the document referred to a 1972 court decision. The court had held that a nightstick is a dangerous weapon under the New York State Penal Law and cited the opinion of the city's Corporation Counsel that auxiliaries should be prohibited from carrying nightsticks in the absence of appropriate legislation. The report concluded that failure to introduce the needed law "could mean criminal charges being raised against an unsuspecting A.P."[4]

The New York City Police Department responded to the report by sanctioning the organization of a Programs and Policy Committee, the establishment of separate training and retention committees and the distribution of a new newsletter. In addition, it was announced on March 15, 1979, that the Deputy Commissioner of Legal Matters had stated that it was "the official policy of the NYCPD to allow its Auxiliary Police officers to carry nightsticks while performing authorized patrol duty in uniform."[5]

The announcement by the Deputy Commissioner of Legal Matters appeared unsatisfactory to the Auxiliary Police Benevolent Association in that its membership could still be arrested and prosecuted for a violation of the penal law which restricted the carrying of dangerous weapons. Moreover, it seemed that no one in the city government was especially concerned over the issue. The association then sought a court order to protect its membership from being placed in jeopardy of arrest as a result of carrying a nightstick. On April 17, 1979, Justice Williams of the Supreme Court, New York County delivered a decision which granted the request of the Association.[6]

Meanwhile, the Auxiliary Police Benevolent Association introduced through members of the State Legislature a bill to grant the city's auxiliaries the necessary power to possess nightsticks. However, at the time of the court decision it had not yet been passed, and without their only real means of self-defense the members of the auxiliary police were urged by the association not to patrol. This position was not changed until July 12, 1979, when information was received that the "nightstick bill" had been signed by Governor Hugh Carey. A local newspaper, *Our Town*, was first to learn about the governor's action as a result of the efforts of Billy Bloom, a reporter for the paper.[7] The bill limited the use of nightsticks to situations calling for the authorized use of "deadly physical force."[8]

It is hard to calculate the mood of every member of the auxiliary during this period of crisis. But it is safe to say that most were disheartened by the governor's inaction and refusal to comment until it appeared that the auxiliary program was likely to fold because of inactivity. However, it was in keeping with their remarkable spirit that within hours after notification of the signing of the bill, most members had returned to full duty.

Prior to the foregoing controversy some positive steps were being taken concerning the Auxiliary Police program. For example, auxiliaries had been granted authority to participate in the Police Academy's physical exercise program[9] and John Jay College of Criminal Justice, a branch of the City University, had agreed to award three general credits in police science for completion of the auxiliary police primary training course.[10] Furthermore, in 1978 an enterprising city police officer received a leave of absence from the police department in order to serve as a teacher at John Kennedy High School in the Borough of the Bronx. He coordinated a program to help students "who may be borderline in their attitude and behavior to see the other side."[11] The primary incentive for these youths was the opportunity to enroll in the city's auxiliary police upon successful completion of their studies. The program was funded under Title IV-C of the Federal Elementary and Secondary Education Act. According to Dr. Ronald H. Bragaw, chief of the Bureau of Social Studies in the New York State Education Department, this program has encouraged some participants to seek careers in law enforcement and has won praise from the New York City Police Department.[12]

After the nightstick controversy had ended, the Police Department began to rebuild the program. This effort began when a full inspector, Benjamin Hellman, was chosen to head the Auxiliary Force Section. He upgraded the primary training class by requiring all participants to perform one tour of "observer field training duty" in the particular command where the volunteer had enrolled. The objective of the duty was to give the new recruit a better understanding of what an auxiliary police officer does while on patrol. In addition, younger volunteers could now qualify at nineteen for promotion to the rank of auxiliary sergeant if they had completed the intermediate training course and at least six months of patrol duty.[13] Moreover, the Police Department agreed to salvage retired radio patrol cars and assign them to the auxiliary police. Inspector Hellman announced that the vehicles would be repainted white to distinguish them from regular police cars and each of the seventy-three auxiliary precinct units would receive one on the basis of a merit plan. The plan consisted of number of unit members and hours of service.[14] Finally, Hellman was able to insure that the regular police officers assigned as auxiliary police unit coordinators in each of the city's precincts would be freed of other tasks in order to devote their schedules to the full-time recruitment, training and supervision of auxiliaries. This could not have been accomplished without the endorsements of Commissioner McGuire and Mayor Koch. In fact, the mayor and the police commissioner did more than approve of these changes. Each enthusiastically praised the role of citizens in police work and encouraged qualified individuals to join the auxiliary police at every forum in which the topic of crime control was discussed.

By the mid–1980s enrollment in the auxiliary police jumped to more than 9,000, the highest total since the early 1950s during the height of the Korean War.[15] Significantly, while the total number of auxiliaries was at its highest level in recent history, the strength of the Police Department had suffered a series of declines as a result of numerous austerity budgets.[16] The Stern and Olivieri report coupled with fiscal necessity and popular municipal leaders helped to save the auxiliaries from extinction.

These unique events also contributed to a new phase in the use of citizens as police volunteers within the city of New York. The auxiliaries were no longer simply being tolerated, but were actually being regularly touted by high ranking police officials and by prominent citizens as a key component in the city's arsenal against aggressive, violent crime. In the process, they were being equipped and trained as genuine peacekeepers. A new role for the auxiliary had emerged. They were now not only community sentinels who watched and reported potential or actual crimes and service providers charged with such menial tasks as patrolling at a church bazaar or aiding a police officer, but preservers and maintainers of public safety. The peacekeeping role has been described as a way "to keep a lid on tensions and troubles in a crime-prone environment so that at least the appearance of stability is maintained."[17] The auxiliaries could be deployed to caution juveniles to behave themselves in public places, inform a noisy crowd to move on, warn a potential prostitute's customer about the dangers in seeking such services, render assistance to intoxicated persons, prevent fistfights and carry out other activities associated with protecting the lives and rights of the public. Although many auxiliaries had undertaken these duties in the past, it was now clear that such work was more of a responsibility than had been the case in earlier times. Significantly, the improved screening, training, equipment and supervision had made it so.

The final chapter in Part II will consider some of the future directions the auxiliary program might take in order to become a more viable adjunct to the Police Department in light of its past history.

12 • The Total Force Concept

Beyond a doubt, the Auxiliary Police Force is the backbone and mainstay of the New York City Police Department's citizen involvement efforts. . . . Originally trained to augment police services in the event of a disaster, they have become a vital part of the police-citizen team.[1]

Benjamin Ward
Commissioner, NYC Police Department

"In the old Wild West days, the sheriff pinned the star on a bystander and made him a deputy. Since the bystander already was equipped with gun and horse, he could easily fit into the new role and take off after the cattle rustlers."[2] But today, before the city fathers elect to pin the deputy's star on thousands of civilians, careful consideration should be given to the exact nature of the authority they intend to bestow, and once having made their decision, they should be prepared to provide the necessary tools for those who may be recruited.[3]

The commentary in favor of the use of police auxiliaries has generally centered on three areas.[4] Foremost is the view which holds that the relief of an overburdened and undermanned police force may be obtained through the utilization of volunteer and salaried civilian manpower. Following closely is the expectation that large savings will be made by the use of such semiprofessionals; and third is the obvious conclusion that such personnel will be a tremendous asset for public relations inasmuch as the volunteers are directly recruited from the neighborhood of local police precincts. Actually, these reasons for promoting the use of citizen police officers, while extremely advantageous, are of only secondary value.

As we have already seen, the use of police volunteers in times of peril has been of strategic importance in the mobilization for civil defense within New

York City. However, of even greater significance when we view New York's auxiliary experience from the standpoint of its long history is the discovery that ultimately our democratic society has been advanced. This phenomenon is an important and unexpected dividend. Briefly stated, the presence of civilian personnel has meant a greater degree of police accountability to the public at large; the cause of civic involvement has been fostered through the participation of community volunteers in their own policing and crime prevention activities; and thirdly, our democratic institutions have been preserved through the provision of standby forces. But this is not all. Newspaper reports and Police Department statistics reveal that more and more minority members of the city are seeking ways to control crime in their communities. In fact, the percentage of black, Puerto Rican, Jewish and Chinese auxiliary police officers is much higher than that on the regular police force.[5] The promise of a more stable community through inner city involvement may prove to be the greatest contribution of the volunteer program. These groups feel less alienated by actively participating in neighborhood police efforts.

However, the survival of New York's volunteer police is not assured. Its history has shown that a change in the office of Mayor has often signaled either an end or a beginning for the city's citizen police. For example, under Mayor Mitchel (1914–1917), Commissioner Woods established the city's first auxiliary police force; Mayor Hylan (1918–1925) and Police Commissioner Enright improved upon Woods' work through the institution of preliminary screening and rudimentary qualifications; Deputy Commissioner Wanamaker, during the same era, tightened the reigns to the extent that only the moderately wealthy could afford to participate; Mayor Walker (1926–1932) let the organization collapse; Mayor La Guardia (1934–1945), perhaps drawing upon his military experiences, inaugurated a significantly new and efficient auxiliary corps; Mayor O'Dwyer (1946–1950) was too preoccupied with personal and postwar problems to become involved with the auxiliary concept; Mayor Impellitteri (1950–1953) saw the auxiliary police only as a branch of the city's civil defense program; Mayor Wagner (1954–1965) inherited the auxiliaries from the Korean War period and did little to change the status quo; Mayor Lindsay (1966–1973) abandoned itis "CD" trappings and took serious stock of its crime-deterrent potential by urging new enrollment and supporting new reforms; Mayor Beame (1974–1977) continued the advances made during the Lindsay years and encouraged the recruitment of auxiliary police during the fiscal crisis; and Mayor Koch (1978–present) has utilized every public forum at his disposal to foster enrollment. Perhaps a trend has been established for the future.

In the years that lie ahead, it is more than likely that present demands for local community control over various public services will grow. Significantly, an official state report has concluded that "more and more people—experts and laymen, public officials and private citizens—have advocated the decentralization of government. Their salient argument has been that government closest to the people is most capable of answering the needs of people."[6] Undoubtedly, such demands will include the fields of law enforcement and public safety. In this regard, the existence of neighborhood auxiliary units will be of additional relevance.

Traditionally, the police function has involved a twofold objective, namely, the arrest of offenders and the general need "to keep the lid on things," through the use of intelligence and understanding in order to maintain order and relative tranquility. The auxiliary police officer of the city of New York is instructed to call for the assistance of the regular police only in the event of serious trouble. Thus, the role of the auxiliaries is closely identified with that function of police work involving the maintenance of order. James Q. Wilson categorizes order maintenance or peacekeeping to include decentralization, neighborhood involvement, foot patrol, wide discretion, the provision of services and the absence of arrest quotas.[7] Clearly, the auxiliary volunteer has to develop many techniques in order to handle his beat, and he has become the foot patrolman of the Police Department in the process, with one key qualification—he does not hold the favored status of "peace officer." If present trends continue, a rare form of police service will have evolved, because as the regular police become better educated and trained, their new found professional status will make it less likely that they will return to walking the beat. Currently, the use of radio motor patrol cars has all but eliminated the sight of regular police on foot patrol, except for a few token posts in high crime areas of the city. However, local community demands for foot patrolmen will not end. According to a 1974 *New York Times* survey of 1,341 city residents, an overwhelming majority wanted more policemen on the beat.[8] This important patrol function is now the primary assignment of each precinct's auxiliary police unit.

In this way, a new species of police personnel is being created. They are being equipped with the latest type of two-way radios and supported by a highly mobile professional police service.

However, whether or not the auxiliaries can remain or should remain an unarmed para-police force is another question. The results of a *New York Times* poll, released at the end of 1981, indicated that 84 percent of city residents believed that crime had worsened since 1977 and 46 percent viewed crime as the most important problem facing the city. Moreover, more persons believed that the police or the courts were less able to do anything about it.[9] In the fall of 1979, Mayor Koch made a decisive effort to bolster the force against crime by seeking to place the Transit and Housing Authority police forces under the direct command of Police Commissioner McGuire.[10] This action was seen as an eventual move toward the complete unification of the three departments. Perhaps, this "total force" concept is also applicable to the Auxiliary Police Force.

The city of Los Angeles utilizes a volunteer reserve police force in order to help in its crime control efforts. Smaller cities have traditionally authorized civilians to serve as part-time law enforcement officers. These communities arm and appropriately train their volunteers in order to supplement the strength of their regular police departments. The volunteers are considered to be equal partners in the crime control process. Similarly, each of the military branches of the United States maintains reserves who become equal partners when activated. Much of the confusion and uncertainty surrounding New York City's Auxiliary Police Force would be ended if the "total force" concept was applied to it.[11] Significantly, the auxiliaries already perform crime prevention, peacekeeping and service roles; therefore, the addition of law enforcement duties would solve once and for all the puzzle of their existence. Problems of retention would be a thing of the past inasmuch as each auxiliary would know the meaningfulness of his or her role. The citizenry would be much better served by the auxiliaries and the lawless element would be on notice that the city was marshalling every resource to contend with crime.

However, the greatest obstacle to overcome before such a goal could be obtained concerns the attitudes of the professional police and their unions. Opposition to any form of civilian supplemental support has already been voiced. Similar proposals in other parts of the nation have been seen as an attempt to rob policemen of employment and as a dilution of their authority and prestige. Yet, in this connection, it is of interest to note that Arthur Woods, the father of New York's volunteer police, and August Vollmer, who established the citizen police of Berkeley, were also among the leading figures behind the development of a professional police service based on college and police academy training. They recognized that efficient law enforcement must always be a joint enterprise of the police and the public. It is to be hoped that just as the auxiliary police originated at the time of the emergence of the first academy trained police officers, they may also come to complement one another through new associations and programs in the future. Their combined efforts could mean a new hope for the survival of our cities.

It would have been easy to fill many pages with accounts of the heroic exploits of individual auxiliary police officers; however, the primary thrust of Part II has been to present a historical overview, in the hope that mayors and police commissioners will not fail to grasp the significance and worth of volunteer police programs. The National Advisory Commission on Criminal Justice Standards and Goals emphasized that responsible citizen involvement is the key factor in reducing crime and recommended that every state and city consider the immediate employment of auxiliary police or reserve officers to supplement their regular police forces.[12]

In concise language, New York City Police Officer James Ryan has summarized their importance in this way:

Inherent in these long hours is the contribution of the Auxiliary Police Force as a crime deterrent . . . whose members do "get involved." New Yorkers—civilians and police—can only benefit.[13]

Throughout the nation, citizen auxiliary police units are becoming a common and accepted part of police planning. Their utilization to assist, support and back up regular police officers is a choice worth making. After studying thirty-seven police-community projects in seventeen cities, George J. Washnis concluded:

There appears to be little question that the mere presence of the Auxiliary Police [in New York City] has helped to maintain order in many areas and deter assailants and burglars. The . . . extra service to the police department is a significant contribution— a program the police department needs and does not wish to lose.[14]

PART III

CURRENT ISSUES IN VOLUNTEER POLICING

Somehow we must let the American public know that neither the police nor other elements in the criminal justice system have anything approaching a complete answer to the problems of crime.

Patrick V. Murphy
President, Police Foundation
In Robert M. Fogelson,
Big-City Police, p. 273.

13 • The Auxiliary Police and the Law

Thus far, the present book has been chiefly concerned with the desirability of establishing auxiliary police units from the standpoint of the chief administrator of a police department or city. However, it is also crucial to be aware of the various pitfalls regarding membership in the auxiliary police. In addition to the specific pressures of being a "voluntary" protector of one's neighborhood (e.g., resentment from some regular police personnel, wonderment of various non-auxiliary family and community members), auxiliaries face many of the problems which are encountered by every regular police officer. The risks of suffering unfavorable publicity, being sued for false arrest and sustaining serious injury are hinged to almost every judgment the regular or auxiliary police officer makes. As a consequence, an additional amount of pressure is placed upon the individual as well as his or her family.

The case of *Buric* v. *McGuire* is illustrative of a few of the foregoing difficulties. Mr. Buric joined the New York City Auxiliary Police Force in 1974 at the age of eighteen. About four years later, a Police Department disciplinary panel found Buric guilty of conduct prejudicial to the efficiency of the department and dismissed him from the force. Specifically, the department determined that Buric had failed to disclose to the first arriving police officer that he had observed a man running and knocking down pedestrians.

Buric sued the city's police commissioner in an effort to be reinstated. On July 19, 1978, Justice Riccobono issued his opinion which eased the penalty for the fired auxiliary. The full text of that decision follows below:

MATTER OF BURIC (McGuire)-This is an application by petitioners for judgment pursuant to CPLR article 78 annulling the determination of respondents dismissing petitioner Buric from the Auxiliary Forces Section of the Police Department of the City of New York.

Petitioner Buric has been a volunteer member of the auxiliary police since March, 1974. On May 24, 1977, at about 6 P.M., while not on regular auxiliary police duty, Buric observed a young male Hispanic running rapidly down 40th Street and Seventh Avenue, bumping into and knocking down pedestrians. He gave chase and followed the individual into a building and up six flights of stairs, after first identifying himself to the building's security guard as an auxiliary police officer and directing the guard to call the police.

Buric found the suspect outside the office of a union located in the building, where the latter was talking with and crying in the arms of a female supervisor of the union. The suspect allegedly stated that he had a pregnant wife at home and had just been fired by his boss and had punched the latter in the face and then ran to the union to have the matter straightened out. Buric, as well as the union supervisor, apparently believed the story, not one word of which was true.

A police car then came to the building in response to the call which the security guard had made at Buric's behest. Buric then told them it was a mistake and the police drove away. He did not inform the police of the suspect's conduct or relate the story given by the latter or even mention that the suspect was still in the building.

Unknown to Buric, the suspect had just mugged an elderly man and was fleeing from the scene of the crime when Buric spotted him. A civilian, Viggo Hanson, observed the victim being yanked into a doorway and then saw the suspect emerge therefrom running rapidly. Hanson went to investigate and saw the victim bleeding badly. He then pursued the suspect into the building, where he came upon the suspect, Buric and the guard. Hanson then told Buric, who identified himself as an auxiliary policeman, that the suspect had just committed a mugging around the corner and that Buric should arrest the suspect. Petitioner responded that he could not do that, but offered to assist Hanson in effecting a citizen's arrest, should the latter desire to be the complainant. This Hanson declined to do, and, frustrated, decided to call a "real cop." By the time a uniformed policeman arrived, the suspect had departed.

The Police Department apparently was chagrined, annoyed, and/or embarrassed by the fact that the alleged perpetrator of a serious crime had slipped through its hands. Buric himself was, in fact, arrested for obstruction of governmental administration for allegedly willfully giving misleading information to the police. However, the arrest was voided by the department. Buric was thereafter suspended from the Auxiliary Police Force and brought up on departmental charges for violation of its regulations. After a hearing, he was acquitted of the charge of visiting a place of business for the purpose of interviewing a person without authority; but was found guilty of the charge of acting in a manner prejudicial to the efficiency of the Police Department. The punishment was dismissal from the Auxiliary Police Force. It is from this determination that the instant proceeding is brought.

Petitioners contend that the dismissal of Buric from the Auxiliary Police Force was arbitrary and capricious and an abuse of discretion and, was, in effect, "Monday morning quarterbacking." It is their contention that, at most, he was guilty of exercising bad judgment, which is not enough, in and of itself, to warrant his dismissal.

In defense of Buric's actions (or inaction), petitioners allege that he did all that he was legally empowered to do. In this regard, they point to the legal impotency of an auxiliary policeman, who but serves as "additional eyes and ears of the police department." Although given a badge for identification purposes, an auxiliary police officer merely possesses the same power to effect a "citizen's arrest" as does any other person.

Under Criminal Procedure Law, section 140.30, "any person may arrest another person (a) for a felony when the latter has in fact committed such felony; and (b) for any offense when the latter has in fact committed such offense *in his presence* (emphasis added; see also McKinney's N.Y. Unconsolidated Laws, section 9186; People v. Foster, 10 N.Y. 2d 99, 102). Mere suspicion and surmise are not enough to justify the arrest of a person by a private person (People v. Williams, 53 Misc. 2d 1086, 1088). A person effecting a citizen's arrest does so under peril of being held civilly liable for false arrest and imprisonment (Sanders v. Rolnick, 188 Misc. 627, aff'd 272 App. Div. 803). Hence, under the facts and circumstances here presented, Buric was justified in not arresting the suspect, since no crime had been committed in his presence, and there was no reason for him to believe that the suspect had, in fact, committed a felony.

However, petitioner was not dismissed for failing to arrest the suspect, but for breach of the rules and regulations governing the conduct of members of the Auxiliary Police Force. Specifically, Rule 11 directs that an Auxiliary Policeman report "without delay . . . anything irregular or offensive, and any *unusual occurrence*, important casualty, or serious crime occurring on their posts or other assigned areas" (emphasis added). It is undisputed that Buric failed to report to the first uniformed police to respond to the call the fact that he had chased a person who was running down a crowded street, knocking over pedestrians, or . . . the story told to him by the suspect. Even in a cosmopolitan, bustling city such as this, that would constitute an "unusual occurrence."

Accordingly, there was a rational basis for respondents' determination, and that determination cannot be said to be arbitrary or capricious.

However, the penalty of dismissal imposed upon petitioner Buric is excessive under the circumstances as set forth in the record (see Matter of Pell v. Board of Education, 34 N.Y. 2d 222, 234; Spencer v. O'Hagan, 60 A.D. 2d 538). Here we have a 21-year-old individual who, without monetary compensation unarmed, risks his life to serve the community as a volunteer auxiliary police officer, and then hires an attorney to fight for the right to continue to serve the public. Perhaps, in this instance, he was a bad judge of human character, or was naively credulous. Undeniably, he was guilty of gullibility. But who is to say that a more experienced person, or even a uniformed police officer, might not have believed the story given by the suspect? Perhaps he has been made more street-wise by this experience. In any event, the court concludes that, under the circumstances, a more appropriate penalty would be directing that he repeat the Primary Training Course given to new Auxiliary Police Officers and/or be placed on probation for one year, or any other penalty which might be deemed reasonable and advisable.

The petition is therefore granted to the extent indicated and is dismissed as against the petitioner-Association for want of standing (cf. Matter of Nassau Educational Chapter CSEA v. Board of Education of Farmingdale UFSD, A.D. 2d [2d Dept.], N.Y.L.J., 3–29–78, p. 13, col. 4). Settle judgment.[1]

The *Buric* case is not as frightening as the case of the *People* v. *Jackson*.[2] Jackson was also involved in a controversial incident which occurred while he was off-duty. However, unlike Buric, Jackson was compelled to stand trial in Criminal Court on the charges of criminal impersonation, resisting arrest, criminal trespass and harassment. At his trial, Jackson stated that a group of community residents urged him to find out what was happening to a woman inside a Housing Authority police office. Holding his badge and identification card in his hand, he knocked on the door of the police room and approached an officer. Judge Berger's decision summarizes the consequences:

Mr. Jackson testified that he identified himself as an Auxiliary Policeman, referred to the crowd outside the office and asked Patrolman Ametrano if he could be of help. Ametrano, he said, told him "get the hell out of here" and when Jackson sought to retrieve the badge and identity card, Ametrano leaped on him. Jackson said he was thrown to the ground, was beaten by Ametrano and his fellow officers both in the police room and on the adjacent sidewalk and was taken to Elmhurst General Hospital by ambulance. There he received seven sutures for a scalp wound.

Two residents of Astoria Houses testified that they saw Jackson remove his shield from his pocket and enter the police room. . . . [3]

Robert Jackson was acquitted of all the charges brought against him.

Interestingly, the *Buric* and *Jackson* cases involved individuals who wanted to continue to participate in the auxiliary program even after having experienced unfortunate treatment. Moreover, it is highly significant that thousands of men and women are still anxious to serve, although the memory of these cases and the tragic death of David Freed must still be present.

All auxiliary police officers should also be acquainted with the nature of their authority to make arrests and conduct searches and the types of appropriate liability insurance available to them. The following three sections will examine these issues.[4]

Arrest Authority

An auxiliary officer out on the street in any capacity is likely to encounter, at some time and place, an emergency situation where merely calling for a regular police officer would be considered an unreasonable response. If that auxiliary officer decides to make an arrest may he or she do so as a peace officer or as a private citizen?

One of the major distinctions between an arrest made by a peace officer and an arrest made by a private citizen can be found in the wording of the *Criminal Procedure Law of New York*. A peace officer may arrest a person for a crime when the officer has "reasonable cause to believe" that such person has committed such crime. On the other hand, a citizen not having peace officer status may only legally arrest a person when that person "has, in fact, committed" the crime.[5] In other words, an officer who makes an arrest is protected from liability for false arrest if his actions are reasonable; a private citizen is so protected only if he is, in fact, correct.

An officer, of course, is better able to make an arrest than is a private citizen. By virtue of his uniform he is more likely to secure the consent and acquiescence of others. By virtue of his training, he is better prepared to deal with those who resist. Statutes are drawn to assist the peace officer. It is a misdemeanor in New York to refuse to aid an officer or to resist an arrest.[6] No similar support exists for the private citizen. In short, although the law empowers a private citizen to make an arrest, it does not encourage him to do so.

In the state of New York, a community can choose to grant peace officer status to its auxiliary unit under section 105 of the Emergency Act. However, according to *PBA* v. *Hitt*, that status is only valid during periods of attack or during duly scheduled drills.[7] Since what does or does not constitute a drill is subject to dispute, an officer to whom such status has been granted is still faced with considerable uncertainty. Moreover, his status is more uncertain in communities which do not exercise their option under the Emergency Act. Unfortunately, most of the legal opinions regarding the exact status of auxiliaries within New York are conflicting.[8]

When an auxiliary officer is on duty, logic would seem to compel us to grant him peace officer status. Any contrary finding would bestow upon the arrestee an ability to resist arrest with impunity. On this precise point, one court stated: "Such a finding would, in fact, legalize mayhem—letting the law smile on the winner."[9]

The most recent authoritative statement on the issue of whether or not auxiliary police are peace officers in New York was made by New York's Attorney General, Robert Abrams. In his "Informal Opinion No. 81–49," Abrams indicated that "the special duties of an auxiliary police officer as a peace officer are limited to those of meeting an enemy attack and do not include tests and training."[10] Clearly, there exists an overwhelming need to clarify the status of the auxiliary police in New York City and in the communities throughout the state of New York.

It must be emphasized that the ambiguity which surrounds the status of auxiliary police within the state of New York may or may not exist elsewhere. Significantly, the 1969 police reserve study conducted by the Arlington County Police Department revealed that 65 percent of the responding departments granted their volunteers "police powers" while on duty. (See Appendix A.)

Search Authority

An important distinction between public and private police authority exists. It is well recognized that the *U.S. Constitution* acts as a major legal limitation on the powers of the public police and on the officially sanctioned activities of volunteer police forces. However, constitutional restrictions are not generally applied to private activities.

One of the most vital constitutional restraints on police behavior concerns the "exclusionary rule." Although subject to various exceptions, the rule requires that illegally seized evidence is to be excluded from the prosecutor's case during the trial of a criminal action.[11] Extensive training in criminal and constitutional law is required in order for any officer to begin to master the complex rules pertaining to arrest, search and seizure. Officers who act in contravention to constitutional procedures stand an excellent chance of having their evidence suppressed forever. This policy also applies to those volunteer officers engaged in authorized duty assignments. Auxiliaries should not be used in a law enforcement capacity until they have had sufficient training. If an untrained private security officer were to make an arrest on insufficient evidence, or conduct an illegal search, or fail to inform a suspect of his or her rights, any evidence thereby obtained might still be admissable against the suspect in court (unless the security officer was employed by government).[12] A volunteer officer's case under similar circumstances would be controlled by the "exclusionary rule." In short, only a properly trained officer, regular or volunteer, can be expected to uphold the civil liberties of private citizens in the pursuit of crime prevention and law enforcement.

However, if an off-duty auxiliary police officer makes an illegal search and seizure of evidence, this, in itself, would not constitute state involvement requiring suppression of the evidence. The evidence will be suppressed upon a finding that regular police officials joined in or ratified the action of the volunteer. In the *Commonwealth of Pennsylvania* v. *Eshelman*,[13] the official involvement by police in a warrantless search conducted by an off-duty auxiliary was in issue. An off-duty auxiliary police officer made an illegal seizure of evidence, namely, a package of marijuana which he had taken from an old automobile located on the defendant's grandmother's property. The volunteer officer brought the package to the local police chief. The chief arranged for the auxiliary officer to take the package to the state police for further investigation and testing of its contents. This action ratified the unauthorized act of the auxiliary officer, making the auxiliary officer's initial illegal actions the actions of the state. In addition, the auxiliary police officer testified that he brought the package to his chief without opening it, thereby indicating that it must have been opened and its contents examined for the first time by the police, in their presence, or at their direction. Thus, the wrongful search initiated by the auxiliary police officer was not completed before the police had participated in it.[14]

Liability Insurance

Under the doctrine of "respondeat superior"[15] communities are increasingly faced with the cost of indemnifying their officers, regular or volunteer. For all but the largest cities, the only solution to this exposure is liability insurance. Once private citizens volunteer to serve on behalf of a public agency, they have a responsibility to exercise care in the execution of that service. Volunteers can expect to be held personally liable for their conduct. However, state and local governments should provide their police volunteers with sufficient liability insurance to protect them against lawsuits.

Generally, states have Workmen's Compensation laws which cover an employee injured on the job. Volunteers must specifically be included as a class in order to be eligible for the compensation coverage. The volunteer must be defined as an employee of the state through legislation or policy amendments. States which do not include volunteers under their Workmen's Compensation coverage usually provide liability insurance through private insurance agencies.

Additionally, volunteer officers should be sheltered from lawsuits associated with the performance of duty, such as false arrest. Coverage is available for conduct related directly to the officer's duty.[16] Premiums are generally evaluated separately for each city. Significantly, a steady flow of claims against a police department can make that department uninsurable. Ultimately, the cost of liability protection to a community for its police, regular or volunteer, is inexorably tied to the quality of screening and training of applicants.

On September 29, 1976, President Ford approved the first federal law designed to provide a death benefit for the families of deceased policemen and firemen. It was of great significance that the provisions of the statute were designed to include volunteer policemen and firemen. The statute, known as "The Public Safety Officers' Death Benefits Act" (42 USC 3796), provides the sum of $50,000 to the family of an officer who has died as the result of a personal injury sustained in the line of duty. However, no benefit is paid if the death was caused by the intentional misconduct of the officer, or if voluntary intoxication was the proximate cause of death.

The issues of volunteer and state/agency liability are not only complex but also changing. Volunteers should be advised about their position and responsibilities early in their training program in order to avoid later misunderstanding. Moreover, it is the burden of each police department which undertakes the recruitment of volunteers to acquaint them with all the realities of the position and to do all that is possible to further their acceptance by regular personnel. The utilization of volunteer legal counsel could keep all concerned advised on any changes in the law regarding volunteers.

14 • Power in the Auxiliary Police

When he was in his nineties, Bertrand Russell, one of the most influential thinkers of the twentieth century, summarized his personal philosophy:

Three passions, simple but overwhelmingly strong, have governed my life: the longing for love, the search for knowledge and unbearable pity for the suffering of mankind.[1]

All people want and need to be admired and to have prestige. In order to achieve these precious satisfactions, many persons have joined groups. In fact, according to a 1974 Census Bureau survey, one out of four Americans over the age of thirteen does some form of volunteer work.[2] More and more people are finding free time on their hands and want to do something with it. John Bonner found a correlation to exist between authoritarianism in auxiliaries and how they viewed their own occupational status:

The lower an auxiliary perceived his occupational station to be, the higher was his degree of authoritarianism. This might help explain why some auxiliaries are drawn to police work. Are they perhaps seeking to identify with a group that they perceive as having high status?[3]

Traditionally, new immigrant groups sought out police work for status and security, but today such positions are scarce. On the other hand, volunteer police positions are readily available. In such programs anyone may gain some status, but generally no monetary security. Moreover, contemporary newspaper reports and police department statistics reveal that greater numbers of minority group members are seeking ways to control crime in their communities. Significantly, the percentage of black, Puerto Rican, Jewish and Chinese auxiliary police officers is higher than that on the regular police force. Currently,

This chapter originally appeared as a part of the author's article entitled: "Auxiliary Civilian Police—The New York City Experience," *Journal of Police Science and Administration* 6 (1978): 92–96. Copyright 1978 by IACP, Inc. Reprinted and adapted with permission.

about 7 or 8 percent of the regular force in the city are black and 2 or 3 percent are Hispanic, while 22 percent of the auxiliaries are black and 13 percent Hispanic.[4] In the city as a whole, the black population is 21.1 percent, and the Spanish-speaking population is 16.2 percent.[5] It is interesting to note that up until the time of the Harlem riots in 1943, black police officers walked foot beats because they were not allowed to ride in radio cars and that the first black policeman's organization, the Guardian Association, did not receive official recognition until 1949, six years after it was founded.[6] Similarly, the auxiliaries in most precincts were prohibited from using radio patrol cars and their organization, the Auxiliary Police Benevolent Association was afforded little official recognition.

We have used the term "status" to refer to the very fact of one's membership in the auxiliary, as distinguished from its use as a description of one's high or low prestige within a particular group. Thus, an individual may have several statuses: healthy, young, male, driving instructor and member of the auxiliary patrol force. Identification of each social category or status is essential before we can examine the "role" or set of norms attached to a given status. For example, we may generally expect a driving instructor to have a knowledge of many safe driving habits. Therefore, by knowing a person's status and role we may be able to predict something about his behavior. Incidentally, there is only some recent evidence which suggests that the status and role of New York's auxiliary patrol force are becoming known to the general public. This problem will be reconsidered at a later point.

Almost all of society's institutions involve a pyramidal system of organization. In particular, police groups have traditionally utilized a semimilitary table of organization. In the regular military, the most significant dividing line falls between officers and enlisted men. Noncommissioned officers—sergeants and corporals—form a buffer between the two. Auxiliary police units adhere to similar patterns of differentiation. For example, auxiliaries with the rank of lieutenant and above generally hold separate meetings and tend to confide among themselves, whereas auxiliary policemen and policewomen primarily form friendships and maintain confidences among themselves.

The nature of an auxiliary's role is most closely aligned to the rank he holds. Fortunately, the role expectations for all ranks have been officially defined according to duties:

AUXILIARY COMMANDING OFFICER [Captain, Deputy Inspector, Inspector]—is a volunteer citizen duly appointed in accordance with these Rules and Regulations and assigned in command by the Commanding Officer, Auxiliary Forces Section, and who has authority over and responsibility for the Auxiliary Police Unit to which assigned.

AUXILIARY EXECUTIVE OFFICER—will assist the Auxiliary Commanding Officer in his duties, and call to his attention all matters of importance such as unusual occurrences and important messages or conditions requiring his attention.

AUXILIARY PATROL LIEUTENANT—will be assigned in Command of the outgoing platoon. Prior to the assignment of members of the outgoing platoon, he will inspect each member to ascertain that each is properly equipped and uniformed and given instructions as may be necessary. He will then post the platoon and be particularly charged with exacting the proper performance of duties by auxiliary patrol personnel under his supervision.

AUXILIARY PATROL SERGEANT—is charged with exacting the proper performance of duties from members assigned to duty under his supervision, and with such other duties as may be assigned to him by competent authority. He shall assist and instruct the Patrolmen in the discharge of their duties and shall report any dereliction of duty on their part to his commanding officer.

AUXILIARY PATROLMEN/POLICEWOMEN—in the performance of patrol duty, shall
A. Be constantly alert, observing everything that takes place within their sight or hearing, and so far as possible within the limits of their posts or other assigned areas. . . .

E. Promptly obey all lawful orders of a superior officer.[7]

Other duties specified for the lowest rank include the procedures for notifying the precinct about a sick or lost person and familiarization as to the locations of telephones, police and fire alarm boxes.

No auxiliary has any authority over any regular police officer, regardless of his or her rank. The ranks within the auxiliary patrol force pertain only to its members. For example, the lowest ranking regular police officer at the scene of an incident is superior to the highest ranking auxiliary. However, among auxiliaries rank is very important. Significantly, since auxiliaries are unsalaried and even pay for extra personal equipment, rank alone becomes the chief means of gaining rewards and prestige.

In the following sections we will consider the role rank plays in our effort to learn who wields power in the auxiliary police. Incidentally, we will not be viewing power in terms of "the ability to make policy"; with respect to the auxiliary program, policy decisions are a political function. For example, the questions of broadened authority, sanctioning of equipment and the use of patrol cars, are matters in the discretion of legislative leaders, the mayor and the police commissioner.

Power is usually sought as a means to an end. It exists whenever one person is able to exercise his will in determining the behavior of another person.[8] It implies responsibilities and burdens. For these reasons, some people do not want to be a chairman, a father or mother, an auxiliary commanding officer, or even an auxiliary patrolman. On the other hand, those who do seek power often cling to it tenaciously. Auxiliary police commanders are no exception. Some have been known to discourage the enrollment of "high caliber" volunteers during their initial screening interviews. Is such a potential recruit a threat to the commander's "status," or does he fear a loss of authority (legitimate power)? Surely, an auxiliary commander's status as a member of the auxiliary is not jeopardized because of the enlistment of one more member, no matter what extra ordinary qualifications he might present. However, he might be justified in the belief that his ability to influence the behavior of others is endangered. Significantly, once the newcomer has achieved the same volunteer status as his commander, he might also seek rank, power and its associated prestige. Through participant observation, this writer has witnessed numerous instances involving precisely such struggles.

People from all walks of life find their way into the various units of the auxiliary patrol force. Butchers, TV producers, taxi drivers, lawyers, stock clerks and even the famous have joined. They each have gained an additional status, but where do the centers of power lie?

In most instances the auxiliaries adhere to their chain of command and positions of authority are maintained. The greatest responsibilities are usually centered at the precinct level insofar as day-to-day command is concerned. Higher echelon auxiliaries are generally figureheads, although their titles may sound impressive to outsiders. Auxiliary commanders on the division level are only required to inspect and prepare biannual evaluations of auxiliary precinct commanders. Both inspection and evaluation reports are generally filed immediately and go unnoticed. Nevertheless, promotion to the division level is usually sought by auxiliary precinct commanders. They may be unaware of the limited functions of the higher rank, or quite aware, and anxious for the rest and the "ego" satisfactions that may accompany such a promotion. However, in this instance, rank and power do not necessarily coincide. Furthermore, the highest rank in the auxiliary, that of inspector, is held by about a dozen individuals. Seven of them hold positions as borough commanders, but none of them has any greater authority than the next. Significantly, they may occasionally work as a committee, but such activity is rare. Here again, rank and authority do not necessarily coincide.

A review of the foregoing analysis would seem to lead us to the conclusion that power in the auxiliary police is localized at the precinct level, and possessed by the auxiliary precinct commander. Through their activities in the auxiliary police, most auxiliary precinct commanders become involved with many segments of their community. They may be called upon to address civic meetings on crime prevention and they often initiate these contacts for purposes of recruitment. Higher echelon personnel also share in these efforts.

Other centers of power, however, are prominent in the auxiliary. Throughout every level of command, regular police officers have been assigned to advise and coordinate. On the precinct level, one police officer is assigned to the auxiliary patrol unit. These assignments are made by the regular precinct captain, who is specifically charged with the responsibility of maintaining an effective auxiliary program in his precinct.[9] Such personnel are called "auxiliary police coordinators." They are responsible for personally enrolling, interviewing, investigating and instructing every new member. Needless to say, they make use of more experienced auxiliaries to aid them in these functions. In most units an accommodation is gradually arranged between the police coordinator and the auxiliary precinct commander. In other words, a direct or tacit understanding is worked out concerning the role each is to play. In some instances, the auxiliary commander becomes a mere figurehead. In other cases, a constant state of friction occurs when the struggle for power cannot be compromised. Thus, the real power centers may vary from precinct to precinct. Significantly, in the key area of making promotions, the auxiliary police coordinator has the edge. All promotions require the endorsement of the regular police precinct commander, and he is generally available only to the coordinator. In most instances, coordinators readily obtain the necessary endorsement, and such recommendations are rarely refused by higher police authorities.

Therefore, the centers of power in the auxiliary patrol force appear to rest in the hands of only a few individuals: auxiliary police coordinators, auxiliary precinct commanders and, to the extent that they take a knowing interest, the regular precinct commanders. At this point, mention should also be made of the role of the commanding officer of the Auxiliary Forces Section. In the past, the incumbents of this office have held the key leadership role for the recruitment and publicizing of auxiliary activities. Their function also involves record keeping, the review of disciplinary matters and the issuance of a series of directives "to assist and direct precinct programs." [10]

A very important ramification of the concepts of rank, status and power concerns how the ordinary citizen perceives or reacts when he or she is confronted by a member of the auxiliary police. Some citizens may be unaware that auxiliaries are merely citizens clothed in a police uniform. Consequently, their actions are only controlled by the laws for citizen arrests and the use of force by ordinary citizens. [11] Moreover, except in the rare instance when an auxiliary may also hold a peace officer position listed under section 1.20 of the Criminal Procedural Law, all auxiliaries are unarmed, except for a nightstick. [12] Furthermore, they may not be assigned to plainclothes duty, strikes, hazardous duty, civil rights demonstrations, or "be used to replace a regular police officer." [13] In 1968, the commanding officer of the Auxiliary Forces Section elaborated:

During their training period they are impressed with the fact that they have no actual police powers and are discouraged from taking any action on their own. In all cases— except where they might see a woman being mugged—they are told to contact the regular police. An auxiliary cop is really just an extra pair of eyes and ears for us. [14]

In 1975 the unarmed volunteer auxiliaries assisted in about five hundred arrests, according to official reports. [15] Moreover, in that year, a twenty-year-old auxiliary sergeant was killed on duty in Central Park. Nevertheless, auxiliaries still attend a preliminary indoctrination of about forty hours, during which time they are repeatedly informed about what they may not do.

It is not very difficult to foresee a public danger arising from the presence of uniformed but relatively untrained and powerless auxiliaries. A citizen might be in need of immediate protection and only be able to find an auxiliary. Fortunately, he usually will not find ''an auxiliary'' because they are required to patrol in pairs. However, even six unarmed auxiliaries are no match for one armed felon.

Another potential problem exists because of the nature of the auxiliary's basic appearance. The auxiliary's uniform is exactly the same as a regular policeman's, except for a star shaped badge and the additional word ''AUXILIARY'' on the armpatch. How many citizens can recognize the difference? Furthermore, if they are able to discern an auxiliary, do they understand his role?[16] Clearly, the role of the auxiliary patrol force is to be supportive to the Police Department. Its members perform support functions with definitely limited areas of responsibility, and they are exclusively under the direction of regular police officers. They are required to serve in a subordinate capacity and may not be used to replace regular officers.

15 • The Origin of the Auxiliary Subway Patrol

The second largest police department in New York City is the Transit Authority Police. This organization ranks among the ten largest police forces in the country and its special purpose is to police "a 237-mile-long subterranean world beneath the streets."[1] The force has its own Police Academy and detective squad. This chapter will consider the difficulties involved in the establishment of an auxiliary police presence within the city's transportation facilities.

The upsurge in crime is particularly noticeable in the city's subway system.[2] On January 8, 1976, the Committee on Transit of the City Council met to discuss this matter. As a combative measure, Manhattan Councilman Theodore S. Weiss suggested the use of an auxiliary police force. In response, Transit Police Chief Sanford D. Garelik stated that he would direct the transit force's legal department to review the legality of such a program. This marked the first time in history that a Transit Authority police chief had publicly promised to work positively for the utilization of auxiliaries.[3]

The idea for utilizing the services of auxiliaries within the city's mass transit system was publicly announced in the mid-sixties by the Auxiliary Police Benevolent Association. The plan was presented to City Council President Garelik[4] on February 16, 1970, at a conference held at the request of the APBA. At that time, the Association's three top leaders argued the merits of the proposal. They were: President Graham Mark Schneider and first and second vice presidents Matthew Evans and Barry Meyers, respectively.

However, the exact origin of the proposal before the City Council dated back to November 2, 1967, when a resolution was introduced calling upon the Transit Authority to provide free public transportation for auxiliary policemen while traveling in uniform.[5] The measure was introduced each year until 1972. The Transit Authority had been responsive to the idea that the auxiliaries could serve as a deterrent to subway crime and lawlessness, but throughout this period of time insisted that the city subsidize the program. The city had been paying for the cost of allowing police and firemen to ride for free, although they were not required to be in uniform. The 1967 resolution had not included any reimbursement provision.

Members of the City Council were at a loss to determine how many auxiliaries would be using the mass transit facilities of the city and with what frequency. Consequently, because the amount of the subsidy could not be readily determined, no further action was taken until March 28, 1972. It was then that various City Council members accepted the figures obtained by the Auxiliary Police Benevolent Association and agreed to support *Resolution No. 770*. This measure called upon the mayor and the Board of Estimate to provide funds and to request the Transit Authority to permit members of the auxiliary police to travel freely to and from their assigned posts while in uniform. The resolution was unanimously approved by the City Council in September of 1972. However, Mayor Lindsay opposed the plan and the Transit Authority still insisted on being paid.

In the spring of 1973, Brooklyn Councilman Theodore Silverman, chairman of the Committee on Civil Service and Labor, sponsored a number of bills on behalf of the auxiliary police. He succeeded in enacting a law to provide their first annual uniform allowance. Attached to this bill was a second section known as *Intro. No. 879-B*. This would have provided the needed funds from the executive expense budget to allow many hundreds of uniformed auxiliary police officers on the city's buses and subways. The members of Silverman's committee debated this bill. They concluded that only the uniform allowance had a chance of overcoming the mayor's opposition. The full City Council readily approved the allowance and Mayor Lindsay eventually signed it into law, but the free transportation measure never left the committee room. The last time the City Council acted on behalf of an auxiliary police free passage proposal occurred on April 30, 1974. On that date Councilmen Silverman and Horwitz drew up bill number 506. It would have had the dual role of providing an auxiliary police presence on all of the city's transit facilities and providing a productivity incentive by requiring the completion of a minimum of 126 hours of service during the preceding year in order to travel in uniform without charge.[6]

Over the years, homeward bound commuters have been subject to numerous subway crises. On May 26, 1971, and August 28, 1973, thousands of passengers were trapped on the IRT Flushing Line. Many New Yorkers were overcome by the oppressive heat while they waited for help. During both incidents auxiliaries aided the injured.[7]

On other occasions, auxiliaries have aided the victims of crime on the city's subways and buses. In 1973 the Transit Authority revealed an upsurge in crimes committed by youths on trains, buses and along station platforms. The report was carried in the *New York Times* in this way:

Many of the youths involved are high school students or truants. They ride in groups, swooping through trains, clustering on platforms, sometimes fighting among themselves and often preying on groups of students from other schools.[8]

On April 19, 1973, a boy was waiting in the Columbus Circle Station with his mother and sister. Three youths began taunting him. Suddenly, one of the three pulled out a pistol and fired at the child. Robert Lewis, an auxiliary policeman grabbed the armed youth and held him until the arrival of the Transit Police.[9]

In the 1970s, the city's buses and subways were equipped with two-way radios and lock boxes in order to reduce the number of drivers who were being victimized. Nevertheless, the harassment and shakedown of commuters continued. A new call for an auxiliary police presence on city buses and trains occurred when Jack Braunstein, the chairman of the Metropolitan Citizens Transit Council, a commuter group, specifically urged the use of auxiliary police throughout the city's transit system in order to help deter crime.[10] A few days after Transit Authority Police Chief Sanford Garelik addressed members of the City Council on the problem of subway crime, Mr. Braunstein stated in a letter to Garelik:

Loiterers are permitted to frequent subway stations, waiting for the opportunity to mug and rob the sick, the lame, the old, women and lone travelers. Bands of potential muggers are permitted to roam the subway trains with impunity looking for likely victims, whom they mug either on the train or follow out to the street and then commit the crime.[11]

The crime problem in the city's transit system has been complicated by the city's fiscal crisis which has, at times, actually necessitated a reduction in the number of transit police officers. There has been some form of separate transportation police since 1936 when the city took over bankrupt private subway systems. These personnel were supervised by Police Department officials until 1953, when an independent transit police force was established. The utilization of auxiliaries could considerably strengthen the patrol capabilities of the transit police department. But, only a Transit Authority decision to allow auxiliaries to ride for free could permit them to be immediately assigned in the subways within their precinct boundaries. In order to insure the safety of the personnel assigned to these posts, a series of familiarization lectures would be needed concerning the special features of working in subways and buses. New recruits would probably enter the ranks of the auxiliary police because of the desire to bring about a safer transit system and to obtain the special free transit privileges. Consequently, there would be no decline in the usual street patrols and in the many other assignments undertaken by the auxiliaries.

Moreover, the establishment of an auxiliary police presence in the subways needed the good will of the rank and file members of the Transit Authority Police. In the summer of 1975, the members of New York City's Auxiliary Police Force stayed away from their precincts for approximately 30 days. There were many reasons for this occurrence, but of particular importance was the atmosphere of hostility occasioned by the layoff of nearly 3,000 regular police officers. Over the years it seems that police disdain for auxiliaries has been almost traditional. Jim Roti-Roti, Auxiliary Police Chief of Colonie, an upstate New York community, has explained that "an auxiliary policeman must get public respect by being as professional as the regulars, yet if he gets too professional, then the regular police will resent him. . . . ."[12]

On the same day that Transit Police Chief Garelik was extolling the virtues of the suggestion made by Councilman Weiss for the establishment of an auxiliary transit police force, John T. Maye, the president of the Transit Patrolmen's Benevolent Association, stated that he would much prefer that the city rehire the 300 transit police who had been previously laid off because of budget cuts.[13] He also asserted that "there would be a risk involved in the use of unarmed auxiliary police when you consider that even our own men who are armed are being assaulted now."[14]

During the first six weeks in 1977 there occurred a 17 percent increase in serious crimes over the same period from the previous year. In a desperate effort to deter crime on the city's subways and buses, the Metropolitan Transportation Authority finally announced on February 25, 1977, that henceforth any uniformed member of the city's auxiliary police could ride free. The same privilege was extended to the city's 3,000 correction officers and 1,300 court officers.[15] However, no attempt was made to mobilize the auxiliaries into regular security patrols or assign them to fixed posts within the transit system.

By 1979, the number of transit police officers had fallen to 800 below their 1975 strength level. Chief Garelik had attempted to compensate for this loss in personnel by securing the services of 144 regular city police officers at a cost of $8.6 million to the city. On September 11, 1979, Mayor Koch announced that he was placing the Transit and Housing Authority police forces under the command of the Police Department. He also replaced Sanford D. Garelik, chief of the transit police since 1975, with James B. Meehan. Mayor Koch described his actions as the first step toward the possible merger of the three police forces. Police Commissioner McGuire stated that he looked upon this opportunity as a way to make "uniform, integrated policy decisions" in fighting crime.[16] Whether or not these moves would lead to the formulation of a plan for the deployment of auxiliaries throughout the city's subways was left unsettled until mid-December of 1981.

The transit police department reported 574 subway robberies for the month of November 1981, a 60 percent increase over the 355 reported for November 1980. Data also showed a similar increase occurred during December 1981.[17] In addition, a poll of New Yorkers conducted during December indicated that transit crime was a dominant concern and it was the most frequently stated reason for riding less often.[18]

In the fall of 1981, Mayor Koch undertook a major initiative in the field of public safety and the involvement of volunteer police. He encouraged Police Commissioner McGuire to survey the city's 7,000 auxiliary police officers in order to learn how many of them would be willing to patrol the subways. This inquiry resulted in an unpublicized experiment within the 46th Precinct of the

Bronx. The Bronx auxiliaries were assigned to protect five subway stations after some orientation on the use of transit facilities. They were issued police radios for contacting the regular or transit police in case of any emergency. When the idea of the patrol experiment was announced publicly for the first time in December of 1981, the leadership of the Transit Patrolmen's Benevolent Association denounced the plan.[19] The Auxiliary Police Benevolent Association warned its members about the inherent dangers of elevated and subway platforms. Moreover, in an unusual show of cooperation the transit PBA and the New York City Transit Police Department brought an article 78 proceeding to prevent the use of auxiliaries for subway patrols. On March 19, 1982, Justice Ira Gammerman made the following decision:

The use of auxiliaries has been previously challenged and found to be proper for such activities as patrolling the streets, [and the] unprotected public parks in the cities of this state during the late hours. . . . There is a need for the auxiliaries to patrol the subways, and it is within the respondents' clear statutory responsibility and authority to utilize civilians for this function. . . . Accordingly, the petition is denied and the cross motion to dismiss the petition is granted.[20]

Thus, the way was now clear to fully utilize the auxiliaries to patrol subway platforms, mezzanines and stairwells throughout the city. In the fall of 1982, Mayor Koch announced that the experimental patrols would become permanent and that the number of volunteer police on subway patrol had grown from 12 to 1,500. The comment of transit PBA officials was that the volunteers were merely "mannequins in uniform," since they lacked adequate training and equipment to protect the public.[21]

The qualifications for becoming an auxiliary police officer in 1983 included: a minimum age of seventeen; citizenship or a declared intent to become a U.S. citizen; residence or work in New York City; no felony or serious misdemeanor convictions; sufficient understanding of the English language; and completion of fourteen sessions of instruction with four extra hours of special subway patrol training. All training sessions were provided during the evening hours and topics studied included: patrol operations, auxiliary police rules and regulations, penal law, first aid and self-defense. Generally, all primary classes of instruction were provided at a local precinct and the local auxiliary police coordinator served as the course instructor. Volunteers who failed to complete self-defense training were assigned to administrative or clerical duties and not permitted to perform patrol duty. Significantly, such duty could be requested by members at any time and automatically applied to any new enrollee over the age of sixty-one. In addition, patrol eligibility was conditioned on satisfactory performance during an annual self-defense and nightstick training class. Optional courses for promotion to the ranks of sergeant and above were also available. A police volunteer could qualify for advanced training by maintaining a satisfactory record of service for a prescribed period. All of this training fell short of the minimum requirements established for training police officers within the state of New York, but it exceeded the training required for various peace officer positions.[22]

One of the chief complaints that transit police officers have had over the years is that passengers either do not report crime when it occurs or they refuse to follow through once having initially filed a criminal charge. John Maye, who headed the transit PBA in the 1970s, estimated that only a third of subway crime was actually reported.[23] Clearly, members of the government, private citizens and community leaders who wish to maintain an auxiliary police presence within the city's transit system will have to contend with some animosity from transit police officers for the present time. However, there are hopeful signs that the police union's antagonism is subsiding. The exclusive use of the transit system's emergency radio frequency by auxiliaries and the restriction that auxiliaries are not to patrol trains or enter tunnels has diminished police criticism. Moreover, improved training programs and the willingness of the city to hire new full-time transit police officers has also alleviated the fears of some regular and Transit Authority police personnel.

In many respects the establishment of the auxiliary subway patrols was tied to several coinciding events. Perhaps, only the concordance of the following historical events led to the auxiliary subway patrols: the efforts of auxiliary PBA and City Council leaders to obtain free transportation for auxiliaries; the receptiveness of a transit police chief to the use of auxiliaries; an upsurge in subway crime; and the initiatives of Mayor Koch. Moreover, the establishment of the Guardian Angels played a significant role in the ultimate sanctioning of auxiliaries in the subways. Surely, if an unrecognized and unauthorized group could board trains for order maintenance, the auxiliaries could at least be assigned to protect subway platforms. New York County Supreme Court Justice Gammerman specifically referred to the Guardian Angels in his judicial opinion dismissing the suit brought by the transit PBA to block the use of auxiliary police in the subways.[24]

16 • Report on New York City's Auxiliary Police

On October 16, 1978, Manhattan Councilmen at Large Henry J. Stern and Antonio G. Olivieri conducted a public hearing on the Auxiliary Police program in New York City.[1] The hearing was called in response to criticisms they had received that the program was not effectively fulfilling its role of having volunteers in uniform aid the Police Department. They were also concerned with the problem of revitalizing the program, as called for by Mayor Koch, in the face of denouncements made by the regular police union. In particular, the Patrolmen's Benevolent Association had complained that auxiliaries took the jobs of regular police officers.

The purpose of the hearing was to gather information on the Auxiliary Police in order to issue a full report of findings and recommendations about the program. Moreover, it was the councilmen's hope to stimulate discussion and to prompt some necessary changes.

On February 11, 1979, Councilmen Stern and Olivieri issued their report based on three months of research and statements made at the public hearing. The document consisted of a twenty-five-page report. Exhibit 3 and Chart 4 present a list of the witnesses at the public hearing and an organization chart of the Auxiliary Police program. The complete report is presented in the remainder of this chapter.

I. Role and Structure of the Auxiliary Police Program

The role of Auxiliary Police (A.P.'s) in New York City traditionally has been described as the "eyes and ears" of the Police Force. Auxiliary Police Officers are civilians who volunteer their time to aid the Police Department in its mission of providing security for the City's population. The A.P.'s receive training and an allowance which is used to purchase a uniform which they wear while on duty. When patrolling in the evening, A.P.'s carry a nightstick, but otherwise they are unarmed. Auxiliary Police are not police officers, although during a state of emergency they have limited status as peace officers. They have no more right to make an arrest than any other civilian, and they call for help from regular police officers when it is needed.

Every precinct commander appoints a regular Police Officer to act as the Auxiliary Police Coordinator for the precinct (there are 73 in the City). The coordinator is directly in charge of the program in his precinct. The coordinator receives staff support for the program from the Auxiliary Forces and Crime Prevention Section, headquartered in Kew Gardens, Queens, and also from a Borough Coordinator appointed by the Borough Commanding Officer.

The program has a rank structure for Auxiliary Police Officers. New recruits start as Auxiliary Officers, and can work through the ranks of Auxiliary Sergeant, Lieutenant, Captain, Deputy Inspector, and Inspector. The Auxiliary Inspector commands the A.P.'s in each police borough (of which there are seven), and an Auxiliary Captain does so in each precinct. Promotion to these positions is based on recommendations of coordinators, and additional training is required.

The number of Auxiliary Police Officers remains small and has been declining. The Auxiliary Forces and Crime Prevention Section estimates that there are about 4000 people in the program, but figures show that active membership is only half that amount. During Fiscal Year 1978, 1590 auxiliaries performed at least 126 hours of service, and an additional 753 recruits completed training and entered the program. However, 1014 resignations were received during the same year. The following chart gives the figures for the last two fiscal years:

	FY 1978	FY 1977
Active members (completed 126 hours in program)	1590	1606
New recruits (completed training)	753	862
Resignations from program	1014	1373
A.P.'s who completed additional or advanced training	194	612

The history of a formalized Auxiliary Police dates back to 1916, during World War I, when a Citizens' Home Defense League was created. The League consisted of 25,000 volunteers who could be sworn in as special patrolmen during an emergency. Membership in the Home Defense League dwindled, and it was reorganized as the Police Reserve in 1918. This program also declined after a decade and ceased to exist.

With the coming of World War II, a City Patrol Corps was created which listed 7,125 members in 1942. This program ended in 1945. In 1950, during the Cold War, the present Auxiliary program was established to aid in civil defense. The State Unconsolidated Law (Sections 9123 and 9185) remains the sole statute authorizing the creation of Auxiliary Police programs in New York State. Even though the civil defense role has decreased, legally this remains the primary purpose of the Auxiliary Police and a major source of funding through Federal civil defense funds. With the reorganization of the Federal civil defense organization, there is a good possibility of changes in this role and funding.

The primary duties of Auxiliary Police Officers are:

●*Foot Patrol*—Auxiliary Police in pairs patrol the City's streets. They report any disturbances to the local precinct via radio or telephone so that a police car can respond to the situation. Patrol assignments are the responsibility of the precinct coordinator in consultation with the precinct commander and the auxiliary captain.

Patrols by A.P.'s can have a significant effect in helping to reduce crime. Auxiliaries received 523 awards for their role in helping with arrests last year, and also 141 awards relating to rescues. Saturation patrols, during which an increased number of A.P.'s patrol a small number of blocks, have proved to reduce street crime. Details of such a saturation patrol by auxiliaries of the 24th Precinct in Manhattan appear below. Saturation Patrol by Auxiliary Police Officers of the 24th Precinct; Limits of Patrol: Broadway to Riverside Drive, West 94 to 86 Streets. Hours: 6:00P.M. to 10:00P.M.

Dates (all 1978)	Complaints of Criminal Activity
Before Saturation Patrol:	
Monday, May 15	burglary; attempted robbery
Tuesday, May 16	burglary
Wednesday, May 17	grand larceny
Thursday, May 18	grand larceny; harassment
Friday, May 19	none
Monday, May 22	assault; attempted robbery
Tuesday, May 23	petty larceny; assault
During Saturation Patrol:	
Wednesday, May 24	none
Tuesday, May 30	none
Tuesday, June 6	petty larceny
Tuesday, June 13	grand larceny
Tuesday, June 20	none
Wednesday, June 21	none
Thursday, June 22	petty larceny
Tuesday, June 27	burglary
Wednesday, June 28	none
Thursday, June 29	none
Friday, June 30	none
Wednesday, July 5	harassment (ongoing complaint)
Friday, July 7	petty larceny
Monday, July 10	burglary
Following Saturation Patrol:	
Tuesday, July 11	robbery; burglary
Wednesday, July 12	none
Thursday, July 13	none
Friday, July 14	assault
Monday, July 17	assault
Tuesday, July 18	leaving scene of accident
Wednesday, July 19	none

Total: During the 14 days of the saturation patrol, there were 7 complaints, 3 of which were street complaints (one ongoing), and the rest of which were inside jobs. During the 14 days of normal patrol which preceded and followed this period, there were 15 complaints.

It is generally acknowledged that a uniformed presence on the streets deter crime. An Auxiliary Police Officer has a distinctive shield and patch on his or her uniform, but otherwise he or she looks like a regular police officer, and it is difficult for any civilian or criminal to distinguish the two.

Despite the risk involved, A.P.'s on patrol have a good safety record. One fatality has been recorded, that of an A.P. on patrol in Central Park in 1975. Injuries suffered while on duty are covered by workmen's compensation.

●*Crowd Control*—Auxiliary Police serve at parades, street fairs, etc., to help in controlling or directing large crowds.

●*Rescue Units*—Auxiliary Police who have received additional training in first aid and rescue techniques may be assigned to an Auxiliary Rescue Unit. There are fourteen such units throughout the City, operating out of various precincts, with their own specially-equipped rescue trucks. They respond to medical or other emergencies when dispatched.

●*Special Task Force*—A Special Task Force, which operates out of the Queens Auxiliary Forces Section headquarters, is available for special assignments in any area of the City. If a precinct coordinator plans a project for which he needs additional auxiliary officers, he can call on the Special Task Force to supply the manpower. Two Radio Motor Patrol (RMP) cars are assigned to the unit to provide transportation to precincts.

●*Clerical and Administrative Tasks*—A.P.'s maintain the records for their own program and help in any duties which may be required in the precinct.

●*Mounted Patrol*—A Mounted Patrol operates on some weekends in Central Park. It performs patrol or crowd control duties on horseback.

●*Harbor Unit*—A Harbor Unit operates to help in police patrol of the waterfront.

●*Traffic Control*—A new unit to help with traffic control and to be trained in traffic control methods is now being organized.

●*Scooter Patrol*—After receiving special training, A.P.'s can patrol on scooters in the few precincts where they are available.

●*Operation ID*—In one Brooklyn precinct, this crime prevention program is handled entirely by Auxiliary Police.

●*Senior Citizen Escort Program*—A.P.'s are performing this service in some areas.

●*Special Staff Support Work*—Auxiliaries who have special skills or interests such as lawyers or social workers can be placed in staff units such as the Legal Division or runaways program. Although only a handful of A.P.'s are now utilized in this way, attempts are being made to expand this program.

II. Findings and Recommendations

1. Role of the Auxiliary Police

The main critique of the program which we received is that there is too little contact between A.P.'s and regular police officers. The "glamor" of police work is the main attraction for joining the program. Unfortunately, this "glamor" is not evident to many A.P.'s. Auxiliaries patrol with other A.P.'s; they are out on foot, not in patrol cars (except for some cars which are available in Central Park, on Staten Island, and in a pilot program in the 24th Precinct), and the one police officer with whom they have regular contact is the precinct auxiliary coordinator. This lack of contact helps to breed animosity between the regulars and the volunteers; many police officers do not care for the auxiliaries (see Section 4).

In conjunction with revised training for A.P.'s, we recommend that:

●Auxiliary police officers should have the opportunity to ride on patrol with police officers on a regular basis. This would give A.P.'s a close look at how a real police officer works and would provide the incentive to volunteer on a regular basis to get this experience. It would give police officers the opportunity to scrutinize the auxiliaries and help to eliminate those who do not belong in the program.

Such a step would have certain disadvantages: an independent patrol by the auxiliaries would be lost; the auxiliaries would have to be ready to leave the police car at a moment's notice in case the officers would be called to a dangerous assignment. But these disadvantages are minor compared to the benefits.

●Police officers who patrol in one-man patrol cars should have the opportunity to request that they be able to patrol with an auxiliary. This would also give an auxiliary the benefit of seeing police work close-up, and it would give a patrolman alone in a car the opportunity to be accompanied by someone with a basic knowledge of police work.

Since one-man patrol cars already are operating in some precincts, and since police officers on such patrols would not be required to patrol with an auxiliary, we feel this program could be successful. The limits of the duties of an auxiliary in such a situation would have to be closely defined.

●Auxiliary officers should be trained to spot violations of the law which are civil offenses, such as violations of Sanitation or parking regulations or of the Health Code, and they should be given the authority to hand out summonses for these offenses. This would require a change in state law.

The most important activity of the auxiliary "eyes and ears" is to spot violent criminals, but non-violent lawbreakers have to be watched too.

●Stolen and abandoned cars are consistent eyesores and hazards. Sanitation Department figures show an average of 1,100 stolen and abandoned cars recovered weekly from the City streets. Auxiliaries should be trained in identifying these vehicles, finding the motor vehicle identification number on them, and reporting so that the vehicle can be removed. A.P.'s can also tour auto dumping grounds to search for stolen vehicles before car strippers get to them.

●During weekdays, auxiliaries patrol almost exclusively during the evenings. Housewives who are free during the day and could participate in the program do not do so. They should be encouraged. But all the precinct coordinators are men, and none of them has shown much initiative along these lines.

●Another problem of the program, which is pointed to in the preceding paragraph, is that when an A.P. arrives at a precinct for patrol, the precinct coordinator or a superior auxiliary officer must be present to assign the A.P. to patrol. If there is no such officer, there is no patrol. One result of this is that there is almost no daytime activity.

In a strange reverse to this, a few precinct coordinators work the day shift and take little part in supervising the A.P.'s who come in during the evening. Precinct coordinators should work the evening shift to ensure that they will be able to supervise the bulk of A.P.'s who volunteer during the evenings. If possible, the regular precinct desk should be instructed to assign patrol during the periods when the coordinator or superior auxiliary officers are not on duty.

2. Management

Police Commissioner Robert McGuire has changed the top management of the Auxiliary Police program, but the basic management structure has remained the same since a decentralization order in 1974. The new managers under McGuire are Deputy Commissioner for Community Affairs William Perry, Deputy Chief Gertrude Schimmel, who is in charge of the A.P. program in the Deputy Commissioner's office, and Captain Donald Roberts, head of the Auxiliary Forces and Crime Prevention Section. The new upper-level managers have tried to revitalize the program through such efforts as Auxiliary Police Week (held October 15–22, 1978) but little is going to change without change in the basic management structure.

At all levels throughout the police boroughs, there is a dual command structure of regular and auxiliary officers. At all times, even the highest-ranking auxiliary officer is required to accept the orders of even the lowliest police officer. The relationship of the two management structures is confused. Who assigns and supervises auxiliaries on patrol? Who performs personnel, recruitment, public relations tasks? Both precinct coordinators and auxiliary officers share the task.

Staff support for the program comes from the Auxiliary Forces Section, which is headed by a Captain who is also in charge of the Crime Prevention Section. The Auxiliary Forces Section (AFS) has a staff of 3 lieutenants, 2 sergeants, 11 police officers, 4 limited-duty police officers on temporary assignment, and 2 civilians. Responsibilities and functions are divided as follows:

- Training & Personnel—1 lieutenant and 4 police officers
- Special Projects, Recruitment & Retention—1 lieutenant and 3 police officers
- Funding, Statistics, Vouchers, Uniforms—1 sergeant and 1 police officer
- Administration—1 lieutenant and 3 police officers.

Queens headquarters has 22 people at a personnel cost of more than $600,000 yearly to provide staff support for the program. Fifty percent of the staff personnel costs are paid by Federal funds channeled through the State Civil Defense program.

Responsibility and authority at various levels in the program are unclear. For instance, the Auxiliary Forces Section can issue an order that all auxiliaries who do not work a minimum number of hours per quarter are to be dropped from the rolls. But a precinct coordinator who wants his enrollment figures to remain high may keep the "ghosts" on the rolls. Since the precinct coordinator is appointed by the precinct commander and not by the head of the Auxiliary Forces Section, the AFS head has little recourse.

Auxiliary superior officers presently have effective lifetime tenure in their positions, and are able to create their own fiefdoms in precincts or boroughs, which lead to inter- and intra-precinct disputes, all to the detriment of the program.

To develop a more effective management and command structure, we recommend:

- Ranks above the rank of auxiliary sergeant should be eliminated. The purpose of ranks is to reward A.P.'s who have performed effectively. But these rewards should come in the form of increased training and responsibility while on patrol, not in rising in a duplicative and unnecessary command structure.

An A.P. who remains in the program for a number of years and gains seniority should be rewarded through greater opportunities to patrol in RMP cars, to issue summonses for a greater variety of civil offenses, and to play a greater role in community service programs. The present command structure does not encourage diverse and imaginative uses of A.P.'s.

●Decrease of fifty percent in the size of the Auxiliary Forces Section and a civilianization of its staff. The Civilian Amateur Radio Patrol program of 8,000 volunteers is coordinated by one police officer. Sixty years ago, the Home Defense League had 8,000 volunteers and a staff of twelve. Although AFS staff has been cut back from 34 in 1972, continued attrition in the program means that cuts in staff support are warranted.

Police officers at AFS handle public relations, personnel, clerical and administrative tasks that could be done by civilians, and the Department's civilianization program should extend to AFS.

●Auxiliary Forces Section headquarters should be located in the Police Academy, or in another location more closely associated with Police Department functions. It is difficult for the Police Department to say it has much interest in a program when the headquarters are located among the pipes in the basement of Queens Borough Hall.

3. Training & Screening of Applicants

Although New York City boasts the largest Auxiliary program in the country, it also has the shortest training period among the programs we surveyed. Recruits who join the program go through a 13-week, 52-hour training course. Training in some other programs encompasses:

Seattle, Washington—120 hours
Los Angeles County, California—381 hours
Los Angeles, California—72 or 300 hours
Oakland, California—72 hours
San Diego, California—114 hours
Willoughby, Ohio—240 hours

Regular police officers in New York City receive approximately six months of training before going out on patrol. It should be noted that part of this time is spent in firearms training, which A.P.'s in New York do not receive.

The AFS staff in Queens has four officers assigned to handle training, yet most basic courses are now taught by precinct coordinators, who are experienced officers but have few or no qualifications to be good instructors.

The manual used in the basic training course can be read easily in an hour. Weekly exams are given in training but they serve little purpose, since almost no one fails. Three college credits are offered by John Jay College, however, for completion of the training course.

An intermediate training course is required for promotion to sergeant, and an advanced course for all higher promotions. These courses are generally more sophisticated, and concepts such as management by objectives are taught. Headquarters personnel are normally the instructors.

Candidates for the auxiliary program initially are interviewed by precinct coordinators, who can reject them if they do not meet basic qualifications (between 17 and 55 in age, good health, U.S. citizenship, no criminal record, read and write English, and live or work in the City). While the recruit is in training, his or her qualifications are supposed to be verified and a character investigation conducted to complete the screening of the applicant.

We recommend the following:

●The program cannot be improved and the recommendations listed earlier cannot be implemented unless training is improved. A.P.'s should receive a basic course before being sworn into the program. After a successful initial, but probationary, period of duty of one year, they should receive further training and authority to enable them to give summonses for civil offenses, ride in one-man patrol cars with regular officers, etc. A.P.'s who do not meet the standards for this additional training should be required to leave the program.

●Training should be done by qualified instructors, preferably through the facilities and instructors of the Police Academy. The training personnel in the Auxiliary Force Section should be transferred to the Police Academy to give the Academy the necessary manpower.

●The 13-week initial training period should be shortened. When it is combined with the period of a month it may take to start in a training course, the four months in training, and another month after finishing training to receive a shield, many recruits become impatient over the six-month delay and never finish training. We recommend that twice-a-week classes be offered, to cut the training period in half.

●Weekly exams should be eliminated and held instead on a more infrequent, but more meaningful, basis.

●Training should include a ride in a police car to give recruits a better idea of what police work is like.

4. Role of the Patrolmen's Benevolent Association

The Patrolmen's Benevolent Association (PBA), the plice officers' union, does not like the Auxiliary Police. A resolution passed at the September PBA convention called A.P.'s "scabs." The PBA has cited four main faults with the program:

●lack of training of A.P.'s

●lack of screening in recruitment

●A.P.'s do jobs regular police officers should be doing

●A.P.'s organize activities or collect funds in ways the PBA is prevented from doing.

There is a great deal of validity to the first two arguments, and we have recommended changes in the program to meet these deficiencies.

Although we have requested additional information on the last two charges, the PBA has been unable to cite instances other than the use of A.P.'s at parades. Parades and similar events are a significant source of overtime for police officers, and they resent anyone taking away the opportunity to make this extra money, as they believe A.P.'s do.

We disagree with the PBA. The commander in charge of policing an event will call out as many police officers as he believes is necessary. He cannot rely on the presence of A.P.'s to call out fewer police officers, since A.P.'s are only volunteers. They have no compulsion to work and it is unknown how many will attend to help police an event.

5. Weapons

There are a number of A.P.'s who would like to carry guns when on duty, just as A.P.'s in many other municipalities do. However, we do not encourage this proposal. A.P.'s with guns would have to have the same training and duties as regular police officers; this is not the purpose of the program.

It should be noted, however, that there are A.P.'s who are licensed to carry guns and do so, although not openly, while on duty. Although this has caused no controversies so far, it could if such a gun were used.

The basic weapon of an Auxiliary is a nightstick, the same nightstick which is carried by regular police officers. A.P.'s are trained in the defensive use of nightsticks and they provide the primary means of defense in case of attack.

The use of nightsticks by A.P.'s is controversial. A 1972 court decision (*People* v. *Schoonmaker*, 40 A D 2d 1066, 3rd Dept.) ruled that a nightstick was the equivalent of a billy, which is defined as a dangerous weapon under Section 265.01 of the Penal Law. A Corporation Counsel opinion (#108,602, dated April 4, 1978) has stated that A.P.'s should be prohibited from carrying nightsticks. Despite these decisions, A.P.'s continue to patrol with nightsticks.

Although the Corporation Counsel in his opinion offers assistance in drafting appropriate legislation to correct this situation, the City has done nothing to introduce the needed legislation.

●We recommend that the City draft appropriate legislation to permit Auxiliary Police to carry nightsticks, and work for its introduction and passage in the State Legislature. Failure to act could mean criminal charges being raised against an unsuspecting A.P., and would add to proof of City disinterest in the program.

6. Uniforms

Each A.P. receives a $75 uniform allowance from the City when he or she enters the program. The allowance is used to purchase a uniform at the Police Department's Equipment Section in Police Headquarters. The Auxiliary also receives a further $75 allowance for each year in which he or she works at least 126 hours in the program.

The allowance is inadequate. In order to pass inspection to enter the program, a male A.P. must spend at least an additional $19.25 to buy parts of the uniform not covered by the base allowance. A female must pay at least $16.90 additional. The reason is the expense of some items: a woman's hat costs $21.75, a scooter coat $45.75. Buying an additional shirt costs nine dollars.

●We recommend that the allowance for uniforms be increased to a maximum of $115, so that all necessary items are covered under it. We intend to introduce legislation to this effect in the City Council.

7. Radios

When A.P.'s are on patrol, they should have a radio walkie-talkie in order to communicate to police dispatchers any signs of criminal activity or assistance they might require. Our investigation has shown that only in Manhattan are there an adequate number of radios to meet the needs of A.P.'s on patrol. In other boroughs A.P.'s either are unable to patrol because there are no radios or else patrol without them, forced to use the nearest phone if trouble occurs.

Even worse, there are numerous reports of interference when an A.P. comes on the air to seek assistance. The interference, caused by regular police officers, takes the form of whistling, calling names such as "toy cop," or threats to get off the air. Although we have been told that it is only a small number of police officers who engage in such activity, almost every A.P. can recount such an experience, which makes it very difficult to get help when needed.

Further evidence we have gathered showed that emergency dispatchers have ignored A.P.'s requests for help. At our public hearing, Melanie Weiss, an A.P. in the 13th Precinct, described how on October 13, 1978, at 8:15 P.M., she had called 911 to request police response to 27th Street & 10th Avenue in Manhattan because of people being threatened by a man wielding two machetes. When she identified herself as an A.P., the emergency operator hung up on her. Response to the situation eventually came from two Housing Police detectives passing the scene on an unrelated call, according to Ms. Weiss. In light of other recent evidence raised about the problems of 911 dispatchers, this incident provides further evidence of the need to upgrade the training and status of dispatchers.

We recommend:

●The Police Department should obtain radios for its A.P.'s in the outer boroughs. The lack of radios means the Department is unable to keep its promise to A.P. recruits that patrols are made with radios. This failure is a main reason for low morale.

●All incidents of interference on radios and nonresponsiveness by dispatchers should be pursued. Similarly, A.P.'s who use radios incorrectly or recklessly should be reprimanded or dismissed from the program.

8. Emergency Rescue Units

Emergency Rescue units consist of people who have additional training in first aid and cardiopulmonary resuscitation, gained at a basic rescue training course. Some members are also Emergency Medical Technicians. Each unit has a van with emergency equipment, and they respond to accidents, either when no other unit is available (a rare occasion) or when permitted to respond by dispatchers (much more frequently). The rescue units provide whatever assistance might be required at the scene.

These units have the highest morale among A.P. units because their small numbers (several hundred) and specific purpose give them an elite status. But their vans, which were purchased through a special grant by the City several years ago, were not designed for their heavy use and frequently break down. Repair by the Department of General Services Motor Vehicle Unit can take up to six months (repairs are not done by the Police Department), and the $1200 budgeted for the job is inadequate. What equipment the vans do have is mainly what has been bought or repaired by the auxiliaries themselves.

●We recommend more material support for the Auxiliary Rescue Units, in terms of greater budget for repair, in-house repair by the Department, and to replace worn-out equipment and eliminate differences in levels of equipment among various units.

9. Mounted Unit

The A.P. Mounted Unit is supposed to operate on weekends in Central Park. However, ever since the elimination of the Police Department stable in midtown, horses have had to be vanned from the Bronx. This has limited the number of horses to four, and because of problems with the van, personnel or the weather, there is no mounted patrol on many weekends and its presence is minimal. The effect on A.P.'s who hope to participate in the mounted patrol is discouraging.

●We recommend that alternatives to strengthen the Mounted Unit be explored. Measures could include other stabling facilities, more or larger vans, better scheduling of personnel to end logistical difficulties, and seeking private contributions to help defer the added cost.

10. Private Funds

One of the complaints of the Patrolmen's Benevolent Association about the program is that A.P.'s can collect funds for various events in ways that the PBA cannot. We received numerous allegations of funds collected by A.P.'s but unaccounted for—at events such as dinner-dances, bus charters, club dues, sale of items such as uniform patches or soft drinks. We have not attempted to verify any of these allegations. We refer to them because of the threatening effect such allegations have on morale and on relations with the PBA.

A non-profit foundation, the Police Foundation, has been established in conjunction with the Police Department in order to develop proposals for aiding Police Department activities and then obtaining private contributions to meet such needs. For instance, the Foundation is funding the project to improve the lounge facilities in the 911 Emergency Center, so that the operators will be able to work in a better atmosphere. The Police Foundation has not expressed a great interest in developing programs to benefit the Auxiliary Police. They recently made their first grant to the program, $700, to help pay for recruiting posters. Little other help appears to be on the way.

●We recommend that an effective method for soliciting private funds for the auxiliary police be developed. Businesses, such as Citibank through the Civilian Radio Motor Patrol, have shown an interest in developing police volunteer programs. Either by convincing the Police Foundation to change its priorities to include the A.P.'s, or by creating another means, a way of obtaining private funds should be found.

11. Affiliated Organizations

The Auxiliary Police Benevolent Association (APBA) is the organization established to represent the A.P.'s. The APBA claims a membership of a majority of A.P.'s. It is headed by John Hyland, a Bronx A.P., and functions through delegates elected from precincts. The organization acts as a vocal pressure group and maintains a phone tape (call 391–0943) to express its views and inform its members. The APBA generates intense dislike among many superior Auxiliary Officers, who belittle its importance.

Religiously based fraternal organizations for A.P.'s have received the blessing of the Auxiliary hierarchy and are currently working to increase their membership. Any organization should develop contacts and relationships outside of strictly formal ones. The A.P. program has not developed many inter-precinct or inter-borough ones, except for the APBA.

12. Other Police Volunteer Organizations

Besides the Auxiliary Police, the Police Department sponsors several other volunteer groups. These are:

- ●Blockwatchers Program
- ●Civilian Observation Patrol
- ●Civilian Radio Motor Patrol
- ●Senior Citizen Escort Program
- ●Civilian Amateur Radio Patrol
- ●Community Councils

These volunteers do not perform their work in uniform, nor do they receive much training. Yet they have been quite successful in attracting volunteers, and their role can conflict with that of A.P.'s since they also serve as "eyes and ears." One particular source of conflict is over radios, which form the basic communication system for three of the volunteer programs, as well as for the A.P.'s.

●We recommend that the Department examine its volunteer programs carefully to make sure that they do not conflict. The A.P.'s, as the best-trained and most visible volunteers, should be the best-equipped and receive the greatest share of the Department's efforts.

13. Discipline and Hearings

Discipline in an all-volunteer program is difficult. There must be an effective way to remove people who do not belong in the program or who have committed acts which require dismissal (an arrest now leads to automatic dismissal, with reinstatement possible if there is no conviction). There are about 25 hearings a year of auxiliaries who have been charged with violating regulations. In 1977, hearings resulted in seven dismissals from the program. The Auxiliary Forces Section has changed the hearing procedure a number of times to meet objections to long delays or unfair trials, and now hearings are to be conducted by superior auxiliary officers.

●We recommend that hearings be conducted by regular police officers, in line with our recommendation that rank in the program be eliminated. We have also proposed earlier that A.P.'s be on a probationary status during their first year in the program, so that they may be dismissed for infractions. After this probation, they should be entitled to a hearing before being dismissed. Since many A.P.'s are young people who are planning a career in law enforcement, they should be given a full opportunity to prove themselves innocent; otherwise, the consequences on their proposed career can be very negative.

14. Legal Rights

The uncertain legal situation of A.P.'s is a definite factor in low morale in the program. The problem with nightsticks was described earlier. But A.P.'s are uncertain of their status if they are sued for their actions while in uniform. Are they employees or officials of the City whom the City will defend?

●We recommend that this situation be clarified either by Corporation Counsel opinion, or by appropriate legislation.

Another legal problem stems from the Civil Defense background of the A.P.'s. State law says that A.P.'s are not to be on duty except in case of emergency or while on drill. Therefore, for A.P.'s to perform legally their duties, a drill must be declared (Opinion of the State Comptroller, 69–87, March 27, 1969). It is unclear whether this "legal fiction'' has been preserved, and if it has not, whether A.P.'s are legally performing their duties.

●We recommend that this situation also be clarified either by regularly declaring drills for A.P.'s or seeking a change in the appropriate statute.

15. Conflict and Outside Employment

A number of auxiliaries either work full-time or moonlight as security guards, court officers, or similar law-enforcement related jobs. The Board of Ethics, in a recent opinion (No. 474, December 12, 1978) dealing with the right of police officers to obtain outside employment as bodyguards, concludes:

It is the opinion of the Board of Ethics that a police officer securing employment as a bodyguard (''personal security'') or other security officer might be engaged in private employment in conflict with the performance of his official duties and that he would be using ''his position to obtain . . . financial gain . . . for himself. . . . '' Seeking or accepting such employment would therefore be a violation of Section 2604, subdivision c (the Ethics Code of the City Charter).

●Due to similar nature of much of the work of A.P.'s, we recommend that the Police Department seek an opinion from the Board of Ethics regarding proper outside employment for A.P.'s.

III. Conclusion

The Auxiliary Police need more effective management, adequate training, higher standards of selection, and a sense of purpose instilled through greater duties in order to end attrition, turn around their demoralized attitude, and create an esprit de corps. Despite the efforts of the new City administration, changes in the program have been ineffective in turning the program around from its downward slide, and more significant changes are needed.

Our report has presented a sketch of a restructured A.P. program. We emphasize quality of participants over quantity. We recommend lack of rank, and a changeover to a program in which rewards will come from innovative, imaginative tasks which will make an individual want to join and stay in the program.

The Auxiliary Police have proven that they can be highly successful. Auxiliaries performed outstandingly during the 1977 blackout and at other times of stress. Proportionally, there are more blacks, Hispanics, and females in the program than in the regular police force. News about an effective, exciting program will travel quickly, and we expect membership to grow. We ask that our recommendations be implemented to help make New York a safer and better place to live and work.

Exhibit 3
Participants in October 16, 1978, Public Hearing

William E. Perry, Deputy Commissioner, Community Affairs, Police Department
Gertrude Schimmel, Deputy Chief, Community Affairs, P.D.
Donald J. Roberts, Captain, Auxiliary Forces & Crime Prevention Section, P.D.
Thomas Velotti, Recording Secretary, Patrolmen's Benevolent Assoc.
Walter Cobin, Patrolmen's Benevolent Association
James E. Eagen, Counsel, Auxiliary Police Benevolent Association
Robert L. Steele, Auxiliary Deputy Inspector, Manhattan South
Robert Gray, Auxiliary Captain, Manhattan South
Harry Junger, Auxiliary Inspector, Manhattan North
John A. Buric, former Auxiliary Police Officer
Melanie Weiss, Auxiliary Police Officer
Dr.James F. Sobrino, Auxiliary Captain, 10 Precinct
Debra Bloom, former Auxiliary Police Officer
Elizabeth Ann Kessler, former Auxiliary Police Officer
Walter Kowsh, Jr., former Auxiliary Police Officer
Edward McBride, Auxiliary Captain, 17 Precinct
Kathryn T. Coughlin, Vice President, Auxiliary Police Benevolent Association
Russell Shewchuk, Auxiliary Police Officer, 78 Precinct
Robert Nunziata, Auxiliary Police Officer, 111 Precinct
John Hyland, President, Auxiliary Police Benevolent Association
P. Greg Allard, Arnis America Organization, Inc.
Anne Fisher, Auxiliary Sergeant, Special Task Force

Written statements from:

Marla S. Perkel, Auxiliary Sergeant, Central Park Precinct
Jeanne DiGangi, Auxiliary Police Officer
Martin Greenberg, Instructor of Police Science, Hawaii Community College
Ted Martino, Auxiliary Captain, Headquarters Unit
Brother Christopher Varley, Auxiliary Police Chaplain, Manhattan South
Gary Wolpow, former Auxiliary Police Officer

Chart 4
Auxiliary Police Organization Chart, 1978

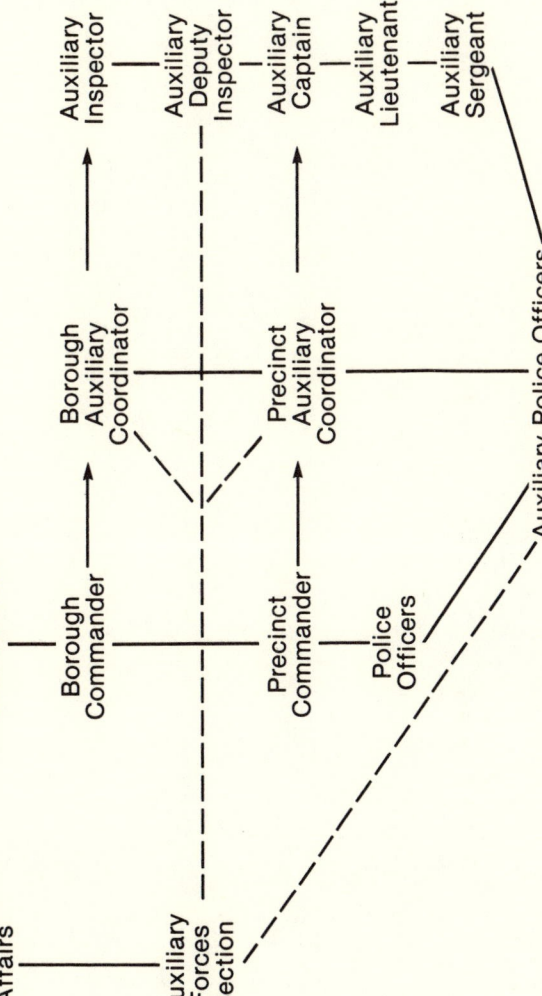

Note: Solid line indicates direct line of command — Dotted line indicates staff support services.

17 • The Guardian Angels

Swear by the blood of the Revolution, never to violate
in the least particular the laws of the country; and
never to tolerate their violation by others.

Abraham Lincoln (1838)[1]

Abraham Lincoln hoped that respect for the laws of society might be obtained by a concerted effort of all of the agencies of social control. His appeals to reason came at one of the most lawless and violent periods in American history. America is still searching for peace on its domestic front. The search continues and it has taken many roads in the past two centuries. The emergence of such "self-help" groups as the Black Panther party, the Jewish Defense League, Newark's North Ward Citizens Committee, the Brooklyn "Maccabees," the Louisiana Deacons and the Guardian Angels have stirred up a wave of controversy since the 1960s.[2]

It is generally believed that the recent groups have not, for the most part, committed violent acts. It is felt that most of these groups have arisen in response to a need for community self-defense and that their major concern has been with self-protection and not with meting out their own style of justice. "Thus, they more closely resemble the early anti-horse thief societies which amplified law enforcement through pursuit and capture, but did not try to substitute for it by administering summary punishments."[3]

The present chapter contrasts the activities and organization of the Guardian Angels with those of the New York City Auxiliary Police. It also examines whether or not all citizen patrol groups could benefit from improved screening and the availability of professional psychological services.

Citizen involvement in crime prevention efforts is epitomized by membership in the Guardian Angels or a unit of the auxiliary police. If each citizen looks out only for himself or herself, community isolation and fragmentation will develop. The lack of community involvement provides a breeding ground for crime.

However, on more than one occasion participation in unarmed street and subway patrols has resulted in disaster. Both an Angel and an auxiliary have been killed.[4] In addition, aggressive and ambitious members have hurt morale and no doubt some members may have emotional problems that have caused some harm. Furthermore, "the fact that private citizens have chosen to involve themselves in police work has meant that the issue, if not often the substance, of vigilantism has reoccurred with them."[5]

A fundamental difference between the Guardian Angels, who claim a national membership of nearly 5,000 and chapters in forty-three cities,[6] and the 9,000 member New York City auxiliary is the lack of governmental support accorded the former group. Auxiliaries are recruited, trained, equipped and regulated by the Police Department; however, Guardian Angels must rely on private donations for their support. The police auxiliaries wear police style blue uniforms with a distinctive seven point star. They are authorized to carry nightsticks, handcuffs, two-way radios and to travel free on public transit lines while in uniform. Angels pay their own transit fares, wear emblematic T-shirts, red berets and sometimes bright red nylon jackets. Auxiliaries are covered by the state Workmen's Compensation Law; the Angels are not. Auxiliaries are supervised by police officers assigned as auxiliary police coordinators in each of the city's precincts. Although there is a rank structure within the auxiliary police program, any auxiliary must follow the lawful orders of any regular police officer. The supervisory roles within the Angel organization below the level of Curtis Sliwa, the group's founder and chief, have not been disclosed.[7] However, officials in New York, Boston and Los Angeles are seeking to establish an identification system for the Angels.

Although the Guardian Angels have been invited to merge with the auxiliaries in New York, they have consistently resisted the opportunity. They may feel more secure in their status as unaffiliated volunteers or it may simply be a case of a leader who is not anxious to lose his army. On the other hand, the Auxiliary Police Force appears to maintain a close working relationship with the New York City Police Department.

Outside of the New York City area, some Angels have been arrested while seeking to enroll additional members. Such an incident occurred in Joliet, Illinois, on August 30, 1983. A group of fifty Angels came to Joliet to patrol the streets and recruit new members in the wake of a series of brutal murders within the community. The Angels put up tents on the lawn of the local courthouse and war memorial. They spoke at a public meeting about police incompetency in the handling of public safety. During the summer of 1983, Joliet was the scene of seventeen murders which included the deaths of two on-duty auxiliary deputy sheriffs and two elderly women. The Will County Sheriff's Office arrested five of the visiting Angels and charged them with disorderly conduct, trespassing and obstructing a peace officer in the performance of his duty. The arrested Angels were jailed for a night and released on individual recognizance the following day. Among those arrested was Lisa Sliwa, the Angel's national director and wife of Curtis Sliwa."[8]

As previously described in Part II, New York's volunteer police have a long history which has revealed an interesting trend in support of civil liberties. For example, excluding the depression period of the 1930s, the only two periods in which they were not utilized, the late twenties and forties coincided with times of serious municipal corruption. On the other occasions, their presence within station houses may have fostered a higher regard for the rights of individuals. On the other hand, the independence of the Angels may pose a future danger to individual liberties should their leadership encourage stronger intimidation tactics.

Currently, there are several points of similarity between the Angels and the auxiliaries. Each group is composed of persons who appear to possess a deep concern for the well-being of their community. In pursuit of this goal, volunteers of both groups patrol city streets, subways and public housing projects. The official use of auxiliaries within New York's subways is a new phenomenon. Neither group employs a licensed psychologist to help screen new members. Both groups tend to adhere, at present, to their avowed roles as observers and reporters of crime. Neither group permits its members to patrol alone. However, whereas auxiliaries usually patrol in pairs, the Angels usually appear in squad strength consisting of ten or more persons.[9]

The members of the Auxiliary Police Force and the Guardian Angels do not possess peace officer status. They have endured repeated criticism and sometimes abuse from members of police unions. The unions charge that the Angels and the auxiliaries interfere with the delivery of professional police services and are used instead of hiring additional police. On the other hand, most community groups have enthusiastically praised and endorsed them.[10] Ironically, a cause for the existence of police resistance to the participation of volunteers may be rooted in the public's enthusiasm for improved protection. For years, the police have built up a distinctive ''subculture'' or ''code'' as a defense against public hostility and apathy. Now faced with a sudden out-pouring of public cooperation, they may be naturally resentful, suspicious and defensive. Clearly, these attitudes need to be altered.

It has long been recognized that foot patrol is a highly effective way of combating such crimes as burglaries, robberies, thefts, purse snatchings and street muggings in crowded areas. Nevertheless, while foot patrol is very useful, most modern police departments have abandoned the practice in favor of radio motor patrol. Research studies have indicated that wherever and whenever citizens patrol, the crime rate has been reduced. For example, Councilmen Stern and Olivieri reported in 1978 that crime was cut by more than 50 percent when auxiliaries were used in saturation foot patrols within the 24th Precinct.[11] However, further research is needed to learn whether foot or radio motor patrols eliminate crime or merely displace it to another neighborhood.

Neither the Angels nor the overseers of the auxiliary police program have opened their files to researchers interested in learning about the background of patrol participants. However, there appears to be general agreement by most observers that there are proportionally more black, Hispanic and female auxiliaries than are in the regular police force. Moreover, most of the Angels appear to reside in high crime and low income neighborhoods. Press interviews with patrol members disclose a consistent feeling for the rights of others and paramount regard for the safety of neighbors.

It has already been noted that neither Guardian Angels nor police auxiliaries possess peace officer powers. However, in many cities outside of New York, volunteers have been sworn in as regular law enforcement officers. In this way, they possess specific legal obligations and all who come into contact with them may be assured of their authority to act. The lack of peace officer status can cause needless confusion for some members of the public, the volunteers, the police and the courts. Significantly, the failure to have delegated the appropriate authority to such volunteers could be dangerous should their efforts to maintain peace ever meet with failure. Some near tragedies have occurred when motorists have disregarded auxiliaries engaged in traffic control.

It is remarkable that the auxiliaries and the Guardian Angels have not experienced greater casualties. A 1968 study involving uniformed patrol officers in the Chicago Police Department described twenty behavioral abilities essential for effective patrol work. More than half of the attributes identified required personal stability, a basic understanding of human relations and above average problem solving skills. Some of the desirable attributes included:

- The ability to tolerate stress in its many forms.
- The ability to maintain a balanced perspective even though being constantly exposed to the worst in human behavior.
- The ability to skillfully question participants of, as well as witnesses to, a crime or incident.
- The ability to endure physical and verbal abuse.
- The ability to deal with people ranging from criminal to noncriminal.
- The ability to react instantly after long periods of monotony.
- The ability to judge out-of-the-ordinary situations.
- The ability to demonstrate mature judgment.
- The ability to take charge of situations, particularly emergencies.
- The ability to work under loose supervision.
- The ability to remain objective.
- The ability to exhibit courage.[12]

In 1977, researchers at Indiana University developed a list of a dozen necessary characteristics to aid in the police selection process. Prominently included were: leadership, integrity, ego control and sensitivity.[13]

Citizen patrol volunteers are in drastic need of better training, improved methods of communication and supervision, as well as appropriate clarification of their legal status. At the very least, government should make available to them the same psychological screening and services that it provides to regular police personnel and their families. Inasmuch as police work is 80 percent social service in most areas, the volunteer patrol members are performing many of the same functions of regular police.[14] A screening process is needed to help weed out those who have sadistic tendencies, those who may be severely prejudiced against racial or religious groups, and/or those who may have emotional problems making them unsuitable for police work. A study conducted in 1978 reported that of 5,000 applicants for police and fire jobs screened over a five year period, 10 to 15 percent were "outright criminals and almost 50 percent were judged psychologically unsuited for the job."[15]

In New York, the Bronx County District Attorney, Mario Merola, has specifically addressed the issue of vigilantism raised by the appearance of the Guardian Angels:

To call them vigilantes is nonsense. The municipal and state governments have not met their obligation to provide the kind of security that's needed on the subway, in the parks or on the streets. It's true, they're not trained. But their mere presence in a uniform is the kind of deterrence factor we're looking for.[16]

Under the four part definition of vigilantism proposed by historian Richard Maxwell Brown, the Guardian Angels satisfy only about half of the criteria for the designation.[17] They patrol in areas with inadequate law enforcement and for the purpose of maintaining order. However, the Angels are an extralegal organization in the sense that no specific legislation has been adopted in their behalf. While the Angels turned down an offer to become an auxiliary of the New York City Transit Police, they have actively sought federal tax-exempt status.[18] Finally, their longevity has surpassed that of many other self-appointed citizen patrol groups and their interest in expansion is regularly documented in the press. Their continued concerns for a favorable public image and growth should enhance their claim to legitimacy. Moreover, they have achieved an enthusiastic acceptance by many elderly and poor citizens in New York City and their political leaders. The auxiliary police are completely integrated into the New York City Police Department. They hold an official status and must conform to the same rules and regulations as regular police. Therefore, they possess a legitimate role in government and are very far from fitting the definition of vigilantism.

The cause of peacemaking could be served through the provision of psychological services to prospective and current members of citizen patrols. When people become conscious of a social problem and/or suffer detrimentally as a consequence of one, they sometimes organize themselves to combat it. The advent of numerous citizen patrols to help prevent crime may be signaling the emergence of a new social movement. Psychological testing could be invaluable in studying the characteristics of the people who claim this interest.

Society's efforts to control crime will not cease if the ranks of volunteer patrol groups are diminished. On the other hand, the overall effectiveness of the justice system has always depended upon the appropriate support and conduct of concerned citizens. In a democratic state, the public's desire for the protection of individual liberties and its concern for the well-being of the justice system are vital. However, both interests are not self-implementing; rather, they are dependent upon the goodwill of governors, mayors, elected representatives, police administrators and other people with power. A resolution seeking the provision of psychological services for police auxiliaries, Guardian Angels and other citizen patrol groups is needed in New York City. A similar resolution is crucial in other locations which have large numbers of volunteer patrols. The resolution might read as follows:

Whereas, the Auxiliary Police program and various privately organized citizen patrol groups have become a valuable adjunct in the fight against crime; and

Whereas, the members of the Auxiliary Police Force total 9,000 and thousands of other unpaid volunteers expose themselves to possible danger, sometimes at the very risk of their lives; and

Whereas, Auxiliaries and citizen patrol volunteers are subject to role conflicts and other stress arising from patrol efforts, regular employment, family and personal problems; and

Whereas, the New York City Police Department recognizes and provides for the psychological screening, testing and counseling of its prospective and current members; and

Whereas, the Auxiliaries and other volunteer patrol groups have responsibilities similar to regular police officers, especially in that they have direct contact with the public; and

Whereas, the Police Department's Psychological Unit has proven its effectiveness; now, therefore, be it

Resolved, That the Council of the City of New York calls upon the New York Police Department to provide the same quality and type of psychological services to the applicants and members of the Auxiliary Police Force and other recognized patrol groups as are made available to prospective and regular members of the Police Department.

The Angels have been described as "a cross between a Special Forces military squad and a street gang" with "little more than their numbers and their poise to defend themselves and others against crime."[19] They are suspicious of attempts to merge them with more formal agencies of social control, such as the auxiliary police. An arrangement has been worked out for the Angels to meet with Transit Police officers on a regular basis for mutual purposes.[20] This is a very sensible development and the eventual creation of guidelines and other controls should promote the objective of public safety.[21]

Moreover, there is some evidence that police animosity towards the Angels has abated since the 1981 shooting death of Frank Melvin. He was killed by a Newark, New Jersey, police officer at a housing project for senior citizens. The incident received wide-spread publicity as a tragic case of mistaken identity. Neither state nor federal officials believed that the incident warranted further investigation and a grand jury found no grounds for lodging criminal homicide charges against the two policemen who were at the scene.[22]

Nationally, Guardian Angel membership requirements currently include attendance at their own in-house three-month training program, three character references, and that the first fifty members of each new chapter be completely free of criminal history.[23] New York City Angels receive an additional four and one-half hours of police training which includes instruction on the lawful use of force by citizens.[24] In 1981, the Angels agreed to permit the New York City Police Department to conduct a criminal records screening of its membership. A roster of 550 names was submitted and only 6 individuals were discovered to have had felony records. Sliwa immediately dismissed these 6 members.[25]

The fact that citizens are willing to contribute their time and effort in the cause of public safety without any expectation of financial gain needs encouragement and not disdain. The spirit of volunteerism is in the best interest of American society today as it was two hundred years ago. The numerous understaffed and underequipped agencies of social control, such as the police, cannot afford to ignore the genuine concerns of the public. The inherent dangers and low pay of most frontline criminal justice positions put all employees into the category of "volunteer." Similarly, even the office of President of the United States must be considered a "volunteer" position in view of the risk involved. Therefore, auxiliaries, Angels, regular police and even presidents, such as Abraham Lincoln, are volunteers. Their ideals of social justice and public service may provoke cynicism, but they shouldn't have to face physical and mental abuse from any source.

18 • The ROTC Police Corps Plan

On August 4, 1982, a private study group, headed by New York attorney Adam Walinsky, proposed the establishment of "The New Police Corps." Walinsky was at one time a top aide to Senator Robert Kennedy and was a former chairman of the New York State Commission of Investigation. The other members of the panel that produced the proposal were: Jan Deutsch, professor of law at Yale University and a former staff member of the President's Commission on Crime and Violence; Lawrence Kurlander, the director of the New York State Office of Criminal Justice under Governor Cuomo and the former district attorney of Monroe County, New York; Monroe Price, dean of the Benjamin A. Cardozo School of Law at Yeshiva University; Jonathan Rubinstein, research director of the Center for Research on Institutions and Social Policy and the author of *City Police*; Neil Welch, the former assistant director of the Federal Bureau of Investigation and secretary of justice for the State of Kentucky; and Jane Walinsky, a New York attorney, who served as research assistant.[1]

The group's proposal is based on the military's Reserve Officer Training Corps (ROTC) program that provides college tuition assistance and other benefits in exchange for an obligation to perform military service after graduation. The group believes that additional police must be made available to communities throughout the State of New York and especially within New York City. The plan envisions the availability of 30,000 extra police officers during the next six to eight years. This number could result in a doubling of the police presence in every area of the state with a serious crime problem. The panel recommends that 20,000 police corps officers be assigned to the New York City Police Department, 7,000 to other suburban forces and 3,000 to rural communities.[2]

The police corps proposal is being studied by governmental committees and civic groups in New York, California, Florida and Maryland.[3] In addition, the police chiefs of San Diego, Atlanta and Minneapolis expressed interest in the proposal in 1982. It was also given a major endorsement by Bart Giamatti, the president of Yale University, who was planning to organize academic support for the project.[4] Editorial praise for the concept appeared in the *New York Times* and in *New York* magazine.[5] Moreover, John Keenan, New York City's criminal justice coordinator, said he had thoroughly studied the plan and endorsed it.[6]

However, New York's Governor Mario Cuomo was said to be unenthusiastic about the idea. New York City's Mayor Edward I. Koch, who on January 1, 1978, succeeded Abraham D. Beame and was reelected for a second four-year term in 1981, feels that the program is flawed because it hasn't worked for the medical profession. Medical students who received tuition grants on a promise to work in deprived communities have not fulfilled their commitments. Mayor Koch stated:

What they demand is the right to pay back money for that education after they're in the field. And this would be true here, with people who wanted to be lawyers or other things, people who won't want to lose three years as police officers—a field in which they have no ultimate desire to serve.[7]

There is considerable debate among law enforcement officials concerning the utility of an associate (two-year) or baccalaureate (four-year) or any level of college work as necessary preparation for police service.[8] Lawrence Sherman, research director of the Police Foundation, has observed that there is no conclusive evidence about the value of higher education for police recruits.[9]

The estimated cost of the program is placed at $840 million (not including equipment or training). The proposal consists of young college graduates serving a three-year obligatory term of police service in exchange for a maximum of $32,000 in college scholarships prior to the beginning of their police duty. They would be compensated at the rate of $20,000 per annum, including fringe benefits, after graduation.[10]

The proposal recommends that the city's Transit Police force should be reorganized in order to accommodate the addition of up to 3,000 of the new police corps members. The corps members would become members of the state police and be centrally administered by them. When crime has been substantially eliminated from the subways, corps members would be assigned to the bus terminals, railroad stations and the city's streets as foot patrol officers.[11]

At the conclusion of the obligatory service, the proposers urge that professional graduate schools (for example, law schools) and private industry provide the former police corps members with opportunities on a preferential basis. Additionally, they would be encouraged "on a purely voluntary but paid basis, to serve for several years of week-ends and summers as members of a newly created Civilian Police Reserve."[12] In this capacity, they would be utilized to rebuild local auxiliary police units throughout the state. The proposal declares that although thousands of unpaid auxiliary police volunteers are currently contributing to the preservation of public order throughout the city and state, they are not well trained, are unarmed and generally do not possess full police powers.[13]

A *New York Times* editorial claims that the proposal merits real interest and represents "a genuine breath of fresh air."[14] The *Times* emphasizes that additional police manpower would help clear the streets of the perpetrators who commit many petty offenses and that members of the new police corps would be well motivated because of their backgrounds to get the job done. Moreover, the plan appears to make the best use of existing state supported higher educational programs in order to pay for part of the expense. Members who return to civilian life would possess "an invaluable understanding of law enforcement and urban crime."[15]

On the other hand, the proposal appears to suffer from a number of significant flaws. The proposal rests on the assumption that a doubling of the police presence in New York City will be a decisive factor in driving fear and crime from the streets. However, merely doubling the number of police in the city may not be enough. Police work in eight-hour shifts, take time off, have illnesses and must appear in court. Consequently, only about a quarter of the 20,000 additional foot patrol officers would actually be on the street at any one time.

The budget figures for the new police corps do not include projected costs for training, equipment, processing new cases, nor cost of living adjustments for living in the city. Such expenses could easily increase the overall amount to $1 billion. Furthermore, overcrowding in the city's correctional system has already reached crisis levels.

The training of the new police corps and their integration into local departments may prove to be an insurmountable difficulty. The proposal refers to use of the summers which occur at the end of the sophomore and junior years as opportunities to conduct training. Reference is also made to the utilization of some law enforcement courses during the regular period of study. These training periods would appear to conflict with the notion that any member's preservice education may consist of "any course of study."[16] Withholding training until after graduation will eat up at least a sixth of the three years of obligatory duty. The resources for training the 30,000 members of the new police corps are not clearly identified.

The proposal envisions that by the end of the second program year, several hundred experienced state troopers in rural areas will be relieved from their routine administrative workload by the new police.[17] Their place will be taken by new police corps members. However, the use of the new police for clerical duties appears to contradict the main thrust of the plan.

The plan states that five hundred experienced state police officers will be reassigned to the city's Transit Police force.[18] Is their replacement by members of the new police corps in upstate areas a meaningful exchange? Will these five hundred officers be provided a cost of living adjustment as a result of their removal to the city? Why would these regular state police be interested in moving to New York City without extra pay?

The original Walinsky plan recommends that the state assistance currently going to New York's private colleges be reallocated to defray a portion of the new police corps' costs. These funds are commonly referred to as "Bundy aid or money'' because of the formula developed by a blue-ribbon committee headed by Dr. McGeorge Bundy. The Walinsky proposal maintains that state funds should not be used to subsidize the expenses of college students at New York's independent colleges and universities, but "rather that money should be paid to students who agree to give the state a period of service in return."[19] The "Bundy money" could supply the financial resources needed to cover over two-thirds of the new police corps' costs.[20] However, the arguments in opposition to the use of this source of aid are noted by the Reverend James C. Finlay, the president of Fordham University and chairman of the Commission on Independent Colleges and Universities. He has indicated that the loss of the "Bundy money" might encourage private college students to enroll at publicly supported institutions, such as the State University of New York and the City University of New York. Currently, 40 percent of the state's higher education students attend the independent schools. President Finlay asserts that "the cost to taxpayers for each of them is about $5,000 a year less than for each student enrolled at SUNY or CUNY," and that students switching to these public institutions "would generate enormous pressure on the state budget."[21] Significantly, the new enrollments would require new and additional taxes that would far exceed the "Bundy money" reallocated for the new police corps.

Jonathan Rubinstein's interest in the new police corps seems to contradict the views he expressed in his well received book on the nature of police work—*City Police*. Rubinstein, a former reporter for the *Philadelphia Evening Bulletin*, graduated from the Philadelphia Police Academy and spent the next year observing police operations and working with police for their entire tour of duty. Rubinstein has observed that the police have only indirect control over the incidence of crime and no direct control over its origins. Rubinstein accurately reveals that the police

cannot prevent crime altogether, and whatever amount of crime they actually do prevent by their presence on the street cannot be demonstrated. . . . All they can do is arrest people. If this does not accomplish the purpose, and it does not, they then must seek to place the responsibility for failure elsewhere.[22]

These facts have been generally understood for some time. For example, the President's Commission on Law Enforcement and the Administration of Justice observed in 1967 that "the ratios of police per thousand population in cities over 500,000 range from 1.2 to 5.4, but that no discernable relationships exist between these ratios and reported rates of crime."[23] However, most authorities in the field would probably agree that the quality of the individual police officer could be enhanced through higher recruitment standards.[24] Furthermore, numerous governmental commissions have recommended at least some higher education as a condition of initial employment on a police force.[25] Thus, a consensus of opinion has emerged that the quality of the police and not the quantity of police is vital. The emphasis in the Walinsky proposal appears to be on both quality and quantity. But, $1 billion in extra taxes for young "quality" police who will leave the force after three years of duty (if they show up in the first place) is an approach to public safety that is extremely shortsighted. It would increase the number of police but risk the hope of raising the overall quality of the police force.

For many years the issue of raising the quality of the police in America has been on the agenda of many of the nation's leading police administrators and police reformers. In the early 1910s, the Bureau of Municipal Research conducted a survey of the existing school for New York City police training and found it to be in a deplorable condition.[26] Since that time giant strides have been made in upgrading the curriculum and instruction of the police academy and in-service training. However, a research project completed in 1975 and funded by the National Institute of Law Enforcement and Criminal Justice, U.S. Department of Justice concluded that the educational levels of police recruits was more a function of "the extrinsic rather than intrinsic characteristics" of a particular agency.[27] The list of significant extrinsic characteristics included: the career and promotional opportunities linked with educational requirements; the police agency's prestige; higher education requirements for initial entry into the agency; and specific incentives for completing various levels of education, such as a salary increment. The study pointed out that "if a real desire exists to improve the caliber of police personnel in a particular agency, the intrinsic nature of the agency is not an excuse for failure to make such improvements."[28]

Thus, the problem of upgrading the quality and educational levels of the police can be addressed by instituting reforms that directly tackle the issue. The establishment of "The New Police Corps" is an unnecessary and very indirect approach for the resolution of the problem.

The concept of "quality" is intimately associated with the idea of police professionalism. However, the dominant theme of the Walinsky proposal is really on "more police," "vast or large numbers," and "30,000 additional police."[29] The word "quality" is frequently used, but the only instance when the plan comes close to the idea of making law enforcement more responsive to the needs of the general citizenry and increasing police efficiency without sacrificing concern for the protection of civil rights is when the subject of "a police executive development program" is mentioned.[30] The Walinsky plan would provide additional educational opportunities and specialized management training for only "the best of the volunteers who wish to remain" after the end of their three-year period of obligatory service.[31] The problem is that the total force of regular police is ignored and yet the responsibility for supervising and providing field training rests with the members of the regular force.[32] Furthermore, the civil service rules and contractual agreements of the police are overlooked.

The new police corps proposal offers more police at a very great cost to taxpayers. Such a proposal should have addressed alternative means for achieving public safety and upgrading the quality of the police. For example:

1. Raising the educational standards for new recruits.

2. Implementing better police procedures, such as the "Beat Commander" project.[33]

3. Fostering genuine police-community relations programs.[34]

4. Linking with college criminal justice departments for the purpose of establishing cooperative work-study programs, such as "police cadets."

5. Reestablishing the federal government's Law Enforcement Education Program (LEEP).[35]

6. Encouraging young persons to take advantage of the Army College Fund program and then to go into police work while attending college or after graduation.[36]

7. Working with the private sector to promote the endowment of more public service college tuition scholarships. For example, the C.V. Starr Foundation of New York has given a $1 million gift to Brown University for recognizing the value of off-campus public service work of student volunteers.[37]

8. Seeking to implement the recommendations of the American Bar Association Criminal Justice Standards and the many advisory commission standards and goals which have been prepared at public expense in recent years.[38]

9. Upgrading the status of the New York City Auxiliary Police to that of an armed volunteer police reserve with full police powers and providing them the basic training required by the New York State Municipal Police Training Council.[39]

10. Placing greater emphasis on the citizens' role in crime prevention. The availability of a continuous series of free courses on security could be a new and effective mechanism for the promotion of public safety.[40]

Each of the foregoing proposals would require enthusiastic public and private support, police initiative and leadership and in most instances the establishment of effective relations with other criminal justice agencies and institutions. However, except for the eighth proposal, each of the alternatives could be implemented at very little cost to the state.

A major alternative to the new police corps idea is the institution of a program of "police cadets." An individual who holds a college degree cannot be immediately accepted into a law enforcement agency. In addition to a qualifying written exam and psychological screening exam, most police applicants must pass a criminal history background investigation and satisfy various physical and medical standards. The Walinsky plan is very unclear about how and when these tests would be administered. However, in a well organized police cadet program such exams and screening devices are administered before accepting anyone into the program. In addition, police cadets are usually required to attend and complete at least a two-year associate degree program in criminal justice. An integral part of the curriculum in criminal justice is field work within a nearby police agency. Cadets perform clerical duties, crowd control and escort service, guard sensitive locations, assist with juvenile aid programs and may even be allowed to complete police academy training. If police cadets have reached the minimum age required to be a police officer and have passed all of their screening and academy exams, they can be immediately assigned as probationary officers upon graduation from college. This is a most attractive alternative to the Walinsky proposal and it has already been endorsed by the leadership of the New York City Patrolmen's Benevolent Association (PBA). In a direct response to the new police corps plan, Phil Caruso, president of the PBA, suggested the development of a police cadet program which would lead to a college degree and a career in police work. He observed that police work cannot be a fleeting experience and that it "requires a unique sense of dedication to a set of values and ideals best fulfilled through a long-term commitment. Less than that brings into question the true motivation of participants."[41]

Ideally, police cadets or police auxiliaries could be granted full tuition and living expense scholarships to attend college. The money could come from a higher tax on the sale of guns and ammunition and the license fee charged on a yearly basis to gun dealers.[42]

Above all, the Walinsky plan avoids or ignores the service of the thousands of men and women who have served and are serving as members of auxiliary and reserve police units throughout the state. For example, the 9,000 police auxiliaries in New York City are used almost exclusively on foot patrol and to maintain order on city streets and subway platforms. Unlike the proposed new police corps recruit, the auxiliary police officer is truly a volunteer and serves his or her community with no expectation of financial return. Furthermore, auxiliaries are able to fulfill their mandate through the use of their uniform, nightstick and two-way radio. A local law permits the police commissioner to declare a state of emergency and to extend "peace officer" status to them.[43] Local control over them has never been an issue and their training has been constantly improving.

The new police corps plan seems to be well intended, but the more appropriate mechanism for expanding the presence of police already exists. Units like New York City's auxiliary police force have been on the scene for most of this century. They have consistently proven their readiness, willingness and ability to do any task assigned. Efforts to upgrade the existing auxiliary police program would not only properly honor these real volunteers but greatly contribute to the safety and security of all New Yorkers.

The presentation and dissemination of "The New Police Corps" proposal poses a problem in decision making for the occupants of New York's executive and legislative branches. They may reject, modify or adopt the proposal.

The proposal pays little attention to the importance of making better use of community, school and juvenile justice resources in order to stem the rise in juvenile delinquency. There has always existed a flexibility for utilizing auxiliary police as aides in a comprehensive delinquency prevention program. Furthermore, the deployment of new police corps members with new diplomas from college and the police academy to the city's subways and streets may be unnecessary. "Buck privates" or infantrymen should be able to handle the job as effectively as an army of "second lieutenants."[44]

19 • Conclusion

In 1982 a young New York lawyer was walking with his girlfriend in a park. He was hit with a baseball bat and stabbed to death.[1] In 1976 an elderly couple in the Bronx were robbed. A few months later they hanged themselves and left a note that said: "We don't want to live in fear anymore."[2] In the same year a couple and their six children were stranded for several moments on Chicago's South Side during a sudden rainstorm. A band of youths approached their car and demanded ten dollars. When the couple refused to pay, they were attacked. As three of the couple's children watched, their father was seriously injured and their mother murdered.[3]

In 1981 approximately 22,000 homicides occurred in the United States and close to 25 million households were touched by a crime of violence or theft. A family in that year was more likely to have one of its members victimized by rape, robbery, or aggravated assault than to have its home catch fire.[4] One of America's leading jurist's has characterized the nation's crime problem in this manner:

City residents are afraid to walk the streets at night; they are afraid to enter their self-service elevators or to venture into the basements of their buildings. They install multiple locks on their doors and windows, and recent reports indicate that sales of burglar alarms, whistles, and household weapons are reaching new peaks.[5]

In 1964 a young woman was killed outside her apartment building. It took the attacker about forty minutes to end her life. Her cries for help were heard by thirty-eight neighbors who failed to come to her aid or call for help.[6] However, four days after this murder two citizens in a different neighborhood became suspicious about a strange man removing a television set from another neighbor's apartment. They called the police and the man later confessed to the young woman's murder.[7] Moreover, there have been many reports of citizens who have aggressively intervened in order to assist crime victims and disaster victims.

Many researchers have tried to explain the phenomenon of bystander conduct. Some have concluded that the failure of onlookers to intervene in emergencies is not simply due to apathy or indifference, but may involve complex social and psychological processes. A process called "pluralistic ignorance" occurs when an individual decides that an emergency situation must not really be an emergency because no one else is responding. The process of ''diffusion of responsibility'' takes place when each member of a bystander group perceives that it is not his or her responsibility to act and no one will be singled out for blame because of the large size of the group.[8] One researcher has discovered that when a bystander has had some interaction with a victim, the likelihood of rendering assistance is vastly improved.[9] Furthermore, bystanders are faced with more than the immediate crisis situation. All bystander conduct takes ''place within a larger framework of norms, values, and prior patterns of behavior, which . . . in the final analysis, may well determine the individual's behavior in the emergency situation.''[10]

A further complication in understanding human conduct is the realization that at one time or another everyone has committed some type of crime and in many of these instances imprisonment was available as a punishment had the individual been arrested and convicted.

The pressing nature of the crime and violence problem in America, the variety of explanations for bystander conduct and the ambiguity of moral development are long standing puzzles. These issues must be appreciated to help destroy the myth that police and other criminal justice practitioners can solve the nation's crime problems. Criminal justice personnel represent only a small segment of society's social control system. The greater part of the forces available are the children, parents, working mothers, single adults, merchants and civil service agency personnel who live and work in the communities across America. The key to achieving neighborhood peace is to find ways to utilize the energies of private citizens. They alone can keep the peace by adhering to widely shared norms of conduct or they may break the peace by disregarding society's approved standards.

The police need support, cooperation and information from community members. The public wants greater safety and fair police treatment. Civilian auxiliaries should be thought of as the most important link between the police and the public. They are in the vanguard of that segment of the community which is committed to the welfare of their neighbors. Moreover, they share and feel the same sense of responsibility as do the police. Significantly, they also wear a badge of office which symbolizes their desire to render spontaneous assistance in any emergency situation. Their uniforms and training periods accentuate this linkage with the police. In New York City and in cities throughout the country, thousands of ordinary men and women are volunteering their extra time to help patrol their communities.

Guardian Angels get more publicity, but their numbers pale beside the ranks of those who have opted to work more anonymously, volunteering an evening a week or more to patrol their communities as the ''eyes and ears'' of the regular police department.[11]

Citizens have much expertise to share and their services contribute to a higher level of participatory democracy. Citizens serving as auxiliary police actually involves the community in its own law enforcement. More avenues of communication are opened and citizens have the opportunity to share in the policing process and to appreciate the extra rules which govern police performance. This affords a greater degree of accountability and represents a vital affirmation of the democratic process.

In a review of the role of police auxiliaries in the United Kingdom, the Royal Commission on Police observed:

We think that the recruitment of special constables is of great value in promoting relations between the police and the public. They provide a natural link between the two. They understand police work and police problems, and in their own homes and places of work they can do much to paint a favorable picture of the police and to dispel the mischievous allegations about police misconduct which tend to circulate in the absence of effective publicity.[12]

Auxiliary police units may strengthen the forces against civil disorder and the rise of a police state. Algernon Black explained how a breakdown in law and order could lead to a negation of human rights:

When disorder and chaos disrupt men's lives, they cannot find security enough to live in freedom. It is then that they turn to a strong man and strict discipline and yield their freedom to a dictator and a totalitarian state.[13]

Every time a criminal is identified, adjudicated and punished, the approved norms of society are reaffirmed. The media brings these cases to the attention of the community and the law-abiding population experiences the sociological processes "norm reinforcement" and "social integration." The cohesiveness of the group is promoted by observing what happens to the nonconformist or criminal. These dynamics must be present for the maintenance of peace within society. If the administration of justice is carried out with due regard for the civil rights and liberties of the accused, the Constitution and other democratic institutions are preserved.

Auxiliary police may be called upon to participate in the same manner as regular police. Therefore, they are in a position to promote social stability, solidarity and the community's sense of justice. The participation of minority group members as well as other community residents greatly enhances a sense of community and provides a magnificent opportunity to foster intergroup relations.

A carefully screened and trained auxiliary police unit should help police departments in at least ten ways:

1. An increase in police professionalism should take place as a result of a better understanding of the police role and the public's role in the achievement of social control.
2. The institutions of American democracy may be better protected because of the additional resources available to defend them.

3. The peace and stability of neighborhoods is preserved by the presence of uniformed civilian auxiliaries on street patrol.

4. The use of auxiliaries provides a pool of qualified personnel for use in emergencies and for any extra assignments.

5. Individuals contemplating a police career may gain valuable insights and the police may recruit better qualified candidates.

6. Individuals desiring to contribute their time and expertise may experience a deep sense of worth and self-respect and also foster social solidarity and norm reinforcement.

7. A constructive alternative to the tendency to engage in vigilantism is provided and the presence of citizens should encourage positive police performance and provide a measure of accountability back to the community.

8. Many police officers and supervisors of auxiliaries should experience a greater sense of job satisfaction as a consequence of their contacts with police volunteers.

9. Auxiliaries can provide feedback regarding policy and programs. They are a unique evaluation resource as a result of their dual statuses.

10. The use of auxiliaries for the delivery of a wide variety of social services is almost unlimited. They can be used to attack the social causes of criminal behavior.

The great potential of citizen involvement in combatting crime has been known by criminal justice practitioners for some time. However, the will to ask them and the act of asking has been delayed a long time. In New York City and in many other population centers, citizens are now being asked and the response has been overwhelming. Moreover, it is reported with increasing frequency that volunteers can perform their assigned duties with skill and competence. The task of recruitment is eased when satisfied volunteers share their experiences with their friends.[14]

Minneapolis Police Chief Anthony V. Bouza has commented:

The creation of an auxiliary police force, serving in uniform, gratis, a few hours a day, several evenings per week, tends to promote a healthy citizen participation in police affairs. These auxiliaries must be given thorough training, close guidance, support, and meaningful assignments.[15]

People will get involved when their self-interest is at stake and they will stay involved when the problem with which they are dealing has been made immediate, specific, realizable, and when tasks are creative and manageable. New members must be made to feel welcome and their special interests and expertise should be considered when assignments are made.[16] Chief Bouza emphasizes that recruitment efforts may be enhanced by providing ''uniform allowances, recognition in the form of awards, letters of commendation or medals, and a useful training program.''[17] Moreover, police auxiliaries can be used to present crime prevention and justice system workshops, to aid elderly persons, to assist juvenile delinquency prevention programs, and trained to investigate and report

environmental hazards.[18] In short, their services can be utilized anytime additional manpower is needed for the purpose of safeguarding the health, safety
and welfare of the community.

It cannot be overemphasized that the recruitment, training and deployment of
minority group auxiliaries serves the most important interests of the police and
the community. The National Advisory Commission on Civil Disorders (1968)
stressed the significance of racial prejudice and discrimination as factors contributing to the outbreak of urban disorders. There is a wealth of documentation
to support the position that too much hostility and antagonism exist between
whites and blacks in the United States and that such feelings have only had a
negative effect on both groups.[19] The selection of police officers and auxiliary
officers of different races and nationalities may help to decrease these tensions
and the occurrence of civil disturbances. The officers may discover that they
share many common bonds and as in the case of bystander intervention, their
contacts may lead to some very positive results. In addition, their interactions
may serve as a guide and role model for the rest of the community. Significantly, such advances are likely because the police/citizen contacts developed
through the creation and support of an auxiliary police force are not fleeting or
temporary. The opportunity for dialogue and the chance to promote greater understanding will be an everyday occurrence. Auxiliaries participate inside the
world of the police and it is precisely this organizational arrangement that makes
for the most effective type of communication. However, as in any close collaboration, the participants must be willing to trust one another.

Finally, police volunteers should be cultivated by police departments because
of the need to evaluate agency service. Auxiliaries are in a unique position to
interpret actual accomplishments and failures. "More and more, social conditions are placing a premium on the competent performance of the law enforcement task."[20] New priorities will be established and new concepts and ideas
will be required to help deal with the pressures placed on the police. Patrick V.
Murphy, who has headed such major American police departments as those of
New York City, Detroit, Washington, D.C., and Syracuse, New York, has
commented on the future of policing and the need for citizen involvement:

If we know that our police cannot possibly take on all the crime problems, which ones
do we want them to go after first? It seems to me that if we go after all of them . . .
we may wind up empty-handed. In essence, the future quality of policing probably depends on the instructions and choices of the citizens as much as anything else. . . .
Some choices have to be made before better police work can proceed.[21]

Auxiliaries can be counted on to support the police. Their long history of dedicated service is appropriate and sufficient evidence for this claim. If asked,
they could also serve as a source of new approaches for improving public safety.

This book has been about ordinary people who cared enough about their
community to become involved and who freely chose to submit to the semi-

military authority of the police in order to evolve a citizen's approach to public safety. Their actions are living testament to the ideas expressed by the late Senator Robert F. Kennedy:

We should also consider ways in which the policeman's job can be lightened by having citizens serve as eyes and ears for the police in their own neighborhoods. There are always problems in trying to cloak ordinary citizens with any aspect of police responsibility, but the idea of a citizen patrol could, in my judgment, be quite constructive and should be explored.[22]

APPENDICES

Appendix A

A Survey of Volunteer Police

Reserve police forces, typically composed of volunteers who operate under the guidance and control of the regular public police organization, serve as an emergency reserve manpower pool for use in the event of civil or natural disaster. The reserves serve as a support or supplement to the regular police force during normal times, especially during peak demands for manpower, such as at shopping centers during the preholiday rush and at atheletic events. Some departments utilize reserve policemen as the second man in a patrol car during busy periods. The reserve force also may serve in a public-relations role, or as a source of recruits for the regular force. Reserve forces sometimes supply specialized services not normally needed, such as mounted patrol or in an underwater search and rescue capacity.

To our knowledge, only meager information is available on the reserve public police in the United States. The best source is a survey conducted in 1969 by the Arlington County (Virginia) Police Department.* That department contacted police departments in all 57 U.S. cities with 1960 population of over 250,000. Of the 48 major city police departments that responded, 34 (or 71 percent) had a reserve police force. There were 10,415 reserve and 75,523 full-time regular officers in those 34 departments. The 75,523 regular officers represent 17 percent of all local regular police in the United States in 1969. On the average, the reserve forces were 14

* Unpublished report, "1969 Reserve Police Survey," Arlington County Police Department, Arlington County, Virginia.

percent as large as the regular force with which they were affiliated. The reserves averaged 14.2 hours of service per man per month and had served an average of 9.9 years. Of the 34 departments with reserve units, 22 (or 65 percent) granted the reserves police powers. Because reserve police in major city police departments may not be "typical" of all departments, the data above may not apply generally.

In addition to being available for use in emergency situations, reserves in 33 of the departments surveyed worked on routine patrol assignments, usually under the direct supervision of a regular patrolman. Reserve units directed traffic in 97 percent of the cities and escorted prisoners in 21 of the cities. Reserves assisted in the Detective and Juvenile Divisions in only two cities, while only 18 percent of the departments routinely allowed two reserves to staff a patrol car without the presence of a regular officer. Most reserves were uniformed and equipped the same as a regular officer (except for badge and patch) and 65 percent were armed on duty.

All of the reserve units required classroom training, while 79 percent required some form of weapon training and qualification. Details of the amount and type of training were not elicited in the survey. Table 1 is a detailed presentation of data obtained in the survey. Those 14 responding major cities that had no reserve force in 1969 were Atlanta, Baltimore, Boston, Chicago, Cincinnati, El Paso, Houston, Louisville, Miami, Oklahoma City, Omaha, Pittsburgh, San Antonio, and Toledo.

This appendix is a reprint of pages 3–5 of the document entitled *Special Purpose Public Police, Vol. V* (February 1972).

It was prepared under a grant from the National Institute of Law Enforcement and Criminal Justice (NILECJ). It is reprinted with the permission of the U.S. Department of Justice. The fact that the NILECJ furnished financial support for the original publication of the report does not necessarily indicate the concurrence of the Institute in the statements or conclusions contained therein.

The more useful type of reserves are those that can function without direct supervision by a regular police officer. To develop the capability of reserves to function independently, it is not uncommon for them to receive 200 to 240 hours of initial training of the same type given regular officers. In contrast, regular officers may receive up to 600 hours of training. In an effort to select quality reserve personnel, careful screening of volunteers resulted in 67 percent of the applicants being disqualified in one city. All major city departments with reserves conducted local background checks on volunteers and 31 of the 34 conducted an FBI check.

Principal arguments against reserves include the "high" cost of recruiting, training, and supervising the volunteers; the difficulty in obtaining volunteers; the rarity of disasters when reserves would be needed; and the possibility a reserve policeman will not perform sufficiently well because of lack of training and experience. While each of these arguments has some validity, a careful screening and extensive training program should result in the effective use of the reserve men on assignments which truly assist and supplement the regular police forces. The worth of the meaningful tasks voluntarily performed by reserves may outweigh the cost of the reserve program while at the same time providing a well-experienced reserve force. In addition, providing quality reserves with important assignments may aid in recruiting. The Arlington County Police Department survey of reserves found that "jurisdictions with most success with reserves, as seen by number of duty hours volunteered per man, appeared to be where the men were trained and used on routine patrol with regular men, even though these same departments imposed the strictest conditions for recruitment and training (both classroom and firing range) and maintained a set number of hours per week or month which the men must work."

Some historical trends are evident when 1969 data are compared with data gleaned from older surveys. In 1960 and 1965, surveys of 18 and 20 major departments were conducted by the Philadelphia and St. Louis Police Departments, respectively. In the ten years from 1960 through 1969, the orientation and control of reserves shifted from civil-defense agencies (53 percent control of reserves in 1960) to police departments. The routine use of reserves shifted from traffic control (only 5 to 20 departments routinely used reserves for tasks other than special-events traffic control in 1960) toward use in a variety of patrol assignments. The percentage of reserve forces granted arrest powers increased from 30 percent of all departments in 1960 to 65 percent in 1969. Recruiting standards for reserves also have been changed (in 1960 only 13 of 20 departments had conditions, such as accepting volunteers or not allowing the applicant to have had a police record, whereas all departments ran background checks in 1969). In short, both the quality and the effective use of reserves appear to be increasing over time.

Much is yet to be learned about reserve police. The available data pertain only to reserves affiliated with major city police departments. Smaller city, county, and rural reserve forces may be distinctly different in terms of organization, functions fulfilled, effectiveness, and so on. Details on the types and expensiveness of training given reserves are not readily available. Nor are details available on overall costs as well as recruiting and screening practices. Data are also unavailable on the degree of discretion given to, and exercised by, reserves as well as on the breakdown of the time spent on various activities. The greatest lack of knowledge concerning reserves has to do with how effective and useful various types of reserve programs are, and with the extent of any possible disbenefits generated by improper reserve police actions. If adequate knowledge of the relationships between alternative reserve program structures (recruiting, selection, training, powers, assignments, etc.) and their effectiveness were available, and if similar knowledge were available for the regular police, cost/benefit analysis would establish definitive guidelines for reserve programs. In the absence of such knowledge, we suggest that an extensive survey be undertaken to reach a larger and more representative sample of police and sheriffs' departments to gather those data readily available but omitted from the surveys cited. Such a survey should include, at least, attitudinal information on effectiveness of reserves as viewed by the regular police, since objective quantitative effectiveness data are almost surely unavailable. The survey should also attempt to uncover particularly effective recruitment and selection programs, so that such successful methods may be widely disseminated and applied.

Table 1

1969 Reserve Police Survey—Arlington County (Virginia) Police Department

Jurisdiction	Full-Time Regular Police Officers	Total Aux. Force	Other Officers	Capt.	Lt.	Sgt.	Min. Age of Recruit	Local	State	FBI	Other	Avg. Length of Service in Years	Avg. Hours per Man/Mo.	Min. Hours Req./Mo.	W/Reg. Officer	Two Aux.	Foot Patrol	2nd Man in Cars	Radio	Direct Traffic	Escort Prisoners	Drive on Occasion	Forms & Reports	Clerical	Radio Dispatch	Ident. Section	Switchboard	Insured	Sworn In	Police Powers on Duty	Classroom	.38	Shotgun	Other (gas)	Uniform	Patch	Badge	Equip.	Sidearm	Shotgun Available in Cars
Akron, Ohio	393	50					30	X	X	X		12	10	8	X		X	X	X	X	X								X	X	X	X	X	X	X		X		X	X
Arlington, Va.	226	12		1	1	1	25	X	X	X	X	8	36	15	X			X	X	X		X	X	X	X			X	X	X	X	X			X				X	X
Birmingham, Al.	520	69					21	X	X	X	X	3	16	8			X	X	X			X	X							X	X	X			X				X	X
Buffalo, N.Y.	1,425	1149		20	60		21	X	X	X	X	19	.5	0				X									X		X	X	X							X	
Charlotte, N.C.	394	98	1 ea. Col. Lt. Col. Maj.	1	5	10	21	X		X		5	45	12	X			X	X	X	X	X						X	X	X	X						X	X	X
Cleveland, Ohio	2,161	500					21	X		X		11	4		X		X			X									X	X						X	X			X	X
Columbus, Ohio	807	101	1 Maj.	4	8	8	21	X			X	5	13	8	X		X	X	X	X	X	X						X	X	X	X		X		X	X		X		X
Dallas, Tex.	1,504	248		8	16	42	19	X	X	X	X		10	8	X		X	X	X	X	X	X	X	X	X	X	X	X	X	X	X		X		X	X		X		X
Dayton, Ohio	427	100											16	16			X	X	X	X	X	X						X	X	X	X		X							
Denver, Colo.	936	50					21	X	X	X	X		20	0	X			X	X	X	X	X	X		X				X	X	X	X		X	X	X		X	X		X
Detroit, Mich.	4,647	1200					23			X	X	1	16	8										X	X		X		X	X		X		X							
Fort Worth, Tex.	580	105		1	7	7	21	X	X	X	X	3	30	24	X	X		X	X	X	X	X	X		X				X	X	X	X	X	X	X	X	X	X	X	X	X
Honolulu, Hawaii	786	103					30	X		X			32	32	X			X	X	X	X	X	X						X	X	X	X		X		X	X	X	X		X
Indianapolis, Ind.	1,023	70	1 Maj.	5	2	6	21	X	X	X		15	1	0	X			X	X	X	X	X		X	X	X		X	X	X	X	X		X		X	X	X	X		X
Long Beach, Ca.	660	90		2	4	12	21	X	X	X	X	10	22	16			X	X	X	X	X	X		X	X	X		X	X	X	X	X		X		X				X	X
Los Angeles, Ca.	5,927	200					21	X	X	X	X		32	16	X			X	X	X	X	X	X	X					X	X	X	X	X		X	X	X	X	X		X
Memphis, Tenn.	1,007	41		1		3	21	X	X	X	X		30	10	X			X	X	X	X	X	X		X	X			X	X	X	X			X	X		X	X		X
New Orleans, La.	1,377	137	3 Maj.	3	9	17	21	X		X		12	32	8	X			X	X	X	X	X	X		X	X			X	X	X	X			X						X
New York, N.Y.	29,939	3433		87	158	178	21	X					3	16	7	X		X		X		X			X	X			X	X		X				X				X	
Newark, N.J.	1,379	487		8	12	25	21	X	X	X		5	5	4		X	X		X	X		X	X						X	X		X				X				X	
Oakland, Ca.	651	70		1	2	6	21	X	X	X	X	2	16	16	X			X	X	X		X	X				X		X	X	X	X	X	X	X	X	X	X	X	X	X
Philadelphia, Pa.	7,319	265		14	15	38	21	X	X	X		8	30	0	X			X	X	X	X								X	X	X	X	X			X					
Phoenix, Ariz.	774	81	Chief	2	5	8	21	X		X	X	8	21	12	X	X		X	X	X	X	X	X	X		X		X	X	X	X	X	X	X		X				X	X Sgts.
Portland, Ore.	722	150		8	12	21	21	X		X	X	3	8	4	X	X		X	X	X	X								X	X	X	X	X	X		X				X	X
Rochester, N.Y.	573	44		3		2	21	X	X			5	5	0	X			X	X	X		X				X			X	X	X	X	X	X		X				X	X
Sacramento, Ca.	449	50					21	X	X	X		5	40	0		X		X	X	X		X							X	X	X	X	X	X						X	X
San Diego, Ca.	875	275		3	7	26	21	X	X	X	X	5	20	8	X			X	X	X	X	X	X	X				X	X	X	X	X	X	X		X	X	X	X	X	X
San Jose, Ca.	456	160		5	5	20	21	X	X	X		2	10	7	X	X	X	X	X	X	X	X	X	X	X	X	X	X	X	X	X	X	X	X		X	X		X	X	X
Seattle, Wash.	1,025	50					21	X	X	X		5	13	16	X	X	X	X	X	X	X	X	X					X	X	X	X	X	X		X				X	X
St. Louis, Mo.	2,016	91					21	X	X	X		3	18	18	X		X	X	X	X	X	X	X	X				X			X	X	X	X	X				X	X	X
St. Paul, Minn.	460	145		6	5	15	21	X		X		15	8	4	X			X	X	X	X	X	X	X	X	X	X	X	X	X		X	X					X	X	X
Tampa, Fla.	522	41		2	4	4	21	X	X	X	X	5	8	8	X			X	X	X	X			X	X	X		X	X			X	X			X				X	
Washington, D.C.	5,220	650		1	27	71	21	X				8	10	12	X		X	X	X	X				X	X			X	X			X				X	X	X	X	X	X
Wichita, Kan.	333	100		6	6	12	21	X	X	X	X	10	40	16		X	X	X	X			X	X							X	X	X				X	X	X	X	X	X

Appendix B

Standards for the Selection and Assignment of Volunteer Police

Every State and every police agency should consider employment of police reserve officers immediately to supplement the regular force of sworn personnel and increase community involvement in local police service.

1. Every State immediately should establish minimum standards for reserve police officer selection and training according to the following criteria:

    a. Reserve officer selection standards should be equivalent to those for regular sworn personnel except that the reserve specialist should be selected on the basis of those limited duties which he will perform. Reserve officer medical and age requirements may differ from those for regular sworn personnel since a retirement liability does not exist.

    b. Reserve officer training standards should be equivalent to those for regular sworn personnel, but reserve specialists should be trained according to the requirements of the specialty which they will perform.

2. Every police agency that has identified a specific need to augment its regular force of sworn personnel to alleviate manpower shortages or to cope with unique deployment problems, should immediately establish a police reserve program. To realize the maximum benefit from such a program, every agency:

    a. Should establish recruitment and selection criteria equivalent to those for regular sworn personnel, with the exception of medical and age requirements;

    b. Should provide reserve generalist training equivalent to that provided regular sworn personnel, and should provide reserve specialist training required by the specialty to which the reservist will be assigned;

    c. Should insure that the reserve training program meets or exceeds State standards that regulate the training of regular, part-time, or reserve officers;

    d. Should assign the reserve generalist to supplement regular police personnel in the day-to-day delivery of police services and assign the reserve specialist to perform services within a particular field of expertise;

    e. Should establish a reserve inservice training program equivalent to that for regular sworn personnel; and

    f. Should furnish the reserve officer with the same uniform and equipment as a regular sworn officer only upon his completion of all training requirements. Until he has completed all training requirements, his uniform should readily identify him as a reserve officer, and he should perform his duties only under the direct supervision of a regular sworn officer.

This appendix is a reprint of pages 263–269 of the document entitled: *Report on Police* (1973). It is one of the reports of the National Advisory Commission on Criminal Justice Standards and Goals, and does not necessarily represent the official position of the U.S. Department of Justice which furnished support for its original publication. It is reprinted with the permission of the U.S. Department of Justice.

Commentary

The term reserve police officer usually is applied to a nonregular, sworn member of a police agency who has regular police powers while functioning as an agency's representative, and who is required to participate in agency activities on a regular basis. A reserve officer may or may not be compensated for his services, depending on each agency's policy. The term reserve is often used interchangeably with auxiliary in referring to nonregular police employees. The auxiliary officer, however, is one whose function is usually related to civil defense activities and whose participation in police functions is usually limited to emergency situations.

The utilization of reserve personnel by police agencies is an extension of a tradition which precedes the existence of structured police forces. This tradition encompasses the historic concept that law enforcement is the responsibility of every citizen. One of the British police principles, as quoted by Charles Reith in *A Short History of the British Police,* states, ". . . the public are the police—the police being only members of the public who are paid to give full-time attention to duties which are incumbent on every citizen. . ." Although this attitude may no longer reflect the thinking of the average citizen, it is part of the rationale for the police reserve concept.

During the settling of the West in the 19th century, deputized citizen volunteers sometimes became vigilante committees, lynching suspected offenders without due process of law.

By the turn of the century, many law enforcement positions, including those of reserve personnel, became political rewards due to nepotism and favoritism. Appointees usually were not required to participate in police-related activities. They did, however, realize the benefits of such positions, including the right to carry a badge and gun, the right to enforce laws on their own premises, and general immunity from arrest.

One of the most glaring examples of the abuse of the citizen-officer concept occurred during World War I. In 1917, the American Protective League, a "citizens' auxiliary" to the Department of Justice, was formed. This organization, without legal authority, conducted "slacker raids" (mass roundups) of suspected draftdodgers, enemy aliens, and deserters. Don Whitehead, in *The FBI Story,* summarized the entire incident by concluding that, "Out of the slacker raid fiasco, there did emerge some good. . . realization within the Department of Justice and the Bureau of Investigation that vigilantism and amateur sleuths have no place in law enforcement, even in the stress of great emergencies."

The history of political favoritism, arbitrary selection standards, and poor training techniques have produced many opponents to the police-reserve concept. Nevertheless, many modern police agencies now utilize reserve officers. The need for standards in this area is evident.

State Standards for Reserve Officers

The April 1969 edition of the *Journal of California Law Enforcement* reported results of a survey of 170 police and sheriff reserve programs in California that involved almost 6,000 reserve personnel. The survey indicated that 90 percent of the agencies employing reserves had training programs of some type. Of these, approximately 55 percent trained their reserves prior to assignment to field duties. Of agencies with inservice training programs, 86 percent included classroom training, and 95 percent trained personnel on the job. Despite these impressive statistics, the average number of training hours for 90 percent of the agencies surveyed was about one-fourth the minimum number of hours (200) required for regular police officers by the Commission on Peace Officer Standards and Training. This training appears inadequate in view of the fact that 89 percent of these agencies deploy reserves in patrol functions for an average of 14 hours per month.

The survey further revealed that although a few agencies provided new reserves with training manuals, structured curriculums, and sophisticated training methods, the great majority lacked efficient training programs. Furthermore, the requirements and qualifications for reserve employment varied widely, and there were no uniform standards for selecting of training reserve officers. The situation remains basically unchanged. Some agencies have no maximum age requirement for reserves. Other agencies assign reserve officers to one-man patrol vehicles without benefit of even 1 hour of formal training in police procedures.

Such undesirable situations serve to strengthen resistance to the use of reserve personnel. Many administrators argue that there is too great a risk in using untrained reserves for police-related duties. They cite legal liabilities, lack of training and experience, and objections from regular police personnel as reasons for their opposition. Advocates of reserve programs, however, claim that with proper selection and training, reserve personnel can perform a useful function.

The most feasible manner of improving the quality of police reserve forces is the establishment of minimum standards for their selection and training by each State. In 1967, the Police Standards Board of Florida's Department of Community Affairs proposed a set of standards for the employment and training of full-time regular police officers. These standards, however, did not apply to auxiliary officers, Florida's term for reserve personnel. This oversight was remedied when the Board approved a similar set of standards for auxiliaries in October 1971. The standards provide a functional definition of an auxiliary officer and the limits of his authority.

The Board established auxiliary officer selection criteria that include many of the qualifications for regular status. The Board also assumed responsibility for approving all auxiliary training programs throughout the State, independent of the agency that administers the program. Auxiliary officers are given 1 year from their appointment date to complete the training program. The Board additionally defined part-time officers and prescribed the same training and selection criteria required of regular full-time sworn personnel. A "grandfather clause" exempted persons then employed.

While most reserve qualifications in the Florida plan are identical to those for regular sworn personnel, age and medical requirements are relaxed. This exemption is offered by most agencies.

Because reserve officers are not career-oriented, their age at entry into the police service is not important as long as a maximum age for active service is established. Similarly, as long as the reserve officer is physically able to perform the duties of his assignment, there is no need for him to be disqualified for the same medical defects that would disqualify a regular officer. Because reserves usually are not salaried, no retirement liability exists, and agencies need not be concerned with medical or pension considerations.

Because some reserve officers perform only specialized functions and not general police work, State selection and training criteria should base employment on the nature of duties, even though such criteria may fall short of those required for the reserve generalist. The Glendora, Calif., Police Department, for example, employs a chemistry professor as a reserve officer to analyze evidence. As long as his duties are limited strictly to evidence analysis, there is no reason why any physical requirements such as height or weight should not be waived.

The Police Reserve Program

Each police agency must determine its own need for a reserve unit, regardless of whether a State has standards for the selection of reserve personnel. Whether the need is predicated on a shortage of available sworn personnel or a particular deployment problem, chief executives are in the best position to evaluate the necessity for reserve personnel. Once a need has been identified, the agency must then determine its selection criteria based on the type of duties to be performed.

The summer season presents unusual law enforcement problems. The Lake County Sheriff's Department in northern California is a 35-man agency authorized to use 40 reserve officers. The area served by this agency is unique because vacationers increase its population each summer from 20,000 to 100,000 persons. Police reports increase by some 200 per month during the season.

Only 17 of Lake County's regular deputies are engaged in patrol or investigative duties; the county has only one incorporated city, Lakeport, with a force of six officers. At the height of the resort season, there are only 23 regular officers to provide police services for a population of 100,000 persons, or one police officer for every 4,300 people in an area of 1,256 square miles.

To provide the necessary police services at minimum expense, Lake County initiated a reserve program administered under a grant from the California Council on Criminal Justice. During the summer, reserves are assigned mainly to beach areas with tourist populations. They are required to work a minimum of 16 hours per month to preserve their status, but most of them average 24 hours. Most reserves function as second men in patrol units, although two units are manned entirely by reserve officers. These units are not allowed to make arrests without the assistance of a regular deputy. Their primary functions are to act as a backup unit or to report observed activities to regular police units for action.

Lake County's reserve program is designed to meet three basic objectives: to provide more effective police service, to have a trained reserve pool of manpower available for emergencies such as natural disasters and civil disorders, and to solve the problems posed by the influx of nonresidents. The program also has served to relieve regular deputies from routine assignments and to improve the police image by involving local residents in police work. Commenting on the program in the February 11, 1972, edition of the *CCCJ Bulletin,* Sheriff Edward L. Anderson stated, "We have a very excellent group of men who have responded to this new reserve unit. Their dedication to the job indicated that many will become full-time deputies with the department."

Reserve Training

One major criticism of reserve programs has

been inadequate training. A successful reserve program must include a structured training curriculum to prepare reserve officers for their police-related duties. If reserve officers perform duties that encompass the full range of police functions, their training should be equivalent to regular sworn personnel training. When reserves are deployed in a limited capacity with singularly specialized duties, training may be geared strictly to those functions. In either case, any State standards for reserve officer training should be met or exceeded.

Under the Indianapolis Police Department's reserve training program, established in 1971, 129 hours of evening instruction are provided over a 10-week period. The program is patterned after the regular recruit training course, and the curriculum is heavily weighted with instruction in criminal law, crowd control, firearms qualification, traffic enforcement, and patrol functions.

Reserve officers in Phoenix, Ariz., undergo 16 weeks of training at their reserve academy. The 181 hours of instruction include 108 hours in general classroom courses, 32 hours in patrol activities, 31 hours in firearms training, and 10 hours in self-defense.

J. T. Jarrell, President of the Police Reserve Unit in Buena Park, Calif., reported in *Police Chief*, October 1971, that his agency had begun to train reserve officers in crime scene investigations, communications, narcotics, intelligence, and traffic accident investigation. The course is designed to provide more flexibility and manpower in emergencies. Even if the majority of the regular force were deployed to support a neighboring city, Buena Park still would have a qualified reserve force to provide regular police services. Two Buena Park reserves recently completed the crime scene investigation course given regular officers, while six others are undergoing on-the-job training as traffic investigators.

Lake County, Calif., reserves also receive the same training curriculum as regular deputies. Courses are administered by Santa Rosa Junior College at the agency's law enforcement academy. They consist of 219 hours of education and training. Reserves receive their training over an extended period of time, usually 1 year, attending two classes per week. During training, reserve officers simultaneously work field assignments with experienced deputies.

The nearby Lakeport, Calif., Police Department has a reserve training program consisting of over 200 hours of a college-sponsored curriculum, as well as an ongoing inservice training program. Lakeport Chief Harry Johnson disagrees with some State officials who advocate sending regular and reserve officers from small agencies to large metropolitan areas for specialized training. He maintains that the problems of a rural agency, such as his six-man department, are not adaptable to big city tactics that need large commitments of personnel. Chief Johnson favors training that emphasizes the needs and capabilities of the small rural agency.

The hazards of police work were major considerations in the development of the Los Angeles Reserve Corps training program. A city ordinance specified that reserves take a minimum of 200 hours of training. The present course calls for 268 hours, which exceeds the minimum established by the State. Instructors who teach regular recruits are used so that uniformity in training standards is maintained. Training, which lasts approximately 7 months, includes subjects ranging from criminal law and human relations to physical defense and firearms procedures. Classes are held two nights each week and two Sundays each month.

The Reserve Deputy Sheriff program in Los Angeles is perhaps the best example of the selective training of reserve generalists and specialists. The bulk of the Uniform Reserve Unit, comprising about 75 percent of the reserve force, receives 300 hours of training in all phases of county police operations. However, highly specialized units, such as the Photographic Reserve Unit, the Mounted Posse, and the Mountain Rescue Team, receive only a 56-hour indoctrination course outlining the duties of a reserve, and pertinent county and State laws. Each member of these specialized units already possesses the necessary expertise.

After initial training, many agencies ignore further development of their reserve officers. Reservists often are not apprised of new patrol techniques or recent legal decisions affecting their duties. To prevent such occurrences, periodic inservice training classes should be instituted.

Lt. Comdr. Robert Buckley, Coast Guard Reserve, has several years of experience as a regular and reserve deputy sheriff, and currently teaches a peace officers' training course in Auburn, Calif. In the October 1970 issue of the *Journal of California Law Enforcement*, he outlined his training program for reserve officers. In addition to the college-oriented course requirements, he suggested the continued use of inservice classes to supplement the basic program.

Assignment

Police reserve forces constitute a manpower alternative, not a substitute for trained full-time sworn personnel. They should not be depended upon to serve such a function. Administrators must realize that reserve units exist primarily to supplement regular sworn personnel and provide a qualified manpower resource to assist in emergency situations. If their selection, training, and use are structured to coincide with this role, reserves may be considered a valuable addition to the public service.

Most agencies use reserves at special events, civil disturbances, or during natural disasters, to supplement regularly deployed patrol forces. Others have expanded the role of the reserve to include patrol, traffic, communications, and other specialized police functions.

The Phoenix reserve force engages in traffic control functions, foot patrol at sports events, and security measures for VIP visits. Phoenix also deploys "R" units manned by two reserve officers. On weekends these units relieve regular beat units from routine radio calls, provide preventive patrol, control traffic accident scenes, and perform other patrol duties. The men in "R" units are certified by reserve commanding officers as capable of performing such duties on the basis of training, experience, and demonstrated abilities. In situations where reserve units are deployed separately from regular officers, reserve supervisors direct reserve patrolmen.

The Phoenix Police Department considers its reserve program successful in supplementing its manpower capabilities. This is understandable in view of the 8,800 man-hours donated by the 95-man reserve unit during 1971. This is equivalent to salary savings for four to five regular officers for the entire year.

A Buena Park reservist with over 3 years experience and certain specified qualifications usually is assigned to such duties as a one-man patrol cover unit to back up regular officers. He must have an accident-free driving record for 3 years to drive a patrol vehicle. The experienced reservist also is trained to function as a dispatcher, a crucial position in any agency. During 1970, the Buena Park reserve force donated 4,783 hours to the city at a savings of $23,915. In addition, the reserves were assigned 1,894 detail hours by the department, resulting in another $2,367.50 in savings. The Buena Park Police Department hopes to reduce agency expenditures, increase flexibility, provide additional manpower at minimal cost, and increase effectiveness in preventing crime through its reserve force.

In 1966, a new concept emerged to revitalize the Los Angeles Police Department's reserve corps. A city ordinance was passed providing for the employment of 2,000 reserve officers to be recruited at a maximum rate of 200 per year. The ordinance further relieved the chief of police from civil liability for the actions of reserves. Los Angeles police expect to derive three major benefits from the program: a decrease in crime, augmentation of the strength of the department's field forces, and the opportunity for concerned citizens to become directly involved in police services. The savings to the city in terms of reservists' salaries is incidental to these benefits.

After completing the training course, Los Angeles Police reserve officers are assigned to one of the department's 17 patrol divisions, where they are supervised by a divisional coordinator who is a sworn officer. To maintain reserve status, personnel must work a minimum of two watches (16 hours) per month, although most work more. The duties of reserve officers consist primarily of patrol operations. As the program expands, reserves will be used in traffic and supportive functions as well as in coping with natural disasters or unusual occurrences.

The Los Angeles Police Department currently employs 199 male and 13 female reserve officers. During 1971, these officers completed 4,336 tours of duty or 34,688 man-hours, saving the city a total of $141,571.

The Los Angeles Sheriff's Department uses more than 1,200 reserve personnel to complement its force of approximately 4,800 sworn personnel; it has probably the largest reserve component in the country. These personnel, paid at the rate of $1 per year, donated 374,867 man-hours of police service to the county of Los Angeles during fiscal year 1970–71. Total savings to the county in police salaries was $2,024,000.

After completing a 5- to 6-month course, most Uniform Reserve personnel are deployed in all stations to supplement patrol forces in the unincorporated areas of Los Angeles County and in the contract cities. Most reserves work as second men in two-man patrol units, with regular officers as partners. Those who are experienced and highly qualified in patrol procedures may be deployed in both one- and two-man reserve units.

Reserve deputies also lend support at the scene of disasters, civil defense exercises, and special events. They are required to work a minimum of one 8-hour tour of duty per month, in addition to attending one monthly reserve meeting. Despite the large size of the unit, there still are not enough reserve officers to fulfill the demand for their services.

Several subunits function under the Uniform Reserve unit to deliver specialized services. These include the Motorcycle Patrol, the Technical Reserve, the Photographic Reserve, the Medical Staff, and the Lady Reserve Company.

The Motorcycle Patrol consists of 25 men who are used in traffic enforcement, traffic control, and crowd control duties. They own their own motorcycles but lease them to the country for $1 per year to obtain county licensing and insurance. These deputies receive 300 hours of training and must work at least 1 year in radio patrol prior to motorcycle assignment. The motorcycle patrol is supported by a six-man reserve team that operates from a radio car.

The Technical Reserve Unit also receives maximum training, but must be skilled in electronics or a related field as well. They perform regular police functions in addition to operating and maintaining communications apparatus for reserve units.

The Photographic Reserve Unit, whose members receive only a 56-hour training course, is even more specialized. These reservists are photographers and film makers who produce training, recruiting, and public relations films for the department. It was estimated that the production of this unit in 1971 would have cost the county $300,000.

The department's Lady Reserve Company has approximately 70 female reserves who are used in jail facilities, transportation units, court functions, and station duties. It is anticipated that this reserve force will be increased to 150 to 200, consistent with the department's plans for using female personnel in all phases of its operations, including uniformed patrol duties.

The 325 reserves who comprise the Mounted Posse also receive 56 hours of training which outlines the duties of the reserve and of county and State laws. This unit supports the regular arm of the department in emergency situations that require trained horsemen. Personnel of the unit are assigned to each of the Sheriff's Stations. They are used primarily by search and rescue services in inaccessible terrain and for crowd control duties under certain special conditions.

The Mountain Rescue Team provides services to citizens who become stranded, lost, or injured in the numerous mountain recreational areas around Los Angeles County. The team receives the 56-hour indoctrination course in the Sheriff's Academy, in addition to continuous specialized mountain and rescue training.

A sworn coordinator of the reserve section has emphasized the department's policy of using reserves as a supplement to the department's regularly deployed personnel, not as substitutes for sworn deputies during special events, disasters, or unusual occurrences. If a reservist is asked to perform such duties without adequate training, he becomes a hindrance rather than a help to the department, and may pose a danger to himself, his partner, and the public.

The extensive training given to reserves by the Glendora, Calif., Police Department facilitates their deployment as one-man patrol units. That department feels that the program has proved highly successful and beneficial to the city.

Lending reservists on a short-term basis to vice, narcotics, and intelligence units may be warranted. Adequately trained and well-screened reserves as "new faces" can assist regular undercover officers in gathering intelligence information, uncovering vice activity, or identifying narcotics dealers. Another innovative idea is the use of female reservists to supplement juvenile units and provide expertise in juvenile matters. Using reserve officers in duties involving jail, property, and deskwork would result in the direct release of sworn personnel for other duties.

The Los Angeles Sheriff's Department has successfully used a limited number of well-trained reservists in substation detective units. Such assignments may well be made for reserve officers who show particular interest or ability in detective work.

Some police administrators have considered forming reserve units to perform riot control duties. This use of reserves might prove more beneficial than calling for outside agencies or Federal troops. They would be more familiar with the general area and would probably elicit less criticism than outside forces. In 1969, the Cook County, Ill., Sheriff formed such a unit, which functions only as a supplement to regular forces and is not intended to be the primary defense force during civil disturbances.

The Compton, Calif., Police Department has developed a chaplain corps whose members have the status of reserves. These clergymen are deployed in full uniform as radio car officers. The program provides the clergymen with an insight into police-community problems, while supplying the department with personnel sensitive to the needs of the community. This communications link between the department and community has received positive response from police and public alike.

Another function usually reserved for regular employees, but suggested for reserve personnel, is training police personnel. It is obvious that only exceptionally qualified individuals should be used in this capacity. This use of reserves could make the academic community aware of the problems and needs of law enforcement, while the agency could be exposed to innovative programs in police training and education. Similar benefits may be realized by using reserve physicians, behavioral scientists, and attorneys in the training function.

Uniforms

There is considerable controversy about whether reserve police officers should wear regular police uniforms. Some experts say that the public pays well for its police service and citizens should always be aware of whether they are being served by a trained police professional or a "weekend warrior." Some police practitioners agree that a visible device should be worn by reservists to facilitate the assignment and assumption of responsibility in field situations. Unless such distinctions are made, they fear a reserve officer may be thrust into a command situation that he is unable to handle.

Police agencies should furnish uniforms and an adequate maintenance allowance to reservists, as they do for sworn personnel.

Other police officials feel that the reservist should wear the same uniform and equipment as regular officers. Because of public distrust, disrespect, and outright derision toward reserve officers, the Buena Park, Calif., Police Department discontinued the use of a shoulder patch designating their status. Citizens and suspects alike had questioned their authority. The reserve officers felt that the reaction to their distinctive identification resulted in the total dilution of their police authority. Those who advocate identical uniforms for reserves and regulars do so to increase acceptance of reserves in their police role.

A compromise seems the most acceptable alternative. Reservists trained on a par with regular officers should be able to handle police situations with the same skill as newly trained regular officers. If selection and training standards for reserves are comparable to standards for regular officers, there need not be a conspicuous difference in their uniforms.

But until a reserve officer has completed his agency's prescribed training course, he should be clearly identifiable as a reservist and should function only under direct supervision of regular sworn personnel. When the agency is satisfied that his training enables him to function efficiently as a police officer, he should be allowed to work under the same conditions, and in the same uniform, as regular sworn personnel.

References

1. Buckley, Robert. "California Law Enforcement Reserve Program," *Journal of California Law Enforcement,* April 1969.

2. Buckley, Robert. "A Minimum Standard of Training for California Law Enforcement Reserves," *Journal of California Law Enforcement,* October 1970.

3. Bushey, Keith D. "Innovative Utilization of Police Reserves." Unpublished Term Report, California State, Los Angeles, December 1970.

4. Indianapolis Police Department. *Indianapolis Police Department Reserve Training Program, Syllabus.* March 20—May 26, 1972.

5. Jarrell, J. T. "Survey and Review of Reserve Police and Reserve Deputy Programs in California," *Police Chief,* October 1971.

6. Lake County, Calif., Sheriff's Department. *First Quarterly Report,* 1971.

7. Lake County, Calif., Sheriff's Department. *Second Quarterly Report,* 1971.

8. Lake County Grant Application to California Council on Criminal Justice—1971.

9. Los Angeles County Sheriff's Department, *Reserve Class Syllabus.* January 9—July 17, 1972.

10. Los Angeles Police Department. "Police Reserve Officers as Manpower Alternatives." Position Paper, 1972.

11. "Reserve Deputies Handle Tough Assignments on Job," *California Council on Criminal Justice Bulletin,* Vol. 5 (February 11, 1972).

12. "Sheriff's Reserves Given $1.00 for Year's Services," *Crime Control Digest,* March 31, 1972.

13. Swanson, C. R., Jr. "Police Minimum Standards and Auxiliary Officers," *Police Chief,* August 1971.

Related Standards

The following standards may be applicable in implementing Standard 10.2:

Appendix C

The Case of the *People* v. *Robert Jackson*

On October 23, 1972, at 9:30 A.M.,[1] the police room of Astoria Houses, a New York City Housing Development, at 420 Astoria Boulevard, Queens, was humming with activity. A man, who earlier that evening had been shot in the chin, was being administered to by two ambulance attendants. At least four New York City Housing Authority patrolmen and two women who had been engaged in a fight were crowded into a small room. According to one prosecution witness, the room was "hectic and noisy."

Outside the ground-floor office, a crowd, curious about the incident involving the two women had collected.

According to the complainant, Housing Patrolman Joseph Ametrano, he was seated at a desk in the police room, when the defendant, Robert Jackson, entered the room.

Ametrano testified that Jackson said he was a police officer and wanted to know what was going on in the police room. Ametrano asked Jackson for identification, which Jackson refused to produce. Another witness for the People, Patrolman Miguel A. Padillo, testified that Jackson said, "I'm on the job" or used "words to the effect that he was a policeman."

In any event, when Ametrano persisted in demanding that Jackson identify himself, Jackson, according to Ametrano, again refused to do so, couching his refusal in profanity and shoved Patrolman Ametrano, who then had to subdue him with the aid of his fellow officers.

The defendant was arrested and charged with criminal impersonation and resisting arrest, both Class A misdemeanors, criminal trespass in the third degree, a Class B misdemeanor and harassment, a violation.

On November 2, the matter came before this court on a preliminary hearing. At the end of the People's case, by consent of the People and the defendant, and with the permission of the court, the hearing proceeded as a trial. It was stipulated that Patrolman Ametrano's hearing testimony would be regarded as having been offered in support of the People's case on the trial.

The defense called as witnesses the defendant and two residents of the Astoria Houses. The testimony of Patrolman Anthony V. Pepe of the New York City Police Department, respecting defendant's completion of a nine-week training course his eight-month experience as an Auxiliary Police Officer and defendant's good reputation for veracity was stipulated. The People called Housing Patrolman Padillo as a rebuttal witness.

Mr. Jackson testified that he had patrolled the neighborhood in his capacity as an

Auxiliary Policeman on many occasions and that his membership on the Auxiliary Force was well known to his neighbors in Astoria Houses. Returning from a friend's house, he saw the crowd outside the police room and was urged by some of the bystanders to find out what was happening to the women who had entered the police room earlier. He was not in uniform at the time, but he removed his badge of office and identification card from his pocket, and holding them in his hand, knocked on the door to the police room. He approached Patrolman Ametrano.

Mr. Jackson testified that he identified himself as an Auxiliary Policeman, referred to the crowd outside the office and asked Patrolman Ametrano if he could be of help. Ametrano, he said, told him "get the hell out of here" and when Jackson sought to retrieve the badge and identity card, Ametrano leaped on him. Jackson said he was thrown to the ground, was beated by Ametrano and his fellow officers both in the police room and on the adjacent sidewalk and was taken to Elmhurst General Hospital by ambulance. There he received seven sutures for a scalp wound.

Two residents of Astoria House testified that they saw Jackson remove his shield from his pocket and enter the police room with the shield in his hand.

The basic charges against the defendant are trespass and criminal impersonation.

As to the charges of criminal trespass, the court entertains reasonable doubt that the People have demonstrated beyond a reasonable doubt that the defendant knowingly entered or remained unlawfully in a building fenced or otherwise enclosed in a manner designed to exclude intruders (sec. 140.10 Penal Law). There is a sharp conflict of testimony as to whether the door to the housing Police Office was open or closed at the time Jackson entered, but there is no contradiction of the defendant's testimony that he knocked on the door and little support for the assertion that he refused to leave the premises. The defendant is acquitted on the charge of trespass.

The charge that the defendant committed the offense of criminal impersonation raises a question—one of first impression, so far as the court and counsel have been able to ascertain, regarding the status of an Auxiliary Patrolman in this state.

So far as it concerns the factual situation in this case, the crime is defined by sec. 190.25 (3) of the Penal Law as the act of a person "who pretends to be a public servant or wears or displays without authority any uniform or badge by which such public servant is lawfully distinguished, with intent to induce another to submit to such pretended official authority or otherwise to act in reliance upon that pretense."

The term "public servant" is defined by section 10.00 (15) of the Penal Law as "(a) any public officer or employee of the state or of any political subdivision thereof or of any governmental instrumentality within the state, or (b) any person exercising the functions of any such public officer or employee."

The Denzer-McQuillan Practice Commentary at page 17 of the McKinney edition of the Penal Law (Vol. 39) states that the term "public servant" is defined broadly enough to include "not only every category of government or public 'officer,' but every 'employee' of every such officer or agency (and) every person specially retained to perform some government service. . . . "

But is the definition sufficiently extensive to cover an auxiliary policeman?

In 1951, during the Korean War the former New York State War Emergency Act, originally enacted in large measure during World War II, was revived in the form of the New York State Defense Emergency Act. (L.1951, c. 784) That law remains in effect at the present time.

Under section 9123, subdivision 22 (McKinney Edition, Unconsolidated Laws) each city and county shall "recruit, equip and train auxiliary police or special deputy sheriffs in sufficient number to maintain order and control traffic in the event of an attack and to perform such other police and emergency civil defense functions as may be required during and subsequent to attack."

Section 9185 of the Emergency Act empowers any county, town, city or village local legislative body to adopt a resolution conferring upon members of the auxiliary police the power of peace officers, subject to such restrictions as the legislative body may impose. Section 9180 defines as a peace officer "any officer mentioned in subdivision 33 of section 1.20 of the Criminal Procedure Law or such other officers duly authorized pursuant to this act to act as peace officers during attack or drill."

On August 14, 1951, the New York City Council enacted Resolution No. 433 reading in part:

Resolved that the City Council pursuant to section 105 of the State Defense Emergency Act confers upon members of the New York City Auxiliary Police the power to act as peace officers, provided however, that such members of the auxiliary police shall exercise such powers only during periods while such members are actually performing duty officially prescribed or ordered by the police commissioner of the City of New York and then only while displaying insignia of their authority.

By the terms of an executive order signed on September 11, 1967, New York City Mayor Lindsay redesignated the Office of Civil Defense as the Emergency Control Board and made it part of the Mayor's Office of Administration. That order assigned to the Police Department responsibility for the organization, administration, training, assignment and discipline of the Auxiliary Police.

The program has been highly successful. From 1971, when Police Commissioner Murphy placed Deputy Commissioner of Community Affairs, Benjamin Ward, in command of the auxiliary force, it has grown from 2,200 to 4,300 men and women devoting some 43,000 hours a month to volunteer police work. Over 22 percent of the force is black and 11 percent Spanish-speaking, helping to dispel the notion that residents of disadvantaged areas are apathetic about crime in their communities.

In June 1972, Mayor Lindsay, in announcing a grant of $162,000 in federal anticrime funds awarded by the Criminal Justice Coordinating Council to the Auxiliary Police program, to help in increasing enrollment to 6,000 by January 1, 1973, said:

The expansion of the Auxiliary Police indicates increased citizen willingness to participate in the safety of our city. The expanded visible presence of Auxiliary Police throughout our city has been a vital factor in the 24.1 per cent decrease in serious crime for the first four months of 1972.

The Auxiliary Police have also brought the Police Department closer to thousands of New York citizens, producing better understanding on both sides. [There has been] increased citizen concern and involvement in police matters and anti-crime work.

And by intelligent planning, especially with increased mobility and supersaturation campaigns, the Auxiliary Police have helped to dramatically reduce crime in target neighborhoods.

All New York City residents owe a real debt of gratitude to these public servants who volunteer their time and pay some of the costs for their uniforms in order to make the city safer for all of us.

It is expected that during the year 1972, some 600 awards will be made to Auxiliary Policemen for outstanding service.

The court notes that a substantial number of awards and commendations have been made to members of the Auxiliary Force for meritorious police work performed while off duty. For example, out of twelve commendations noted in Auxiliary Forces Section Directive No. 119, dated June 12, 1972, seven covered off-duty feats.

Yet, it seems clear that New York City Auxiliary policemen are not normally to be regarded as police or peace officers.

Page 4 of the Auxiliary Police Rules and Regulations issued by the Police Department states: "Auxiliary Policemen, while training, are not peace officers or police officers, and do not possess any powers above and beyond those of the private citizen."

A recruiting pamphlet prepared by the department and entitled, "Why Should I Volunteer for the Auxiliary Police?" notes: "The Auxiliary Policeman does not hold peace officer status. We do not carry guns, nor do we have the power of arrest beyond those of regular New Yorkers. We are trained to patrol, observe and report."

Peace officers and police officers are defined in section 1.20 of the Criminal Procedure Law. In general, according to Professor Denzer's annotations (Criminal Procedure Law-McKinney Ed. Vol. 1, p. 23), police officers are such genuine law enforcement officials as members of organized police forces, sheriffs, district attorney's investigators, New York City fire marshals and the like. Peace officers are members of law enforcement or quasi-law enforcement bodies, such as court officials (including judges), certain court attendants and clerks, parole and probation officers, humane society agents, prison guards, certain state and city tax inspectors and railroad police. Police officers are included in the enumeration of peace officers, but peace officers are not police officers.

The distinction between an auxiliary policeman and a peace officer is underlined by the provisions of section 9186 of the Emergency Defense Act stating that a member of a municipal or volunteer agency "in the course of his duty and while wearing or displaying a distinguished brassard or other insignia of authority" may stop and detain a person committing a misdemeanor or infraction in his presence and turn such person over "to a peace officer who may arrest him without a warrant on the charge of committing the misdemeanor or infraction." This confers on the auxiliary policeman the same rights he already possesses as a citizen—a limited right of arrest.

At this point one might well inquire as to the legal basis for assigning a New York City Auxiliary Patrolman functioning in emergency situations to such duties as foot patrol, station house security, precinct clerical duty, telephone switchboard duty, radio motor patrol car observation, taxi task forces and rescue squads.

The answer appears to lie in a free reading of the Emergency Defense Act supported by opinions of the Attorney General and Comptroller of the state.

In an informal opinion dated August 13, 1970, the Attorney General states that under the authority of section 209-0 (2) of the General Municipal Law, upon threat of a natural disaster emergency such as flood, drought, tidal wave, fire, earthquake, hurricane, windstorm or other storm, landslide or causes other than enemy attack, the chief executive of the city may use all facilities, equipment, supplies, personnel and other resources of his political subdivision in such manner as may be necessary to cope with the disaster. Subdivision 5 of the same section provides that "any and all personnel or other forces while engaged in rendering assistance pursuant to this section shall be deemed civil defense forces holding a civil defense drill-training exercise."

Volume 20 of the Opinions of the State Comptroller (1964) contains an opinion (No. 64-728) to the effect that auxiliary police may be used to direct traffic, control parking for parades and can also assist or relieve regular police in maintaining order in various types of emergencies. Such duty could reasonably be regarded as a "drill" within the meaning of the Defense Emergency Act, thus qualifying the auxiliary police officers as peace officers when performing such a drill.

To the same effect is an opinion reported in Vol. 17, Opinions of the State Comptroller (No. 61–440) (1961) and Vol. 18, Opinions of the State Comptroller (No. 62–519) (1962).

In summary, it would appear that the authority of an auxiliary policeman is limited to performing many police or quasi-police activities designated as drills or training on the basis of the twenty-one-year-old "emergency" declared by the Legislature and subject to repeal at any time. This seems to be a rickety foundation on which to rest the public-spirited efforts of a substantial number of citizens engaged in a commendable civic activity.

The status of auxiliary policemen is complicated by the fact that under the provisions of section 434a–7.0 of the Administrative Code of the City of New York, the Police Commissioner, upon "an emergency or apprehension of riot, tumult, mob, insurrection, pestilence or invasion may appoint as many unpaid patrolmen from among the citizens as he may deem desirable." Such patrolmen "shall possess the powers, perform the duties and be subject to the orders, rules and regulations of the department in the same manner as regular patrolmen."

Under the same section, the Commissioner, on the application of a person or corporation showing the need therefor, may appoint any number of special patrolmen to do special duty in behalf of the person or corporation paying for their services. Such special patrolmen "shall during the term of their holding appointment possess all the powers and discharge all the duties of the force, applicable to regular patrolmen." In fact, under Police Department Regulation 17/142.0 (Licenses, Permits and Privileges) upon certification by a special patrolman's employer that a pistol is required in the performance of his duties and approval by the Patrol precinct commander, he may be authorized to carry a revolver.

Perhaps, in view of other provisions of law authorizing maintenance of a uniformed police force for New York City housing projects (Public Housing Law, sec. 402, subdiv. 5); of a New York City Transit Authority uniformed police force (Public Authorities Law, sec. 1204, subdiv. 16); and of Port of New York Authority police and such para-police units as "meter-maids" and school crossing guards,[2] the Legislature should examine and codify the scattered laws dealing with regular, special purpose and supplementary policemen.

Certainly, the exemplary work performed by Auxiliary Police Forces deserves some special legislative definition. Crime will not disappear from our midst overnight and local and state governments should encourage citizens under proper guidance and direction to supplement and assist in the work of professional law enforcement officers.

Returning now to the instant cases, the court feels constrained to acquit the defendant on the remaining charges.

As to the charge of criminal impersonation, despite doubt that the defendant was acting in the capacity of a peace officer at the time of this unfortunate incident, the evidence falls far short of establishing his guilt beyond a reasonable doubt. Assuming that the defendant was making his inquiry to satisfy his curiosity or that of his neighbors, rather than seeking to be of assistance, what possible benefit could accrue to him from pretending to be a police officer? Eliciting an answer from Patrolman Ametrano was not equivalent to making him submit to pretended official authority within the prohibition of Sec. 190.25 of the Penal Law. The court doubts that the defendant disregarded Rule 14 of Chapter 8 of the Auxiliary Police Rules requiring a volunteer, when identifying himself to state his rank as "auxiliary" in order to avoid "misunderstanding of identity," and Rule 3 of Chapter 9 directing members of the Auxiliary Police to "promptly give their name, command, identification and shield number, if any, to any person requesting the same."

The weight of the credible testimony likewise fails to convince this court that the defendant, faced with the formidable array of uniformed housing patrolmen in the police room, was resisting arrest or harassing the complainant.

The genesis of this unhappy occurrence may rest in the possibility of friction generated between a group of professional police officers, doing a creditable job in protecting the lives and property of residents of city housing developments and unpaid volunteers patrolling the same areas under the command of New York City Police Department officers. If that is the case, there is an urgent need for better liaison between the Police Department which supervises Auxiliary Police forces and the Housing Police.

The defendant stands acquitted of all charges brought against him.[3]

• Notes

Foreword

1. See Appendix C.
2. Ramsey Clark, *Crime in America* (New York: Simon and Schuster, 1970), p. 145.
3. Ibid., p. 126.

Introduction

1. The National Manpower Survey of the Criminal Justice System (1978) projected that in 1985 state and local police employment would reach 718,000. See *Volume Two: Police, The National Manpower Survey of the Criminal Justice System* (Washington, D.C.: Government Printing Office, 1978).

2. *Omnibus Crime Bill of 1968* created the Law Enforcement Assistance Administration (LEAA). The LEAA was terminated on April 15, 1982, and all continuing functions were transferred to the Office of Justice Assistance, Research, and Statistics. From 1969 through 1980, LEAA's appropriation to contend with the nation's crime problems amounted to $7.7 billion. The *Model Police Standards Council Act* stresses higher education for police as a goal toward achieving professional status.

3. Charles Reith, *The Blind Eye of History: A Study of the Origins of the Present Police Era* (Montclair, N.J.: Patterson-Smith, 1975), pp. 25–29.

4. *Law Enforcement News*, May 23, 1983, p. 2.

5. *Law Enforcement News*, September 27, 1982, pp. 1 and 12.

6. Authority to confer peace officer powers upon the members of the NYC Auxiliary Police is granted to the Police Commissioner. See *New York City Council Res. No. 433*, August 14, 1951 in *The Auxiliary Police Rules and Regulations*, Police Department, City of New York, October 1972. However, a significant controversy exists over when peace officer status can be granted. It may apply only during a period of attack by enemy forces. See *Informal Opinion No. 81–49* (April 7, 1981) of New York State Attorney General; see also *New York Times*, June 21, 1981, pp. 1 and 10, sec. XXII.

7. *New York Sunday Daily News*, May 1, 1983, n.p. and March 6, 1983, p. 52.

8. See Peter C. Unsinger, *Personnel Practices of Reserve/Auxiliary Law Enforcement Programs* (Springfield, Va.: National Technical Information Service, 1973), p. 6. In a letter to the author dated June 10, 1976, Albany, New York, Arnold W. Grushky, the deputy director of the New York State Office of Civil Defense, was unable to pro-

vide any materials concerning the number or use of auxiliary police units within the state of New York.

9. President's Commission on Law Enforcement and Administration of Justice, *Task Force Report: Police* (Washington, D.C.: Government Printing Office, 1967), p. 123; James M. Erikson, "Community Service Officer," *Police Chief* 40 (June 1973):40–46; James M. Erikson and Matthew J. Neary, "The Community Service Officer—A+ or A-?" *Police Chief* 42 (March 1975):36–40.

10. V. A. Leonard and Harry W. Moore, *Police Organization and Management*, 3d ed. (Mineola, N.Y.: Foundation Press, 1971), p. 139; James E. Rice and Henry C. Zavislak, "Police Paraprofessionals in Jackson, Michigan," *Police Chief* 44 (January 1977):47–49.

11. John Renyhart, "Law Enforcement Explorers Get Involved," *Police Chief* 42 (December 1975):54.

12. *New York Times*, July 25, 1979, p. B3.

13. "Citizen Crime Patrols Active in Urban Areas," *Target* 5 (September 1976):3; R. K. Yin et al., *Patrolling the Neighborhood Beat: Residents and Residential Security* (Santa Monica, Calif.: The Rand Corporation, 1976).

14. George J. Washnis, *Citizen Involvement in Crime Prevention* (Lexington, Mass.: D. C. Heath and Co., 1976), p. 133.

15. Under the reorganization plan for the LEAA the National Institute of Law Enforcement and Criminal Justice became the National Institute of Justice.

16. *Law Enforcement News*, May 23, 1983, p. 13.

17. *The Practice of Crime Prevention, Vol. 1: Understanding Crime Prevention* (Lexington, Ky.: The National Crime Prevention Institute Press, 1978), p. 1.2.

18. J. T. Skip Duncan, *Citizen Crime Prevention Tactics: A Literature Review and Selected Bibliography* (Washington, D.C.: Government Printing Office, 1980), p. 2.

19. For a copy of the current schedule of courses contact: Admissions, National Crime Prevention Institute, School of Justice Administration, University of Louisville, Louisville, Ky. 40292. Telephone:(502) 588–6987.

20. Since 1978, the coalition has distributed over one million crime prevention booklets. The Crime Prevention Coalition is composed of forty-four national nonprofit organizations, fourteen federal agencies, and thirty state organizations. For current information about the work of the coalition contact: National Crime Prevention Council, Room 718, 805 15th Street, N.W., Washington, D.C. 20005. Telephone:(202) 393–7141. See *Security Systems Digest* 14 (July 4, 1983):7–8.

21. Additional organizations and groups involved in the promotion and implementation of community crime prevention projects include: The Young Lawyers' Division of the American Bar Association; the Chamber of Commerce of the United States; the National Association on Volunteers in Criminal Justice; the National Association of Citizens Crime Commissions; the National Association of Town Watch; the National Center for Community Crime Prevention; We Tip, Inc.; and Crime Stoppers. For descriptive information and/or the address of any of the organizations cited, see the latest edition of the *Encyclopedia of Associations*, Gale Research Company, Detroit, Mich. 48226.

22. Ralph A. Rossum, *The Politics of the Criminal Justice System: An Organizational Analysis* (New York: Marcel Dekker, Inc., 1978), pp. 71–72; David Patrick Geary, *Community Relations and the Administration of Justice* (New York: John Wiley and Sons, Inc., 1975), p. 46.

23. The focus of the present study of auxiliary police is on the New York Police

Department. Of course, New York is not the United States or the world. Moreover, the New York Police Department is not typical of any other American municipal police system, but then this author is unaware of any city which could be considered typical. In any case, the author is preparing a companion volume on the subject of comparative auxiliary police systems.

1. The Early History of Law Enforcement

1. J. Ross Eshleman and Barbara G. Cashion, *Sociology: An Introduction* (Boston: Little, Brown and Co., 1983), pp. 88–90.

2. Robert S. Clark, *The Criminal Justice System: An Analytical Approach* (Boston: Allyn and Bacon, Inc., 1982), pp. 58–59.

3. It is common to think of the law in terms corresponding to a particular profession (for example, business law), but this is an error. "There are but two distinct divisions of the law: (1) *substantive law* which defines rights and duties and (2) *adjective law*, or the *law of procedure*, which provides for the enforcement of rights or the performance of duties and the punishment of wrongs." See Carey Kierstead Ganong and Richard Warren Pearce, *Law and Society* (Homewood, Ill.: Richard D. Irwin, Inc., 1965), p. 6.

4. Ibid., p. 18.

5. Thomas J. Gardner and Victor Manian, *Criminal Law: Principles, Cases and Readings*, 2d ed. (St. Paul, Minn.: West Publishing Co., 1980), pp. 9–10. A familiar expression of the moral law is: "If I am not for myself, who will be for me? But if I am for myself alone, what am I? And if not now, when?"

6. See Charles Reith, *The Blind Eye of History: A Study of the Origins of the Present Police Era* (Montclair, N.J.: Patterson-Smith, 1975), pp. 18–21. See also *The President's Commission on Law Enforcement and Administration of Justice Task Force Report: The Police* (Washington, D.C.: Government Printing Office, 1967), p. 2.

7. J. Norman Swaton and Loren Morgan, *Administration of Justice: An Introduction* (New York: D. Van Nostrand Co., 1975), pp. 8–9.

8. Clark, *Criminal Justice System*, pp. 62–63.

9. Ibid., p. 64.

10. Ibid., pp. 66–69.

11. Erik Beckman, *Law Enforcement in a Democratic Society: An Introduction* (Chicago: Nelson-Hall, Inc., 1980), pp. 5–6.

12. See Clark, *Criminal Justice System*, p. 71; see also Frank R. Prassel, *The Western Peace Officer* (Norman: University of Oklahoma Press, 1972), p. 25.

13. Edward Eldefonso, Alan Coffey and Richard C. Grace, *Principles of Law Enforcement: An Overview of the Justice System*, 3d ed. (New York: John Wiley and Sons, 1982), pp. 9–10.

14. Ganong and Pearce, *Law and Society*, p. 32.

15. See Samuel Sandmel, *The Hebrew Scriptures: An Introduction to Their Literature and Religious Ideas* (New York: Alfred A. Knopf, 1963), pp. 3–4; see also Beckman, *Law Enforcement*, pp. 3–5.

16. Swaton and Morgan, *Administration of Justice*, p. 10.

17. Gardner and Manian, *Criminal Law*, p. 32.

18. Beckman, *Law Enforcement*, p. 14.

19. Ibid., pp. 24–25.

20. Alan Kalmanoff, *Criminal Justice: Enforcement and Administration* (Boston: Little, Brown and Co., 1976), p. 246.

21. The origins of the inquest, early trials and the oath *ex officio* are discussed and amplified in Leonard W. Levy, *Origins of the Fifth Amendment: The Right Against Self-Incrimination* (New York: Oxford University Press, 1968), pp. 5–10, 20–35, 271–282.

22. Beckman, *Law Enforcement*, p. 16.

23. Alan Dershowitz, "Stretch Points of Liberty," *The Nation*, March 15, 1971, p. 330.

24. An invaluable summary of the historical distinctions between the accusatorial and inquisitorial models appears in Levy, *Origins of the Fifth Amendment*, pp. 39–40. An important overview of the present European and American systems of justice appears in Marian Neef and Stuart Nagel, "The Adversary Nature of the American Legal System from a Historical Perspective," *New York Law Forum* 20 (Summer 1974):123–164.

25. T. A. Critchley, *A History of Police in England and Wales*, 2d ed. (Montclair, N.J.: Patterson-Smith, 1972), p. 1.

26. *The President's Commission*, p. 3.

27. Critchley, *History of Police*, pp. 2–3.

28. Ibid.

29. Ibid., p. 5.

30. *The President's Commission*, p. 3.

31. Critchley, *History of Police*, p. 29. "Unity of command," a major principle of personnel supervision, refers to the concept that an employee should be under the control of only one superior.

32. Ibid., p. 6.

33. *The President's Commission*, p. 4; see also Critchley, *History of Police*, pp. 3, 7–8.

34. Critchley, *History of Police*, p. 9.

35. See A. C. Germann, F. Day and R. Gallati, *Introduction to Law Enforcement and Criminal Justice* (Springfield, Ill.: Charles C. Thomas, 1977), p. 56.

36. Ibid.; see also Beckman, *Law Enforcement*, p. 14. Beckman writes that at the time of William the Conqueror, *serjeants* or servants "later became servants of the king at law."

37. See *The President's Commission*, p. 4; see also Randall G. Shelden, *Criminal Justice in America: A Sociological Approach* (Boston: Little, Brown and Co., 1982), p. 90.

38. Jonathan Rubinstein, *City Police* (New York: Ballantine Books, 1973), p. 5.

39. Alan J. Butler, *The Law Enforcement Process* (Port Washington, N.Y.: Alfred Publishing Co., 1976), p. 33.

40. Ibid.

41. See Critchley, *History of Police*, pp. 38–42.

42. Mark H. Moore and George L. Kelling, " 'To Serve and Protect': Learning from Police History," *The Public Interest* 70 (Winter 1983):52.

43. Douglas G. Browne, *The Rise of Scotland Yard: A History of the Metropolitan Police* (Westport, Conn.: Greenwood Press, 1977), pp. 79–80.

44. See Reith, *Blind Eye of History*, p. 83; see also Leonhard Felix Fuld, *Police Administration: A Critical Study of Police Organizations in the United States and Abroad* (Montclair, N.J.: Patterson-Smith, 1971), pp. 24–26. The Fuld book was originally published in 1909, but is considered a landmark resource alongside the works of August

Vollmer, Bruce Smith, Orlando W. Wilson and others who have written notable textbooks on the subject of police administration and management.

45. Clark, *Criminal Justice System*, p. 89; Swaton and Morgan, *Administration of Justice*, p. 16.

46. Ramsey Clark, *Crime in America: Observations on Its Nature, Causes, Prevention and Control* (New York: Pocket Books, 1975), p. 109.

2. The Early History of New York City's Police

1. James J. Green and Alfred J. Young, " 'The Finest'—A Brief History of the New York City Police Department," *FBI Law Enforcement Bulletin* 45 (December 1976):17.

2. Ibid. Evidently, the first *schout-fiscal*, Hendrick Van Dyck, felt the stress of his many duties since he was dismissed from his position because of drunkenness. See William J. Bopp and Donald O. Schultz, *A Short History of American Law Enforcement* (Springfield, Ill.: Charles C. Thomas, 1972), p. 16.

3. N. Gary Holten and Melvin E. Jones, *The System of Criminal Justice*, 2d ed. (Boston: Little, Brown and Co., 1982), p. 125.

4. Green and Young, " 'The Finest,' " p. 18.

5. Robert S. Clark, *The Criminal Justice System: An Analytical Approach* (Boston: Allyn and Bacon, Inc., 1982), p. 84.

6. Green and Young, " 'The Finest,' " p. 17; see also Douglas Greenberg, *Crime and Law Enforcement in the Colony of New York 1691–1776* (Ithaca, N.Y.: Cornell University Press, 1976), pp. 156–157.

7. Clark, *Criminal Justice System*, p. 84.

8. James F. Richardson, "The History of Police Protection in New York City 1800–1870," Ph.D. dissertation, New York University (Ann Arbor, Mich.: University Microfilms International, 1961), p. 10.

9. J. W. Peltason, *Corwin and Peltason's Understanding the Constitution*, 8th ed. (New York: Holt, Rinehart and Winston, 1979), p. 24.

10. Henry W. Wrobleski and Karen M. Hess, *Introduction to Law Enforcement and Criminal Justice* (St. Paul, Minn.: West Publishing Co., 1979), pp. 32–33.

11. Peltason, *Understanding the Constitution*, p. 117.

12. *The President's Commission on Law Enforcement and Administration of Justice Task Force Report: The Police* (Washington, D.C.: Government Printing Office, 1967), p. 7; see also Wrobleski and Hess, *Introduction to Law Enforcement*, pp. 204–205.

13. See Wrobleski and Hess, *Introduction to Law Enforcement*, pp. 16 and 24; see also Larry D. Ball, *The United States Marshals of New Mexico and Arizona Territories, 1846–1912* (Albuquerque: University of New Mexico Press, 1978), pp. 3–7. Ball distinguishes the work of the early U.S. marshal from the county sheriff or other local law enforcement officer. The frontier U.S. marshal dealt not only with robbery, murder, feuds, and range wars but also with political chicanery, land frauds, alien smuggling, labor disputes, Indian matters, racial troubles and international boundary problems.

14. *The President's Commission*, pp. 6–7.

15. See Richardson, "History of Police Protection," pp. 1–3 and 9–11.

16. Ibid., pp. 3–4.

17. Ibid., pp. 2–3.

18. Ibid., pp. 30–31 and 12. "Roundsmen" or "sergeants of the watch" were introduced in the mid–1830s. See Richardson, "History of Police Protection," p. 95.

19. Erik Beckman, *Law Enforcement in a Democratic Society: An Introduction* (Chicago: Nelson-Hall Inc., 1980), p. 34.

20. Richardson, "History of Police Protection," pp. 40 and 51–52.

21. See *Report of the National Advisory Commission on Civil Disorders* (New York: Bantam Books, 1968).

22. Allan E. Levett, "Centralization of City Police in the Nineteenth Century United States," Ph.D. dissertation, University of Michigan (Ann Arbor, Mich.: University Microfilms International, 1975), pp. 77–80.

23. Ibid., p. 81. The concept of "nativism" refers to the attitude or policy of favoring the native inhabitants of a country as against immigrants and a "nativist" is one who believes in or advocates nativism. The nativists of the early 19th century in the United States held hostile attitudes toward all but native-born Protestant Americans. See *Webster's Third New International Dictionary of the English Language Unabridged* (Springfield, Mass.: G. and C. Merriam Co., 1971), p. 1506.

24. Richardson, "History of Police Protection," pp. 128–129.

25. Ibid., p. 124. However, it was not until 1862 that the constables assumed the duties of the city marshals and all laws relating to the election of constables were repealed. See Augustine E. Costello, *Our Police Protectors: A History of the New York Police* (1885; reprint ed., Montclair, N.J.: Patterson-Smith, 1972), p. 155.

26. Ibid., pp. 124–126, 147–150, 179–182.

27. Costello, *Our Police Protectors*, p. 100.

28. Ibid., p. 102. However, Green and Young attribute the reference to Mayor William Havemeyer. The confusion may have to do with the fact that Matsell was Havemeyer's police chief. See Green and Young, " 'The Finest,' " pp. 19 and 25.

29. Richardson, "History of Police Protection," pp. 218–221.

30. Ibid., p. 130.

31. David R. Johnson, *American Law Enforcement: A History* (St. Louis, Mo.: Forum Press, 1981), pp. 28–29.

32. Richardson, "History of Police Protection," pp. 239–241.

33. Ibid., pp. 251–252.

34. See Costello, *Our Police Protectors*, pp. 138 and 151.

35. Richardson, "History of Police Protection," pp. 266–269.

36. Ibid., pp. 272–288.

37. James F. Richardson, *The New York Police: Colonial Times to 1901* (New York: Oxford University Press, 1979), p. 107.

38. See Wilbur R. Miller, *Cops and Bobbies: Police Authority in New York and London, 1830–1870* (Chicago: University of Chicago Press, 1977), pp. 51–52. However, "even as late as 1880, the police of Brooklyn, New York, then a separate city of five hundred thousand persons, did not carry firearms." See Samuel Walker, *Popular Justice: A History of American Criminal Justice* (New York: Oxford University Press, 1980), p. 64.

39. Richardson, *New York Police*, p. 263.

40. Lee Kennett and James LaVerne Anderson, *The Gun in America: The Origins of a National Dilemma* (Westport, Conn.: Greenwood Press, 1975), pp. 169–170.

41. Ibid., p. 151.

42. Bopp and Schultz, *Short History*, pp. 54–55.

43. Johnson, *American Law Enforcement*, p. 27.

44. George R. Wilson, "Historic Guardians of Our Nation's Capital," *FBI Law Enforcement Bulletin* 45 (April 1976):18.

45. Ibid.

46. See Levett, "Centralization of City Police," pp. 138–139.

47. Randall G. Shelden, *Criminal Justice in America: A Sociological Approach* (Boston: Little, Brown and Co., 1982), p. 98, see also pp. 95–97.

48. Samuel Walker, *A Critical History of Police Reform: The Emergence of Professionalism* (Lexington, Mass.: D. C. Heath and Co., 1977), p. 17. Walker's book examines the history of police reform from the 1850s through the end of the 1930s. Throughout the nineteenth century and into the twentieth, the nation did not appreciate "that unemployment was a function of the market; rather it was considered to arise from laziness and other attributes of individuals, or from the life-styles of many immigrants. . . . The poor and the immigrants were viewed as objects for control, benevolence and commiseration." See Levett, "Centralization of City Police," p. 139.

49. Eric H. Monkkonen, *Police in Urban America 1860–1920* (Cambridge: Cambridge University Press, 1981), p. 55.

50. Ibid., p. 56.

51. Ibid.

52. Green and Young, " 'The Finest,' " pp. 22–23.

53. See Richardson, "History of Police Protection," pp. 370–371, 400, 408–410, 415–416.

54. Green and Young, " 'The Finest,' " p. 24. "Some departments had employed women as matrons to supervise women in the jails and lockups as early as the 1840s, and the practice became widespread in most of the larger cities by the 1880s." See Walker, *Popular Justice*, p. 138. See also Peter Horne, *Women in Law Enforcement* (Springfield, Ill.: Charles C. Thomas, 1975).

55. Robert M. Fogelson, *Big-City Police* (Cambridge, Mass.: Harvard University Press, 1977), pp. 1–3, 29. Fogelson's book examines the changes in structure, personnel and function of numerous big-city departments since the 1890s.

56. Ibid., pp. 5–6.

57. Walker, *Critical History of Police Reform*, pp. 44–45. Theodore Roosevelt (1858–1919) served as governor of New York for two years following his exploits in the Spanish-American War and was elected vice-president of the United States in 1900. On September 14, 1901, he became the twenty-fifth president of the United States following the death of William McKinley. He was elected president in 1904, but lost in the election of 1912 when he was the Progressive party's candidate for the presidency.

58. See Richardson, *New York Police*, pp. 263–266.

59. See Green and Young, " 'The Finest,' " p. 24; see also Walker, *Critical History of Police Reform*, pp. 28, 46–47.

60. "A Capsule History of the Police Department," *Spring 3100* 40 (February 1969):25.

61. See Joyce V. Anenson, "The FBI's First 75 Years," *FBI Law Enforcement Bulletin* 52 (July 1983):2–11; see also Walker, *Critical History of Police Reform*, pp. 77–78.

62. Kennett and Anderson, *The Gun in America*, p. 140.

63. Ibid., pp. 171–183.

64. Ibid., p. 183.

65. See Daniel L. Schofield, "The Fourth Amendment Exclusionary Rule and the

United States Supreme Court," *FBI Law Enforcement Bulletin* 46 (March 1977):26–31.

66. Lyndol Wilkinson, "Gun Control Legislation Experts Think Law Limiting Ownership 'Too Difficult to Accomplish,' " *Security Systems Digest* 13 (February 24, 1982):4.

67. Walker, *Critical History of Police Reform*, p. 131.

68. Ibid., p. 154.

69. *Brooklyn Daily Eagle*, October 17, 1915, p. 5.

70. Leonhard F. Fuld, *Police Administration* (1909; reprint ed., Montclair, N.J.: Patterson-Smith, 1971), pp. 120–125; see also Walker, *Critical History of Police Reform*, pp. 66, 136–137.

71. Fogelson, *Big-City Police*, p. 231; see also Albert J. Reiss, Jr., *The Police and the Public* (New Haven, Conn.: Yale University Press, 1971), p. 73.

72. Patrick V. Murphy and Thomas Plate, *Commissioner: A View from the Top of American Law Enforcement* (New York: Simon and Schuster, 1977), p. 234.

73. "World News Tonight," ABC-TV, February 17, 1983.

3. Vigilantism and the Police

1. Quoted in *Parade Magazine*, June 22, 1975, p. 10. Edward H. Levi was the Attorney General of the United States from February 1975 until January 20, 1977.

2. See William E. Burrows, "The Vigilante Rides Again," *Harvard Magazine*, December 1974, pp. 36–41.

3. See Richard Maxwell Brown, *Strain of Violence: Historical Studies of American Violence and Vigilantism* (New York: Oxford University Press, 1975), pp. 305–319.

4. Ibid., p. 110.

5. Ibid., pp. 95–97.

6. Ibid., pp. 110–111.

7. H. Jon Rosenbaum and Peter C. Sederberg, eds., *Vigilante Politics* (Philadelphia: University of Pennsylvania Press, 1976), p. 4.

8. Brown, *Strain of Violence*, pp. 130 and 96.

9. Ibid., pp. 114–115.

10. Ibid., pp. 98–101.

11. Lew L. Callaway, *Montana's Righteous Hangmen* (Norman: University of Oklahoma Press, 1982), p. xvi.

12. Michael Feldberg, *The Philadelphia Riots of 1844: A Study of Ethnic Conflict* (Westport, Conn.: Greenwood Press, 1975), pp. 3–16.

13. Ibid.

14. Michael Feldberg, *The Turbulent Era: Riots and Disorder in Jacksonian America* (New York: Oxford University Press, 1980), pp. 120–121.

15. Brown, *Strain of Violence*, p. 124; see also pp. 127–128 and 134–143.

16. Burrows, "The Vigilante Rides Again," p. 38.

17. Feldberg, *The Turbulent Era*, pp. 74–75.

18. Brown, *Strain of Violence*, p. 141.

19. Irving J. Sloan, *Our Violent Past: An American Chronicle* (New York: Random House, 1970), p. 163; see also pp. 157–162.

20. Ibid., pp. 6 and 33.

21. Brown, *Strain of Violence*, pp. 125–126.

22. Ibid., p. 126.

23. Philip Taft and Philip Ross, "American Labor Violence: Its Causes, Character,

and Outcome,'' in *Violence in America: Historical and Comparative Perspectives*, ed. Hugh D. Graham and Ted R. Gurr (Beverly Hills: Sage Publications, Inc., 1979), pp. 204 and 215.

24. Samuel Walker, *A Critical History of Police Reform: The Emergence of Professionalism* (Lexington, Mass.: D. C. Heath and Co., 1977), p. 150.

25. Joan M. Jensen, *The Price of Vigilance* (Chicago: Rand McNally and Co., 1968), p. 180. See also pp. 17–18, 28, 52, 61, 84, 145–157.

26. Ibid., p. 288; see also pp. 246, 254–259, 265, 276–291.

27. Ibid., p. 296.

28. Ibid., p. 289.

29. See Sloan, *Our Violent Past*, pp. 34–35; Samuel Walker, *Popular Justice: A History of American Criminal Justice* (New York: Oxford University Press, 1980), pp. 119–120. In *Plessy* v. *Ferguson*, 163 U.S. 537 (1896) the U.S. Supreme Court held that a state could compel racial segregation in the use of public facilities, provided equal facilities were available for all races. However, the facilities provided for blacks were kept separate and seldom equal. It was not until *Brown* v. *Board of Education*, 347 U.S. 483 (1954) that public school segregation was declared unconstitutional. Later cases declared unconstitutional laws that required segregation in recreational facilities, public transportation, places of public accommodation and courthouses. For example, see *Gayle* v. *Browder*, 352 U.S. 903 (1956).

30. Walker, *Popular Justice*, pp. 119–120.

31. For a detailed account of Klan activities see: David M. Chalmers, *Hooded Americanism* (Garden City, N.Y.: Doubleday, 1965); Paul J. Gillette and Eugene Tillinger, *Inside the Ku Klux Klan* (New York: Pyramid, 1965); Arnold S. Rice, *The Ku Klux Klan in American Politics* (Washington, D.C.: Public Affairs Press, 1962).

32. Sloan, *Our Violent Past*, p. 37.

33. See Arnold Madison, *Vigilantism in America* (New York: Seabury Press, 1973), pp. 55–70.

34. Brown, *Strain of Violence*, p. 148.

35. Ibid., pp. 148 and 150. See also Herbert L. Packer, *The Limits of the Criminal Sanction* (Stanford, Calif.: Stanford University Press, 1968), pp. 149–173.

36. See Kanti C. Kotecha and James L. Walker, ''Vigilantism and the American Police,'' in Rosenbaum and Sederberg, *Vigilante Politics*, pp. 158–172; Paul Chevigny, *Police Power: Police Abuses in New York City* (New York: Pantheon Books, 1969).

37. For a succinct overview of some of these ghetto riots and many other episodes of domestic violence in the history of the United States see Richard Hofstadter and Michael Wallace, eds., *American Violence: A Documentary History* (New York: Vintage Books, 1970).

38. Steven M. Cox and Jack D. Fitz, *Police in Community Relations: Critical Issues* (Dubuque, Iowa: William C. Brown Co., 1983), pp. 116–117.

39. ''World News Tonight,'' ABC-TV, February 17, 1983.

40. Donald Robinson, ''Neighborhood Watch: Potent Weapon Against Crime,'' *Readers's Digest*, December 1981, p. 144; interview with Mortimer Kashinsky, Auxiliary Inspector, New York City Auxiliary Police, June 18, 1983.

41. Robinson, ''Neighborhood Watch,'' p. 141.

42. Jane Jacobs, *The Death and Life of Great American Cities* (New York: Vintage Books, 1961), pp. 31–32.

4. The Citizens Home Defense League

1. New York City Police Commissioner, April 1914 to December 1917.

2. *Brooklyn Daily Eagle*, April 12, 1914, p. 3.

3. *New York Herald Tribune*, May 13, 1942, n.p.

4. William Hard, "Statesman and Ex-Cop," *New York Herald Sunday Magazine*, May 17, 1931, p. 7.

5. Gertrude Mathews, "Police Preparedness," *Outlook*, February 16, 1916, p. 398.

6. *New York Times*, April 27, 1916, p. 8.

7. "A Voluntary Police Force," *Outlook*, February 16, 1916, pp. 362–363.

8. James E. Wales, "A City's Volunteer Police Force," *American City*, February 1917, p. 201.

9. *New York Times*, April 27, 1916, p. 8.

10. *New York Times*, July 6, 1916, p. 9.

11. Frank H. Potter, "The Home Defense League," *Outlook*, March 21, 1917, p. 505.

12. *New York Times*, February 11, 1917, p. 8.

13. Potter, "Home Defense League," p. 505.

14. *New York Sunday Times*, July 9, 1916, p. 1.

15. Editorial, "Assuming a Personal Responsibility," *New York Times*, April 28, 1916, p. 10.

5. The New York Police Reserves

1. Laws of New York, 1917, Chap. 651. See Exhibit 1 for the complete text of this Act.

2. Frederick Boyd Stevenson, "Backing Up the Police in Guarding New York," *Brooklyn Daily Eagle*, August 25, 1918, sec. 3, p. 1.

3. New York City Police Commissioner, January 1918 to December 1925.

4. *New York Times*, February 20, 1918, p. 1.

5. Stevenson, "Backing Up the Police," p. 1.

6. James F. Richardson, *The New York Police* (New York: Oxford University Press, 1970), pp. 9–10.

7. *New York Times*, February 21, 1918, p. 22.

8. *Brooklyn Daily Eagle*, May 29, 1918, p. 18.

9. *Brooklyn Daily Eagle*, June 25, 1918, p. 4.

10. Editorial, "A Police Reserve of Women," *Brooklyn Daily Eagle*, May 10, 1918, p. 6.

11. *Brooklyn Daily Eagle*, June 23, 1918, p. 4.

12. *Brooklyn Daily Eagle*, August 20, 1918, p. 5.

13. *New York Times*, January 3, 1919, p. 7.

14. *New York Times*, September 24, 1925, p. 23.

15. *Brooklyn Daily Eagle*, June 1, 1919, p. 9.

16. Richard Hofstadter, William Miller and Daniel Aaron, *The United States*, 3d ed. (Englewood Cliffs, N.J.: Prentice-Hall, 1972), p. 653.

17. Laws of New York, 1920, Chap. 711. See Exhibit 2 for the complete text of this Act.

18. *Brooklyn Daily Eagle*, May 16, 1920, p. 13.

19. *New York Times*, September 19, 1920, sec. 2, p. 8.

20. Ibid.

21. *New York Times*, November 26, 1921, p. 14.

22. *New York Times*, April 11, 1922, p. 1.

23. *Brooklyn Daily Eagle*, April 10, 1922, p. 1.

24. *Brooklyn Daily Eagle*, April 11, 1922, p. 1.

25. *Brooklyn Daily Eagle*, June 27, 1926, p. 4.

26. *Brooklyn Daily Eagle*, June 20, 1926, p. 6.

27. *Brooklyn Daily Eagle*, January 17, 1928, p. 3.

28. *Brooklyn Daily Eagle*, April 13, 1918, p. 5.

29. Incidentally, the plane was commanded by Richard E. Byrd, the great Arctic explorer. As early as 1914, Wanamaker had financed the construction of a plane for the express purpose of demonstrating the feasability of transatlantic flight. However, the war effort led him to turn over his aircraft for use by the Allies. See *Brooklyn Daily Eagle*, March 9, 1928, p. 3.

30. It is of interest to note that several years after the reserves were discharged, the National Commission on Law Observance and Enforcement (1931) found that the obtaining of confessions through physical violence was a widespread police practice. See President's Commission on Law Enforcement and Administration of Justice, *The Challenge of Crime in a Free Society* (Washington, D.C.: Government Printing Office, 1967), p. 93.

31. *Brooklyn Daily Eagle*, March 31, 1934, p. 19.

6. The New York City Patrol Corps

1. *Brooklyn Daily Eagle*, May 30, 1921, p. 2.

2. Gerald Astor, *The New York Cops* (New York: Charles Scribner's Sons, 1971), p. 143.

3. *New York Times*, February 15, 1936, p. 1.

4. *New York Times*, February 28, 1936, p. 23.

5. Brig. Gen. Ames T. Brown was the Adjutant General of the N.Y. State Guard, assigned to the Division of Military and Naval Affairs within the Executive Department of the State of New York.

6. *New York Times*, March 7, 1942, p. 18.

7. Telegram, February 9, 1942, N.Y.C. Municipal Archives. In addition, an opinion of the Attorney-General of February 19, 1941, stated that the formation of local military organizations apart from the active militia or U.S. troops was expressly forbidden by former section 241 of the N.Y. State Military Law (currently, Article II, Section 240), as military authority is of state and not local concern and local subdivisions have no authority to appropriate money for military purposes in the absence of express legislative authority. See 1941, *Op. Atty. Gen.* 390; *U.S. Constitution*, Article 1, sec. 8 and Article IV, sec. 4.

8. Letter, February 10, 1942, N.Y.C. Municipal Archives.

9. *New York Times*, April 16, 1942, p. 11.

10. *New York Herald Tribune*, March 30, 1942, p. 2.

11. Arthur R. Macoskey, ed., *City Patrol Corps Manual* (New York: Eagle Library, Inc., 1942), p. 3.

12. See Laws of New York, 1942, Chap. 445.

13. *Brooklyn Eagle*, April 22, 1942, p. 5.

14. *Brooklyn Eagle*, October 17, 1942, p. 2.

15. *Brooklyn Eagle*, June 11, 1942, p. 3.

16. *New York Times*, June 27, 1942, p. 12.

17. A typical one, for instance, was the Eighth Avenue subway powerhouse operating day and night at Greenwich Avenue and Horatio Street next to the Jackson Square Public Library. Sabotage hitting there would have dislocated the city's transportation system; had you passed that way in 1943, you would have seen a khaki uniformed sentinel on duty with the Corps insignia on cap and arm. See *The Villager*, April 15, 1943, p. 7 (a local newspaper published in Greenwich Village, New York).

18. *The Villager*, April 15, 1943, p. 7.

19. *New York Times*, June 27, 1942, p. 12.

20. *Brooklyn Eagle*, June 27, 1942, p. 1.

21. *Brooklyn Eagle*, December 20, 1942, p. 8.

22. *Brooklyn Eagle*, January 10, 1943, p. 6.

23. Charles Reed Jones, "Want to Be a Cop?" *New York Herald Tribune Sunday Magazine*, May 30, 1943, p. 5.

24. *New York Times*, June 5, 1943, p. 32.

25. *Brooklyn Eagle*, March 7, 1943, p. 7.

26. *Brooklyn Eagle*, June 13, 1945, p. 1.

27. *Brooklyn Eagle*, November 23, 1945, p. 1.

28. Editorial, "Call City Patrol Corps To Meet Crime Crisis," *Brooklyn Eagle*, November 21, 1945, pp. 1 and 10.

29. Ibid., p. 10.

30. *New York Times*, August 20, 1945, p. 21.

31. President Roosevelt appointed La Guardia to head the national Office of Civilian Defense in May 1941; however, La Guardia resigned from this post in February 1942. For further details regarding La Guardia's last years in office see Charles Garrett, *The La Guardia Years* (New Brunswick, N.J.: Rutgers University Press, 1961), pp. 281–294.

32. Garrett, *The La Guardia Years*, p. 284.

33. Perhaps, La Guardia's egotism was the overriding reason for the corps demise. Some persons have theorized that "at heart La Guardia wanted the Democrats to come back because he felt that when they got through his own administration would shine by comparison" (Garrett, *The La Guardia Years*, p. 296). If this be correct, he was certainly not inclined to leave behind his successful auxiliary police corps to help the next mayor.

7. The Civil Defense Auxiliary Police

1. Gerald Astor, *The New York Cops* (New York: Charles Scribner's Sons, 1971), pp. 156–158.

2. A State Civil Defense Law had been approved by the Governor on April 18, 1950. Under its provisions the New York City Director of Civil Defense was appointed on July 10 of the same year. When the New York State Legislature was next convened, the State Emergency Act was passed and signed by the Governor on April 12, 1951, giving New York unprecedented powers to deal with the protection of life and property in the event of enemy attack. *Appendix C*, a court opinion by Judge M. Marvin Berger, has

been included in order to present an outline of the major legal references in auxiliary police history since 1951.

3. *Brooklyn Eagle*, August 7, 1950, p. 1.

4. This proclamation has never been rescinded.

5. *New York Times*, January 3, 1951, p. 17.

6. "Enrollment of Auxiliary Police," Police Department, City of New York, A.P. No. 3, November 9, 1950. (These qualifications are still in effect, although seventeen-year-olds may now enroll as trainees, and a person need only be employed in the city to qualify.)

7. Newton H. Fulbright, "Mayor to Broadcast Call Today for Million Civil Defense Aids," *New York Herald Tribune*, January 21, 1951, pp. 1 and 12.

8. *Long Island Daily Press*, March 26, 1952, p. 2.

9. On at least one occasion a new twist in the familiar "looter routine" was introduced. It consisted of having a supposed looter pose as an air warden to escape detection. (See *Long Island Star Journal*, April 4, 1952, p. 8.) During these realistic drills smoke bombs sometimes caused workers to be temporarily knocked out and fire hoses aimed off target soaked participating volunteers. (Interview with Auxiliary Inspector Eunice Faust, the commanding officer of the Auxiliary Women's Unit, until its elimination in the summer of 1973.)

10. *New York Times*, January 16, 1952, p. 14.

11. *New York Herald Tribune*, December 6, 1953, p. 1.

12. *Long Island Press*, May 20, 1964, p. 4.

13. Ibid.

14. In 1973, the Administrative Code of the City of New York was amended by Local Law 19. Section U51–11.0 provides an annual $75 uniform allowance for each auxiliary police officer upon the completion of a minimum number of service hours.

15. *World-Telegram*, June 20, 1964, p. 2.

16. Formerly, Assistant Corporation Counsel, New York City and founder and first president of the Auxiliary Police Benevolent Association, 1964–1972. Mr. Schneider is currently engaged in the private practice of law in New York City.

17. The benefits of New York State's workman's compensation laws are available to auxiliary policemen who sustain injuries while performing authorized duties. See section U51–10.0 of the Administrative Code of the City of New York.

18. *New York Times*, October 31, 1971, p. 9.

8. The Auxiliary Police Force

1. "Reorganization of Civil Defense," A Report to Mayor Lindsay by Timothy J. Cooney, March 18, 1966, pp. 39–42.

2. Sy Safransky, "Could We Cope With a Major Disaster on LI?" *Long Island Press*, September 29, 1966, p. 23.

3. See Hon. John V. Lindsay, Executive Orders No. 29 of August 19, 1966 and No. 51 of September 11, 1967.

4. Stephen Cohn, "City Police Seek More Auxiliaries," *New York Times*, May 28, 1967, p. 43.

5. "McKiernan Hits Civilianization for '911' Errors," *The Chief*, January 30, 1974, p. 3.

6. Advertisement, *Daily News*, March 12, 1968, p. 45.

7. *Daily News*, Sunday, May 7, 1967, Brooklyn Section, p. 1.

8. "With Mayor Lindsay Television Program," Channel 5, Sunday, November 26, 1967.

9. *Long Island Press*, April 16, 1967, p. 3.

10. *Long Island Press*, February 23, 1968, p. 2.

11. Emil Hroch and Fred Carpenter, "Pay for Auxiliary Police? Study in Jamaica Urged," *Long Island Press*, February 4, 1968, p. 18.

12. See *New York Times*: March 15, 1968, p. 43; March 19, 1968, p. 28; March 21, 1968, p. 32.

13. David Burnham, "Youths to Patrol a Brooklyn Area," *New York Times*, January 1, 1970, p. 72; see also J. M. Erikson and M. J. Neary, "The Community Service Officer," *Police Chief* 42 (March 1975):36–40.

14. See Chief Inspector's Memo No. 39, 1969, N.Y.C.P.D.

15. *New York Times*, Sunday, May 6, 1973, p. 68.

16. Ibid.

17. In April 1973, Donald F. Cawley became police commissioner. New changes instituted included the designation of a Chief of Field Services to replace the position of Chief of Patrol. The Auxiliary Forces Section was placed under the new office of Chief of Field Services.

18. In addition, in 1973 the Police Department redesignated all Patrolmen and Patrolwomen to the title of "Police Officer." At the same time, all Auxiliary Patrolmen and Patrolwomen became "Auxiliary Police Officers."

19. Richard Rothbard, "Auxiliary Police Help Cop on the Beat," *The Queens Tribune*, September 7, 1972.

20. Clive Lawrence, "New York's Unarmed 'Finest,' " *The Christian Science Monitor*, March 7, 1972.

21. Raymond A. Joseph, "The Civilian Cop Helps Fight the Crime Rise, Or Is He 'Plain Nuts'?" *The Wall Street Journal*, February 20, 1973, p. 1.

22. See "Auxiliary Cop to Get City's Aid," *New York Post*, April 24, 1976, p. 7; N.Y.P.D., *Aux. Forces Sec. Directive No. 4–1*, May 18, 1976.

23. See Joseph P. Fried, "Auxiliaries Told to Adopt a Low Profile," *New York Times*, February 2, 1975, p. 35: Frank Emerson, "The Private Citizens Who Wear a Badge," *New York Post*, February 24, 1973, p. 25.

24. Robert Daley, *Target Blue* (New York: Dell, 1971), p. 527.

25. Mary O'Flahery, "Park Duty Eyed for Auxiliary Copettes," *Daily News*, Sunday, March 24, 1974, p. 3B.

26. Catherine Calvert, "What It's Like To Be a Woman Cop," *Mademoiselle Magazine*, September 1973, p. 88.

9. City in Crisis

1. For a complete record of the city's financial crisis see Fred Ferretti, *The Year the Big Apple Went Bust* (New York: G. P. Putnam's Sons, 1976).

2. Frank Lombardi, "Abe Tilts With Fiorello, OKs Pinball," *Daily News*, June 7, 1976, p. 5.

3. *Daily News*, February 28, 1975, p. 3.

4. *Daily News*, June 26, 1975, p. 65.

5. *Open Door*, No. 50, December 18, 1975.

6. *New York Times*, August 8, 1976, p. 27.

7. *Long Island Press*, July 15, 1976, p. 8.

8. *The Star*, newsletter published by the Auxiliary Forces Section of the Police Department, City of New York, undated.

9. New York City Police Department, "Decentralization of the Auxiliary Forces Program," *Interim Order No. 9*, January 24, 1974. Reprinted with permission.

10. Auxiliary Police in Crisis

1. Carl J. Pelleck, "Auxiliary Police Are Gone," *New York Post*, July 18, 1975, pp. 1 and 79; Robert D. McFadden, "Auxiliary Police Fade Under Layoffs," *New York Times*, July 21, 1975, p. 26.

2. *Daily News*, July 3, 1975, p. XQ5.

3. *Daily News*, July 10, 1975, p. XQ1.

4. William T. Slattery, "Park Patrols To Resume," *New York Post*, July 22, 1976, p. 6.

5. William T. Slattery, "Auxiliary Cops Debate a Return to the Streets," *New York Post*, July 25, 1975, p. 50.

6. Jerry Adler, "Auxicops Mull Further Protest," *Daily News*, August 6, 1975, p. 37.

7. N.Y.C.P.D., Auxiliary Forces Section, Temp. Procedure Order No. 15, August 14, 1975. (Published by permission.)

8. Peter Coutros, "No Harvest for Brave David," *Daily News*, September 3, 1976, p. 28.

9. The *Auxiliary Police Rules and Regulations, October 1972*, states on page eight that only auxiliary police assigned to a Park Unit are authorized to perform motor patrol "in private autos." This provision was the only reference for the use of automobiles. Central Park contains 840 acres and attracts approximately 12.5 million visitors each year. For these reasons, it is probable that the Park Unit was singled out for special attention. In 1973, the Central Park Precinct began using auxiliary personnel to man idle police radio cars at key, fixed locations in order to contribute to an atmosphere of police omnipresence. This program was apparently expanded to include the use of police cars by supervising auxiliary officers. See John William Bonner, "Authoritarianism in Auxiliary Police," Master's Thesis, John Jay College of Criminal Justice, 1974, p. 33.

10. Stewart Ain and Paul Meskil, "Clubbed by Nudie in Park, Auxiliary Cop Dies," *Daily News*, September 1, 1975, p. 5.

11. Justice Irving Lang warned that "extreme caution" should be exercised before releasing him. *New York Times*, May 15, 1976, p. 29.

12. In 1919, Adam Mang, a member of the volunteer Police Reserves, was killed during election riots. See *Brooklyn Daily Eagle*, May 30, 1921, p. 1. In 1973, Roger McCottrie, a black-belt Karate expert, was killed by gunfire while off-duty. See Milton Adams, "Cop's Killer 'Known,' But Witnesses Are Silent," *New York Post*, November 16, 1973, p. 15.

13. Barry Cunningham, "The Auxiliary Police: Death and Conflict," *New York Post*, September 6, 1975, p. 21.

14. Hank Roden, "PBA Puts 'Cuffs' on Auxiliaries," *Long Island Sunday Press*, September 14, 1975, p. 1.

15. *Brooklyn Daily Eagle*, January 20, 1918, p. 4.

16. Roden, "PBA Puts 'Cuffs' on Auxiliaries," p. 1.

17. Cunningham, "The Auxiliary Police," p. 21.

18. *Daily News*, October 12, 1975, p. 16Q.

19. Editorial, "The Cutback of the Auxiliary Forces," *Our Town*, July 25, 1975, p. 6.

20. "Civilian Gets Inspector's Funeral," *The Police Officers Journal*, October 1975, pp. 1 and 14.

21. Irving Spiegel, "Auxiliary Police Death Raises Doubt Over Training," *New York Times*, September 2, 1976, p. 32.

22. Lucinda Franks, "Slain Auxiliary Is Given a Police Funeral," *New York Times*, September 3, 1975, p. 40.

23. N.Y.C.P.D., Auxiliary Forces Section, Directives No. 23, December 4, 1975 and No. 23–1, December 12, 1975.

24. In "Operation Identification" the Police Department supplies an electric etching tool to mark personal property. Owners are encouraged to engrave their social security number followed by the letters "N.Y.C." In this way, theft is discouraged, unauthorized resale is more difficult and the chance to recover stolen property is improved.

11. The Auxiliary Peacekeeping Force

1. "A Message from Mayor Koch," *Auxiliary Police Newsletter II*, P.O. Box 5258, Grand Central Station, New York, N.Y. 10017, April 1979, p. 1.

2. Barbara Gelb, "The Purge of the Chiefs," *The New York Times Magazine*, April 16, 1978, p. 103.

3. The complete list of participants and the full report are found in Chapter 16.

4. Henry J. Stern and Antonio G. Olivieri, "Report on New York City's Auxiliary Police Program," p. 16.

5. New York City Police Department, *Auxiliary Forces Section Directive No. 11*, March 15, 1979.

6. *New York Law Journal*, April 23, 1979, p. 12.

7. See Billy Bloom, "2300 Auxiliary Police Return to the Street," *Our Town*, July 22, 1979, p. 5.

8. Deadly physical force is defined as the physical force which, under the circumstances in which it is used, is readily capable of causing death or other serious physical injury. The "nightstick bill," or as it was more officially known bill 5616-A, added a new subdivision to section 265.20 of the Penal Law of the State of New York. Its provisions are reported below:

Section 1. Section 265.20 of the penal law is amended by adding a new subdivision c to read as follows:

c. Section 265.01 shall not apply to possession of that type of billy commonly known as a "police baton" which is twenty-four to twenty-six inches in length and no more than one and one-quarter inches in thickness by members of an auxiliary police force of a city with a population in excess of one million persons when duly authorized by regulation or order issued by the police commissioner of such city. Such regulations shall require training in the use of the police baton including but not limited to the defensive use of the baton and instruction in the legal use of deadly physical force pursuant to article thirty-five of this chapter. Notwithstanding the provisions of this section or any other provision of law, possession of such baton shall not be authorized when used intentionally to strike another person except in those situations when the use of deadly physical force is authorized by such article thirty-five.

§. This act shall take effect immediately.

9. New York City Police Department, *Auxiliary Forces Section Directive No. 14,* April 16, 1979.

10. New York City Police Department, *Auxiliary Forces Section Directive No. 3,* February 1, 1979.

11. *New York Law Journal,* July 10, 1978, p. 2.

12. Ibid.

13. New York City Police Department, *Auxiliary Forces Section Directive No. 11,* March 31, 1980.

14. New York City Police Department, *Auxiliary Forces Section Directive No. 14,* May 12, 1980.

15. Some 5,000 auxiliaries were performing over 100 hours of service each year. Interview with Mortimer Kashinsky, Auxiliary Inspector, New York City Auxiliary Police, June 18, 1983.

16. In 1981, membership in the New York City Police Department declined to 22,170, its lowest point since 1954. This figure was expected to rise to 24,095 by the summer of 1984. The total number of transit, housing and regular police was expected to reach 30,173 by 1984. See *New York Times*: December 24, 1981, p. B3; April 16, 1983, p. 1; April 27, 1983, p. 1.

17. Elmer H. Johnson, *Crime, Correction and Society,* 4th ed. (Homewood, Ill.: The Dorsey Press, 1978), p. 284.

12. The Total Force Concept

1. Benjamin Ward, "The Search for Safety—A Dual Responsibility," in *Deterrence of Crime In and Around Residences* (Washington, D.C.: Government Printing Office, 1973), pp. 116–117.

2. H. Leith, "Civilians Taking Bigger Role in City's Police Work," *Long Island Press,* April 24, 1968, p. 33.

3. On this point, Professor Unsinger has stated: "For agencies currently deploying reserve/auxiliary peace officers or contemplating doing so in the future, it behooves them to determine the jobs or tasks that will be required of the volunteer. In industry, this practice of developing job descriptions and setting the specifications is standard practice. By knowing fully what is expected, being equipped and trained to do it and having the authority to accomplish it, the volunteer will be in a position to contribute to the achievement of the goals of law enforcement. By choosing men wisely and training them for the task, the satisfaction that comes from a real contribution will help in the retention of quality reserve/auxiliary personnel." Peter C. Unsinger, *Personnel Practices of Reserve/Auxiliary Law Enforcement Programs* (Springfield, Va.: National Technical Information Service, 1973), pp. 8–9.

4. For a summary of the advantages and disadvantages of police reserve/auxiliary programs see G. Douglas Gourley and Allen P. Bristow, *Patrol Administration* (Springfield, Ill.: Charles C. Thomas, 1971); Everett M. King, *The Auxiliary Police Unit* (Springfield, Ill.: Charles C. Thomas, 1960).

5. See Chapter 14.

6. State Charter Revision Commission for New York City, *Revising the New York City Charter: Introductory Report*, 1973, p. 6.

7. James Q. Wilson, "What Makes a Better Policeman," *Atlantic Monthly*, March 1969, p. 135.

8. David Burnham, "Most Call Crime City's Worst Ill," *New York Times*, January 16, 1974, pp. 1, 20. The Flint, Michigan Neighborhood Foot Patrol Program was initiated in January 1979 in order to foster community crime prevention. The Charles Stewart Mott Foundation granted $2.6 million to the city of Flint for the implementation of regular police foot patrols in fourteen experimental neighborhoods. Over the three years of the experiment, crime was down by 8.7 percent and calls for service were down 43.3 percent in the areas where foot patrols were used. The success of the program prompted the Mott Foundation to provide funding for a National Neighborhood Foot Patrol Center. Currently, the center is located in the School of Criminal Justice at Michigan State University, East Lansing, Michigan 48824. The center disseminates information, technical assistance, education and training. The following toll free number is available for additional information about the services and activities of the center. 1 800–892–9051

9. *New York Sunday Times*, December 27, 1981, p. 6E.

10. *New York Times*, September 11, 1979, pp. 1, B9.

11. See James H. Scheuer, *To Walk the Streets Safely* (New York: Doubleday and Company, 1969), p. 131.

12. The National Advisory Commission on Criminal Justice Standards and Goals, *Report on Police* (Washington, D.C.: Government Printing Office, 1973), p. 263. See Appendix B for the Commission's full report on the selection and assignment of reserve police officers.

13. James E. Ryan, "Auxiliary Police," *Spring 3100* (N.Y.P.D. Publication), July–August, 1972, p. 20.

14. George J. Washnis, *Citizen Involvement in Crime Prevention* (Lexington, Mass.: D. C. Heath and Co., 1976), pp. 88–89.

13. The Auxiliary Police and the Law

1. *Buric v. McGuire*, New York County Supreme Court, Special Term, Part 1, *New York Law Journal*, July 19, 1978, pp. 6–7.

2. The full text of *People v. Jackson* is presented in Appendix C.

3. *People v. Jackson*, Queens County Criminal Court, Part 3A, *New York Law Journal*, December 29, 1972, p. 19.

4. The materials presented under the headings of "Arrest Authority," "Search Authority," and "Liability Insurance" are primarily adapted from Ronald E. Dow, *Volunteer Police: Community Asset or Professional Liability* (Albany, N.Y.: New York Conference of Mayors, 1978), pp. 11–16. They are reprinted with the permission of the N.Y. Conference of Mayors and Municipal Officials.

5. *New York Criminal Procedure Law*, Sections 140.25 (1); 140.30 (1).

6. *New York Penal Law*, Sections 195.10; 205.30.

7. *PBA v. Hitt*, 75 Misc. 2d 565 (1972) at 568.

8. See *Opinions of the Attorney General* (Albany: State of New York, 1970), p. 157; *Opinions of the Comptroller Relating to Municipal Government* 18 (Albany: State

of New York, 1962), p. 265; *Opinions of the Comptroller Relating to Municipal Government* 30 (Albany: State of New York, 1974), p. 570.

9. *New York* v. *Perez*, 79 Misc. 2d 88 (1974) at 92.

10. *Attorney General's Informal Opinion No. 81–49*, April 7, 1981, addressed to Charles A. Bradley, Corporation Counsel, City of White Plains, New York, p. 3; see also letter to author from James D. Cole, Assistant Attorney General, State of New York, June 15, 1983, which declared that this opinion "interprets current law governing status and powers of auxiliary police."

11. *Mapp* v. *Ohio*, 367 U.S. 643 (1961).

12. James S. Kakalik and Sorrel Wildhorn, *The Private Police: Security and Danger* (New York: Crane Russak, 1977), pp. 253–255 and pp. 323–325; also see the landmark case of *Burdeau* v. *McDowell*, 256 U.S. 465 (1921).

13. *Commonwealth* v. *Eshelman*, 383 A. 2d 838 (1978).

14. The court concluded: "It is fundamental agency law that an act outside the scope of one's authority may be ratified by the subsequent conduct or behavior of the principal on whose behalf one purports to be acting. . . . In our view, the conduct of [the auxiliary police officer's] superior [the police chief] in the police department upon receiving the package from [the auxiliary police officer] in effect ratified [his] unauthorized acts on behalf of the commonwealth." *Commonwealth* v. *Eshelman*, 383 A. 2d 838 (1978).

15. Literal translation: "let the master respond."

16. The cost per "class A officer" (with power of arrest) with one company approximates $200 per year (for $100,000 each person, $300,000 each incident, $1,000 deductable coverage) while the same coverage for a "class B officer" (without power of arrest) is about $100. The differential between class A and B officers for another company providing essentially similar coverage is about $68. These figures were in effect on September 19, 1977. The information was provided by Beatrice W. Haskins, Program Director at James F. Jackson Associates, Inc., Woodbine, Maryland 21797.

On February 27, 1979, Council members Stern and Olivieri introduced a local law to amend the Administrative Code of the City of New York in order to indemnify auxiliary police officers for any act performed within the scope of their duties and so long as they were not grossly negligent. The bill, *Introduction No. 602*, was referred to the Council's Committee on Finance. The bill had not been approved as of the time of the submission of the author's final draft of this book to the publisher.

14. Power in the Auxiliary Police

1. *Long Island Press*, December 16, 1976, p. 21.

2. *Americans Volunteer 1974* (Washington, D.C.: Government Printing Office, 1975), p. 3.

3. John William Bonner, "Authoritarianism in Auxiliary Police," Master's thesis, John Jay College of Criminal Justice, City University of New York, 1974, p. 60. Bonner was surprised to find that auxiliary and regular police are quite similar in their respective degrees of authoritarian makeup. Another finding revealed that the regulars held an unusually high view of their own occupational status.

4. See the following issues of the *New York Times*: June 17, 1973, p. 25; September 4, 1973, p. 33. Also see *New York Post*, February 24, 1973, p. 25.

5. *New York Daily News*, January 10, 1974, p. 20.

6. *New York Post*, March 6, 1976, p. 20.

7. *Auxiliary Police Rules and Regulations*, Police Department, City of New York, October 1972, pp. 23–24.

8. Max Weber, *The Theory of Social and Economic Organization*, trans. by A. M. Henderson and Talcott Parsons (New York: Oxford University Press, 1947), p. 152.

9. *Interim Order No. 9*, Police Department, City of New York, January 24, 1974, pp. 1–2. See Chapter 9 for the complete text of this order.

10. Ibid., p. 3.

11. *Rules and Regulations*, p. 22.

12. See New York City Police Department, *Auxiliary Forces Section Directive No. 28*, October 22, 1980.

13. *Rules and Regulations*, p. 21.

14. *New York Post*, October 5, 1968, p. 28.

15. *New York Times*, April 22, 1976, p. 37.

16. This dilemma was strikingly illustrated by Dr. Bernard Donovan, the School Superintendent for the City of New York. In 1968, he recommended the hiring of security guards for New York's public schools and reportedly stated in an article which appeared on page 6 of the *Long Island Press*, January 23, 1968: "I will speak to the Police Commissioner about getting security aides auxiliary police power."

15. The Origin of the Auxiliary Subway Patrol

1. Robert Lindsay, "The Men on the Turnstile Beat," *New York Times*, Sunday, October 29, 1972, sec. 4, p. 8.

2. See Jan M. Chaiken, Michael W. Lawless, and Keith A. Stevenson, *The Impact of Police Activity on Crime: Robberies on the New York City Subway System* (New York: New York City Rand Institute, 1974). This report reviews an eight-year period of robberies in the subway. Among other purposes, the study examined the impact of Mayor Wagner's decision in 1965 to nearly triple the strength of the Transit Authority Police Department, from 1,219 to more than 3,100 men. The report shows that a decrease in the felony crime rate was due to the deterrent effect of the increased number of police. However, the cost to the city for each felony crime deterred was calculated to be $35,000!

3. Edward Ranzal, "Transit Police Auxiliary is Suggested," *New York Times*, January 9, 1976, p. 35; Howard Reiser, "Auxiliary Cops for Subways?" *Long Island Press*, January 9, 1976, p. 5.

4. Sanford D. Garelik served as chief inspector of the regular New York Police Department from 1966 to 1969 and was president of the City Council from 1970 to 1974.

5. A proposal which was made in early January of 1967 may have provided the stimulation for the APBA's requests for Council action. At that time, a group known as the "Community-Wide Panel for a Better City" recommended that auxiliary police should be assigned to protect every subway station and all frequently used bus stops during the evening hours. A chief spokesman for the group was Vincent L. Broderick, a former Police Commissioner. In 1976 he was appointed a Judge of the U.S. District Court by President Ford. See Erwin Savelson, "Patrols Urged for Bus Stops," *World Journal Tribune*, January 3, 1967, p. 1; *The Council's Res. No. 1035* of November 2, 1967, had the weight of a mere request.

6. A bill was also put before the Committee on Corporations, Authorities and Commissions in the Assembly of the State of New York. This bill sought to amend the Public Authorities Law in order to permit uniform members of New York City's auxiliary

police to ride for free on all facilities operated by the Metropolitan Transportation Authority. The bill was introduced by Assemblyman Hochberg and sponsored by Assemblyman Delli Bovi on March 24, 1975.

7. "It was hot as hell," said Bob Tripp, an auxiliary policeman who made his way to the first car to help the injured. *New York Times*, August 29, 1973, p. 44.

8. *New York Times*, October 10, 1973, p. 93.

9. *New York Times*, April 20, 1973, p. 11.

10. *Long Island Press*, April 13, 1973, p. 8.

11. Bernard Rabin, "Subway Crime Drop Disputed," *Daily News*, January 13, 1976, p. 7.

12. Albert Lee, *Crime-Free* (Baltimore: Penguin Books, 1974), p. 193.

13. Significantly, Maye's view received some consideration by Chief Garelik about a week later. In remarks on a television interview program, he stated: "When you have fired as we have 300 men and when the men in the department are cooperating with you in reducing the overtime and in making arrests, certainly I think that some assurance should be given those men that the employment ultimately of auxiliaries would not affect their jobs in the future." (ABC-TV, "Eyewitness News Conference," January 18, 1976, p. 22 of typed transcription.)

14. Ranzal, "Transit Police Auxiliary is Suggested," p. 35.

15. *New York Times*, February 26, 1977, p. 34.

16. *New York Times*, September 11, 1979, pp. 1 and B9.

17. *New York Times*, January 1, 1982, p. 27.

18. *New York Times*, December 31, 1981, p. B4.

19. *New York Times*, December 17, 1981, p. B3.

20. *In re PBA* v. *Koch*, 113 Misc. 2d 882–884. The decision was rendered on March 19, 1982, Supreme Court, Special Term, New York County.

21. *New York Daily News*, November 16, 1982, p. XQ4.

22. At the time of the preparation of this book, the New York State Municipal Police Training Council had established 285 hours as the minimum police officer training requirement. Persons holding "peace officer" positions had no minimum training requirements. See *General Municipal Law*, Sec. 109-g; *Executive Law*, Sec. 840; and 9 *NYCRR* Subtitle U.

23. *New York Times*, October 10, 1973, p. 93.

24. See *In re PBA* v. *Koch*, 113 Misc. 2d 883 (1982).

16. Report on New York City's Auxiliary Police

1. Henry J. Stern was appointed Parks Commissioner during Mayor Koch's second term as the city's mayor. Antonio G. Olivieri (1941–1980) died at age 39 on November 4, 1980 from cancer. He had maintained an active schedule throughout his fight against the disease and his courage inspired all who knew about his condition. Councilman Olivieri graduated from Harvard College and Columbia University's School of Law. He prepared comprehensive reports on health, tenant and environmental matters during his careers as a member of the City Council and as a two-term Assemblyman. At a memorial service in his honor, it was said that he was a person who "instinctively sided with the disadvantaged and the weak." See *New York Times*: November 5, 1980, sec. II, p. 16; November 8, 1980, p. 28.

17. The Guardian Angels

1. Quoted in Richard Hofstadter and Michael Wallace, eds., *American Violence: A Documentary History* (New York: Vintage Books, 1971), p. 476.

2. See Arnold Madison, *Vigilantism in America* (New York: Seabury Press, 1973), pp. 141–151; see also Gary T. Marx and Dane Archer, "Community Police Patrols and Vigilantism," in *Vigilante Politics,* ed. H. Jon Rosenbaum and Peter C. Sederberg (Philadelphia: University of Pennsylvania Press, 1976), pp. 129–157.

3. Marx and Archer, "Community Police Patrols and Vigilantism," p. 131.

4. See Michael Norman, "Guardian Angel is Killed by an Officer in Newark," *New York Times*, January 1, 1982, p. 26; see also *New York Times*, September 2, 1976, p. 32.

5. Marx and Archer, "Community Police Patrols and Vigilantism," p. 131.

6. Interview with Curtis Sliwa, "Crossfire," Cable News Network (CNN) Television Program, August 12, 1983. Angels patrol in such cities as Boston, Philadelphia, Newark, Cleveland, Miami and Los Angeles.

7. Curtis Sliwa founded the Guardian Angels in 1979. The original press release announcing the formation of a citizens' group to patrol the city's subways declared: "The Magnificent 13 is just the start. We intend on working toward having patrols organized for all subway lines . . . 13 today BUT 1300 tomorrow!" See Nicholas Pileggi, "The Guardian Angels: Help—or Hype?" *New York Magazine*, November 24, 1980, p. 19.

8. See *Sacramento Union*, September 2, 1983, p. A8; see also *Chicago Tribune*, September 2, 1983, Sec. II, p. 5.

9. See Bernard Edelman, "Does New York Need the Guardian Angels?" *Police Magazine* 4 (May 1981):51.

10. In an opinion research survey of sixty-seven civilians, thirty Transit Authority police and eighty-six PBA delegates, the civilians rated the Guardian Angels quite favorably while the police rated them unfavorably. The survey instrument contained twenty-seven items to test the attitudes of the subjects. However, three civilians compared the Angels to "Nazis." One of the civilian subjects explained how he had changed his attitude about the Angels after encountering about thirty of them near a subway entrance. He said: "I got an eerie feeling about them. Then when I heard that there were already 700 of them and they aim to double that number I really started having my doubts about the whole thing." See Brian B. Ostrowe and Rosanne DiBiase, "Citizen Involvement as a Crime Deterrent: A Study of Public Attitudes Toward an Unsanctioned Civilian Patrol Group," *Journal of Police Science and Administration* 11 (June 1983):186–192.

11. *New York Times*, December 28, 1980, p. 36.

12. *Psychological Assessment of Patrolman's Qualifications in Relation to Field Performance* (Washington, D.C.: Government Printing Office, 1968), pp. 7–11.

13. "Indiana University Develops Police Selection Procedure," *Target* 6 (September 1977):1.

14. See Larry T. Hoover, *Police Educational Characteristics and Curricula* (Washington, D.C.: Government Printing Office, July 1975), pp. 7–8.

15. See *Time*, August 22, 1978, pp. 32–33.

16. Quoted in Judith Cummings, "Should Subway 'Angels' Get a Halo?" *New York Sunday Times*, December 21, 1980, p. 6E.

17. See Richard Maxwell Brown, *Strain of Violence: Historical Studies of American Violence and Vigilantism* (New York: Oxford University Press, 1975), pp. 95–97. The

characteristics identified by Brown as relating to the phenomenon of vigilantism included: 1. an extralegal organization; 2. existence for a definite (often short) period of time; 3. in an area with inadequate or absent law enforcement; 4. for the purpose of establishing law and order.

18. See Cummings, "Should Subway 'Angels' Get a Halo?" p. 6E and Pileggi, "The Guardian Angels," p. 15. On August 12, 1983, Sliwa stated that the Guardian Angels had formed a not-for-profit corporation known as the Alliance of Guardian Angels, Inc. See Sliwa, CNN Interview.

19. Edelman, "Does New York Need the Guardian Angels?" pp. 51–52.

20. Cummings, "Should Subway 'Angels' Get a Halo?" p. 6E.

21. On August 12, 1983, Sliwa stated that nine of the cities in which the Angels were in operation had entered into a "memorandum of understanding" with them. These agreements included provision by the police for background investigations of new Angel recruits, identification cards and some training. See Sliwa, CNN Interview.

22. See James Haskins, *The Guardian Angels* (Hillside, N.J.: Enslow Publishers, 1983), pp. 46–48.

23. Ibid., pp. 52 and 40.

24. Ibid., p. 58.

25. Ibid., p. 31.

18. The ROTC Police Plan

1. Adam Walinsky et. al., *The New Police Corps*, August 4, 1982, p. 12 (a pamphlet); see also *Law Enforcement News*, September 27, 1982, p. 12.

2. Walinsky, *The New Police Corps*, p. 8.

3. Adam Walinsky in a speech before the Metropolitan New York Chapter of the American Academy for Professional Law Enforcement, March 10, 1983.

4. Michael Kramer, "The National Interest: More Cops for Your Money," *New York Magazine*, December 6, 1982, p. 32.

5. See *New York Times*, August 6, 1982, p. 22 and January 11, 1983, p. 18; *New York Magazine*, December 6, 1982, pp. 30 and 32.

6. *The Christian Science Monitor*, January 4, 1983, p. 6.

7. Kramer, *The National Interest*, pp. 30 and 32.

8. In a survey of every police chief in cities of 50,000 and over and of a random 25 percent sample of chiefs in cities from 25,000 to 50,000 population, conducted by the International Association of Chiefs of Police (IACP), less than half of the respondents reported feeling that two years of college should be the minimum educational level for police; and only 15 percent said they thought the requirement should be four years of college. See Charles W. Tenney, Jr., *Higher Education Programs in Law Enforcement and Criminal Justice* (Washington, D.C.: Government Printing Office, June 1971), p. 34.

9. "ROTC for the Nation's Cops?" *Newsweek*, April 4, 1983, p. 78.

10. Walinsky, *The New Police Corps*, pp. 21–24.

11. Ibid., pp. 14–15.

12. Ibid., p. 12.

13. Ibid., p. 19.

14. Editorial, "A Breath of Fresh Air for Police," *New York Times*, August 6, 1983, p. 22.

15. Ibid.

16. Walinsky, *The New Police Corps*, p. 9.

17. Ibid., pp. 15–16.

18. Ibid., p. 14.

19. Ibid., p. 22.

20. Ibid.

21. Letter, James C. Finlay, "Wrong Source of Funds for a New York State Police Corps," *New York Times*, September 10, 1982, p. 22.

22. Jonathan Rubinstein, *City Police* (New York: Farrar, Straus and Giroux, 1973), p. 368.

23. Larry T. Hoover, *Police Educational Characteristics and Curricula* (Washington, D.C.: Government Printing Office, July 1975), p. 2.

24. Ibid.

25. Ibid., pp. 1 and 2.

26. Robert M. Fogelson, *Big-City Police* (Cambridge, Mass.: Harvard University Press, 1977), p. 103.

27. Hoover, *Police Educational Characteristics*, p. 32.

28. Ibid., p. 33.

29. Walinsky, *The New Police Corps*, pp. 6, 9–10, 17–18.

30. Ibid., p. 11.

31. Ibid.

32. Walinsky, Speech.

33. See Patrick V. Murphy and Thomas Plate, *Commissioner: A View from the Top of American Law Enforcement* (New York: Simon and Schuster, 1977), pp. 130–131.

34. See *Report of the National Advisory Commission on Civil Disorders* (New York: Bantam Books, 1968), pp. 319–320; Pamela D. Mayhall and David Patrick Geary, *Community Relations and the Administration of Justice*, 2d ed. (New York: John Wiley and Sons, 1979), pp. 308–340.

35. The 1968 Omnibus Crime Control and Safe Streets Act established the Law Enforcement Assistance Administration (LEAA) and within LEAA the Law Enforcement Education Program (LEEP). Under this program thousands of criminal justice practitioners received funds for college tuition and students who intended to pursue careers in the field also received tuition assistance.

36. The U.S. Army College Fund Program encourages high school graduates to save money for college tuition, room and board, and books while serving in the military. For every $1 they put in, they receive $5 or more. After two years in the Army, they can have up to $15,200 or after three years, up to $20,100. It is believed that prior military service helps students obtain the maturity, discipline and confidence it takes to succeed in college or in the business world. The most current information about the Army College Fund and related programs is available from any local armed forces recruiting office. Veterans who select a criminal justice degree program which includes attendance at a police academy may substantially increase their chances of obtaining a police officer position. Information about higher education degree programs in the field of criminal justice may be obtained at most public libraries.

37. See *The Christian Science Monitor*, January 3, 1983, p. 16.

38. The latest printing of the *American Bar Association Criminal Justice Standards* is available from the Circulation Department, American Bar Association, 1155 East 60th Street, Chicago, Ill. 60637 and the *Report on Police, Report on Corrections, Report on*

Courts, Report on Community Crime Prevention, Report on the Criminal Justice System, and others of the 1973 National Advisory Commission on Criminal Justice Standards and Goals are available from the U.S. Government Printing Office, Washington, D.C. 20402.

39. In 1983, New York City Council Member Susan D. Alter introduced a local law to amend the Administrative Code of the City of New York which would create an armed "Volunteer Reserve Unit" to serve as back-up to the regular police force. It was referred to the Committee on Public Safety. See *Int. No. 478,* New York City Council; *New York Daily News,* March 6, 1983, p. 52 KL.

40. See Martin A. Greenberg, "Volunteer Crime Prevention Program: A Proposal for Survival in America's Third Century," *The Police Chief* 44 (April 1977):60–61; for an overview of many different kinds of individual and collective crime prevention initiatives see J. T. Skip Duncan, *Citizen Crime Prevention Tactics: A Literature Review and Selected Bibliography* (Washington, D.C.: Government Printing Office, April 1980).

41. Letter, Phil Caruso, "Police Corps, No; Police Cadets, Yes," *New York Times,* January 28, 1983, p. 26.

42. See *The New Republic,* December 6, 1982, p. 9.

43. See New York City Council *Res. No. 433,* August 14, 1951; but see also *Informal Opinion No. 81–49* (April 7, 1981) of the New York State Attorney General and *New York Times,* June 21, 1981, pp. 1 and 10, sec. XXII. Auxiliary Police in Westchester County are seeking to amend Section 2.10 of New York State's Criminal Procedure Law in order to obtain "peace officer" status on a permanent basis. See *NY Senate Bill No. S. 2970,* February 17, 1983, introduced by Sen. Joseph R. Pisani.

44. In the 1970s, Adam Walinsky supported a police draft. In this way, the ranks of the nation's police forces would always be filled at far less cost than at present. Moreover, the drafted police officer would be likely to have more roots to the community and therefore be less likely to abuse the rights of citizens. A police draft is used in at least two nations, Israel and Argentina. Walinsky's proposal for conscripting police officers is never mentioned in the "New Police Corps" plan. It is a puzzle to this author why Mr. Walinsky has shifted his emphasis in the 1980s. See Irving Piliavin, "Police–Community Alienation: Its Structural Roots and A Proposed Remedy," in *Police Community Relations: Images, Roles, Realities,* ed. Alvin W. Cohn and Emilio C. Viano (Philadelphia: J. B. Lippincott Co., 1976), pp. 597 and 602, note 17.

19. Conclusion

1. *Wall Street Journal,* November 9, 1982, p. 1.

2. *New York Times,* October 7, 1976, p. 51.

3. *New York Daily News,* June 15, 1976, p. 2.

4. "Households Touched by Crime 1981," *Bureau of Justice Statistics Bulletin,* September 1983, p. 1.

5. Bernard Botein, *Our Cities Burn: While We Play Cops and Robbers* (New York: Simon and Schuster, 1972), p. 20. Numerous self-protection books have been published; for example, see Judith Fein, *Are You a Target?* (Belmont, Calif.: Wadsworth Publishing Co., 1981); Anthony Greenback, *The Book of Survival* (New York: Harper and Row, 1967); Ira A. Lipman, *How to Protect Yourself from Crime* (New York: Avon Books, 1982); and Hugh C. McDonald, *Survival* (New York: Ballantine Books, 1982).

6. See A. M. Rosenthal, *Thirty-eight Witnesses* (New York: McGraw-Hill, 1964); *New York Times*, March 12, 1965, p. 35.

7. See Albert A. Seedman and Peter Hellman, *Chief!* (New York: Avon Books, 1975), pp. 111–150.

8. See Bibb Latane and John M. Darley, *The Unresponsive Bystander: Why Doesn't He Help?* (New York: Appleton-Century-Crofts, 1970); see also *New York Times*, August 19, 1983, p. 6.

9. William L. Claiborne, "New Yorkers Fight Back: The Tilt Toward Vigilantism," *New York Magazine*, October 15, 1973, p. 53.

10. Leon S. Sheleff, *The Bystander: Behavior, Law, Ethics* (Lexington, Mass.: D. C. Heath and Co., 1978), pp. 18 and 25.

11. Philip Ross, "Have Nightstick, Will Walk," *New York Magazine*, November 15, 1982, p. 56.

12. George E. Berkeley, *The Democratic Policeman* (Boston: Beacon Press, 1974), p. 175.

13. Algernon D. Black, *The People and the Police* (New York: McGraw-Hill, 1968), p. 12.

14. Maria B. Taylor, "Volunteerism—A Police Department's Response to Changing Times," *FBI Law Enforcement Bulletin* 51 (January 1982):20.

15. Anthony V. Bouza, *Police Administration: Organization and Performance* (New York: Pergamon Press, 1978), p. 280.

16. The only other book known to the author on the subject of auxiliary police is Everett M. King, *The Auxiliary Police Unit* (Springfield, Ill.: Charles C. Thomas, 1961). It contains a wealth of practical information on financing, staffing, recruiting, training, maintaining interest and discipline within an auxiliary police force.

17. Bouza, *Police Administration*, p. 280.

18. See Martin A. Greenberg, "Volunteer Crime Prevention Program: A Proposal for Survival in America's Third Century," *The Police Chief* 44 (April 1977):60–61; Martin A. Greenberg, "Know Your Rights: A PCR Program in Justice Education," *The Police Chief* 47 (March 1980):56–60; Ellen C. Wertlieb and Martin A. Greenberg, "The Police and the Elderly (Conclusion)," *FBI Law Enforcement Bulletin* 52 (October 1983):1–7; Martin A. Greenberg, "The Police Role in Foster Care: A Lesson Plan," *The Police Chief* 45 (August 1978):64–67; and Martin A. Greenberg, "The Police Role in Environmental Safety," *The Police Chief* 46 (November 1979):48–49.

19. See Angus Campbell and Howard Schuman, "Police in the Ghetto," in *Police Community Relations: Images, Roles, Realities*, ed. Alvin W. Cohn and Emilio C. Viano (Philadelphia: J. B. Lippincott, 1976), pp. 192–220.

20. Charles B. Saunders, Jr., *Upgrading the American Police: Education and Training for Better Law Enforcement* (Washington, D.C.: The Brookings Institution, 1970), p. 171.

21. Patrick V. Murphy and Thomas Plate, *Commissioner: A View from the Top of American Law Enforcement* (New York: Simon and Schuster, 1977), pp. 267–268.

22. Robert F. Kennedy, "Improving the Administration of Criminal Justice," *Case and Comment* 73 (May-June 1968):5.

Appendix C

1. *People* v. *Jackson, New York Law Journal,* vol. 168, No. 123, December 29, 1972, p. 19. Also, reported in 339 N.Y.S.2d 429. The defendant was represented by Peter F. Vallone, who prepared a thirteen-page memorandum of law on behalf of his client. Mr. Vallone is presently a member of the Council of the City of New York.

2. Currently, we may add the titles of civilian traffic control coordinator and public school security officer to the growing list of emerging para-police units within the City.

3. On April 9, 1973, a few months after this decision was rendered, Daniel J. Daly, Chief of the New York City Housing Authority Police, issued Memo No. 23 in which he wrote: "New York City Auxiliary Policemen frequently perform their duties in and about Authority projects. . . . Its personnel are responsible citizens organized and equipped for the specific purpose of helping the police deter crime in their communities. . . . If the goals of Law Enforcement and the Communities are to be realized, it is most important that Members of the Force fully cooperate with the Auxiliary Police. They must be made to feel that they are members of an overall team pledged to provide protection and render a necessary service to the Community. . . . Members of the Force coming in contact with Auxiliary Policemen shall extend proper courtesies to these citizens who are volunteering their time and services in an effort to assist the police in suppressing undesirable conditions."

• Bibliography

Books and Articles

Anenson, Joyce V. "The FBI's First 75 Years." *FBI Law Enforcement Bulletin* 52 (July 1983).

Astor, Gerald. *The New York Cops*. New York: Scribner's, 1971.

Ball, Larry D. *The United States Marshals of New Mexico and Arizona Territories, 1846–1912*. Albuquerque: University of New Mexico Press, 1978.

Beckman, Erik. *Law Enforcement in a Democratic Society*. Chicago: Nelson-Hall Inc., 1980.

Berkley, George E. *The Democratic Policeman*. Boston: Beacon Press, 1974.

Black, Algernon D. *The People and the Police*. New York: McGraw-Hill, 1968.

Bonner, John W. "Authoritarianism in Auxiliary Police." Master's thesis, John Jay College of Criminal Justice, 1974.

Bopp, William J., and Schultz, Donald O. *A Short History of American Law Enforcement*. Springfield, Ill.: Charles C. Thomas, 1972.

Botein, Bernard. *Our Cities Burn: While We Play Cops and Robbers*. New York: Simon and Schuster, 1972.

Bouza, Anthony V. *Police Administration: Organization and Performance*. New York: Pergamon Press, 1978.

Brown, Richard M. *Strain of Violence: Historical Studies of American Violence and Vigilantism*. New York: Oxford University Press, 1975.

Browne, Douglas G. *The Rise of Scotland Yard: A History of the Metropolitan Police*. Westport, Conn.: Greenwood Press, 1977.

Burrows, William E. "The Vigilanti Rides Again." *Harvard Magazine*, December 1974.

Butler, Alan J. *The Law Enforcement Process*. Port Washington, N.Y.: Alfred Publishing Co., 1976.

Callaway, Lew. L. *Montana's Righteous Hangmen*. Norman: University of Oklahoma Press, 1982.

Calvert, Catherine. "What It's Like To Be a Woman Cop." *Mademoiselle Magazine*, September 1973.

Campbell, Angus, and Schuman, Howard. "Police in the Ghetto." In *Police Community Relations: Images, Roles, Realities*, edited by Alvin W. Cohn and Emilio C. Viano. Philadelphia: J. B. Lippincott, 1976.

"A Capsule History of the Police Department." *Spring 3100* 40 (February 1969).

Chaiken, Jan M., et al. *The Impact of Police Activity on Crime: Robberies on the New York City Subway System.* New York: New York City Rand Institute, 1974.

Chalmers, David M. *Hooded Americanism.* Garden City, N.Y.: Doubleday, 1965.

Chevigny, Paul. *Police Power: Police Abuses in New York City.* New York: Pantheon Books, 1969.

Claiborne, William L. "New Yorkers Fight Back: The Tilt Toward Vigilantism." *New York Magazine,* October 15, 1973.

Clark, Ramsey. *Crime in America: Observations on Its Nature, Causes, Prevention and Control.* New York: Pocket Books, 1975.

Cooney, Timothy J. "Reorganization of Civil Defense: A Report to Mayor Lindsay." March 18, 1966.

Costello, Augustine E. *Our Police Protectors: A History of the New York Police.* 1885. Reprint. Montclair, N.J.: Patterson-Smith, 1972.

Cox, Steven M., and Fitz, Jack D. *Police in Community Relations: Critical Issues.* Dubuque, Iowa: William C. Brown, 1983.

Critchley, T. A. *A History of Police in England and Wales.* 2d ed. Montclair, N.J.: Patterson-Smith, 1972.

Daley, Robert. *Target Blue.* New York: Dell, 1971.

Dershowitz, Alan. "Stretch Points of Liberty." *The Nation,* March 15, 1971.

Dow, Ronald E. *Volunteer Police: Community Asset or Professional Liability.* Albany, N.Y.: New York Conference of Mayors and Municipal Officials, 1978.

Duncan, J. T. Skip. *Citizen Crime Prevention Tactics: A Literature Review and Selected Bibliography.* Washington, D.C.: Government Printing Office, 1980.

Edelman, Bernard. "Does New York Need the Guardian Angels?" *Police Magazine* 4 (May 1981).

Edwards, George. *The Police on the Urban Frontier.* New York: Institute of Human Relations Press, 1968.

Eldefonso, Edward, et al. *Principles of Law Enforcement: An Overview of the Justice System,* 3d ed. New York: John Wiley and Sons, 1982.

Erikson, James M. "Community Service Officer." *Police Chief* 40 (June 1973).

————, and Neary, Matthew J. "The Community Service Officer—A + or A-?" *Police Chief* 42 (March 1975).

Eshleman, J. Ross, and Cashion, Barbara G. *Sociology: An Introduction.* Boston: Little, Brown and Co., 1983.

Fein, Judith. *Are You a Target?* Belmont, Calif.: Wadsworth Publishing Co., 1981.

Feldberg, Michael. *The Philadelphia Riots of 1844: A Study of Ethnic Conflict.* Westport, Conn.: Greenwood Press, 1975.

————.The Turbulent Era: *Riots and Disorder in Jacksonian America.* New York: Oxford University Press, 1980.

Ferretti, Fred. *The Year the Big Apple Went Bust.* New York: G. P. Putnam's Sons, 1976.

Fogelson, Robert M. *Big-City Police.* Cambridge, Mass.: Harvard University Press, 1977.

Fuld, Leonhard F. *Police Administration: A Critical Study of Police Organization in the United States and Abroad.* 1909. Reprint. Montclair, N.J.: Patterson-Smith, 1971.

Ganong, Carey K., and Pearce, Richard W. *Law and Society.* Homewood, Ill.: Richard D. Irwin, 1965.

Gardner, Thomas J., and Manian, Victor. *Criminal Law: Principles, Cases and Readings.* 2d ed. St. Paul, Minn.: West Publishing Co., 1980.

Garrett, Charles. *The La Guardia Years*. New Brunswick, N.J.: Rutgers University Press, 1961.

Geary, David P. *Community Relations and the Administration of Justice*. New York: John Wiley and Sons, 1975.

Germann, A. C., et al. *Introduction to Law Enforcement and Criminal Justice*. Springfield, Ill.: Charles C. Thomas, 1977.

Gillette, Paul J., and Tillinger, Eugene. *Inside the Ku Klux Klan*. New York: Pyramid, 1965.

Gourley, G. Douglas, and Bristow, Allen P. *Patrol Administration*. Springfield, Ill.: Charles C. Thomas, 1971.

Green, James J., and Young, Alfred J. " 'The Finest'—A Brief History of the New York City Police Department." *FBI Law Enforcement Bulletin* 45 (December 1976).

Greenback, Anthony. *The Book of Survival*. New York: Harper and Row, 1967.

Greenberg, Douglas. *Crime and Law Enforcement in the Colony of New York 1691–1776*. Ithaca, N.Y.: Cornell University Press, 1976.

Greenberg, Martin A. "Auxiliary Civilian Police—The New York City Experience." *Journal of Police Science and Administration* 6 (March 1978).

———. "Auxiliary Police Forces: Altruism or Authoritarianism?" *Law Enforcement News* 3 (April 19, 1977).

———. "Know Your Rights: A PCR Program in Justice Education." *Police Chief* 47 (March 1980).

———. "The Police Role in Environmental Safety." *Police Chief* 46 (November 1979).

———. "The Police Role in Foster Care: A Lesson Plan." *Police Chief* 45 (August 1978).

———. "Police Volunteers: Are They Really Necessary?" In *Critical Issues in Criminal Justice*, edited by Dae H. Chang and R. G. Iacovetta. Durham, N.C.: Carolina Academic Press, 1979.

———. "Volunteer Crime Prevention Program: A Proposal for Survival in America's Third Century." *Police Chief* 44 (April 1977).

———. "Volunteers Against Crime: New York's Auxiliary Police Force." *New York Journal of Crime and Justice* (November 1–15, 1974).

Hard, William. "Statesman and Ex-Cop." *New York Herald Sunday Magazine*, May 17, 1931.

Haskins, James. *The Guardian Angels*. Hillside, N.J.: Enslow Publishers, 1983.

Hofstadter, Richard, and Wallace, Michael, eds. *American Violence: A Documentary History*. New York: Vintage Books, 1971.

Hofstadter, Richard, et al. *The United States*, 3d ed. New Jersey: Prentice-Hall, 1972.

Holten, N. Gary, and Jones, Melvin E. *The System of Criminal Justice*, 2d ed. Boston: Little, Brown and Co., 1982.

Hoover, Larry T. *Police Educational Characteristics and Curricula*. Washington, D.C.: Government Printing Office, 1975.

Horne, Peter. *Women in Law Enforcement*. Springfield, Ill.: Charles C. Thomas, 1975.

Jacobs, Jane. *The Death and Life of Great American Cities*. New York: Vintage Books, 1961.

Jensen, Joan M. *The Price of Vigilance*. Chicago: Rand McNally and Co., 1968.

Johnson, David R. *American Law Enforcement: A History*. St. Louis: Forum Press, 1981.

Johnson, Elmer H. *Crime, Correction and Society*, 4th ed. Homewood, Ill.: The Dorsey Press, 1978.

Kakalik, James S., and Wildhorn, Sorrel. *The Private Police: Security and Danger*. New York: Crane Russak, 1977.

Kalmanoff, Alan. *Criminal Justice: Enforcement and Administration*. Boston: Little, Brown and Co., 1976.

Kennedy, Robert F. "Improving the Administration of Justice." *Case and Comment* 73 (May-June 1968).

Kennett, Lee, and Anderson, James LaVerne. *The Gun in America: The Origins of a National Dilemma*. Westport, Conn.: Greenwood Press, 1975.

King, Everett M. *The Auxiliary Police Unit*. Springfield, Ill.: Charles C. Thomas, 1960.

Kotecha, Kanti C., and Walker, James L. "Vigilantism and the American Police." In *Vigilante Politics*, edited by H. Jon Rosenbaum and Peter C. Sederberg. Philadelphia: University of Pennsylvania Press, 1976.

Kramer, Michael. "The National Interest: More Cops for Your Money." *New York Magazine*, December 6, 1982.

Latane, Bibb, and Darley, John M. *The Unresponsive Bystander: Why Doesn't He Help?* New York: Appleton-Century-Crofts, 1970.

Lee, Albert. *Crime-Free*. Baltimore: Penguin Books, 1974.

Leonard, V. A., and Moore, Harry W. *Police Organization and Management*, 3d ed. Mineola, N.Y.: Foundation Press, 1971.

Levett, Allan E. "Centralization of City Police in the Nineteenth Century United States." Doctoral thesis, University of Michigan, 1975.

Levy, Leonard W. *Origins of the Fifth Amendment: The Right Against Self-Incrimination*. New York: Oxford University Press, 1968.

Lipman, Ira A. *How to Protect Yourself from Crime*. New York: Avon Books, 1982.

Macoskey, Arthur R., ed. *City Patrol Corps Manual*. New York: Eagle Library, Inc., 1942.

Madison, Arnold. *Vigilantism in America*. New York: The Seabury Press, 1973.

Marx, Gary T., and Archer, Dane. "Community Police Patrols and Vigilantism." In *Vigilante Politics*, edited by H. Jon Rosenbaum and Peter C. Sederberg. Philadelphia: University of Pennsylvania Press, 1976.

Mathews, Gertrude. "Police Preparedness." *Outlook*, February 16, 1916.

Mayhall, Pamela D., and Geary, David P. *Community Relations and the Administration of Justice*, 2d ed. New York: John Wiley and Sons, 1979.

McDonald, Hugh C. *Survival*. New York: Ballantine Books, 1982.

Miller, Wilbur R. *Cops and Bobbies: Police Authority in New York and London, 1830–1870*. Chicago: University of Chicago Press, 1977.

Monkkonen, Eric H. *Police in Urban America 1860–1920*. Cambridge: Cambridge University Press, 1981.

Moore, Mark H., and Kelling, George L. " 'To Serve and Protect': Learning from Police History." *Public Interest* 70 (Winter 1983).

Murphy, Patrick V., and Plate, Thomas. *Commissioner: A View from the Top of American Law Enforcement*. New York: Simon and Schuster, 1977.

National Advisory Commission on Civil Disorders. *Report*. New York: Bantam Books, 1968.

National Advisory Commission on Criminal Justice Standards and Goals. *Report on Police*. Washington, D.C.: Government Printing Office, 1973.

Neef, Marian, and Nagel, Stuart. "The Adversary Nature of the American Legal System from a Historical Perspective.'' *New York Law Forum* 20 (Summer 1974).

Ostrowe, Brian B., and DiBiase, Rosanne. ''Citizen Involvement as a Crime Deterrent: A Study of Public Attitudes Toward an Unsanctioned Civilian Patrol Group.'' *Journal of Police Science and Administration* 11 (June 1983).

Packer, Herbert L. *The Limits of the Criminal Sanction.* Stanford, Calif.: Stanford University Press, 1968.

Peltason, J. W. *Corwin and Peltason's Understanding the Constitution,* 8th ed. New York: Holt, Rinehart and Winston, 1979.

Pileggi, Nicholas. ''The Guardian Angels: Help—or Hype?'' *New York Magazine,* November 14, 1980.

Piliavin, Irving. ''Police-Community Alienation: Its Structural Roots and A Proposed Remedy.'' In *Police Community Relations: Images, Roles, and Realities,* edited by Alvin W. Cohn and Emilio C. Viano. Philadelphia: J. B. Lippincott Co., 1976.

Potter, Frank H. ''The Home Defense League.'' *Outlook,* March 21, 1917.

Prassel, Frank R. *The Western Peace Officer.* Norman: University of Oklahoma Press, 1972.

President's Commission on Law Enforcement and Administration of Justice. *The Challenge of Crime in a Free Society.* Washington, D.C.: Government Printing Office, 1967.

———. *Task Force Report: The Police.* Washington, D.C.: Government Printing Office, 1967.

Psychological Assessment of Patrolman's Qualifications in Relation to Field Performance. Washington, D.C.: Government Printing Office, 1968.

Radelet, Louis A. *The Police and the Community.* Beverly Hills, Calif.: Glencoe Press, 1973.

Reiss, Albert J., Jr. *The Police and the Public.* New Haven: Conn.: Yale University Press, 1971.

Reith, Charles. *The Blind Eye of History: A Study of the Origins of the Present Police Era.* Montclair, N.J.: Patterson-Smith, 1975.

Renyhart, John. ''Law Enforcement Explorers Get Involved.'' *Police Chief* 42 (December 1975).

Rice, Arnold S. *The Ku Klux Klan in American Politics.* Washington, D.C.: Public Affairs Press, 1962.

Rice, James E., and Zavislak, Henry C. ''Police Paraprofessionals in Jackson, Michigan.'' *Police Chief* 44 (January 1977).

Richardson, James F. ''The History of Police Protection in New York City 1800–1870.'' Doctoral thesis, New York University, 1961.

———. *The New York Police: Colonial Times to 1901.* New York: Oxford University Press, 1979.

Robinson, Donald. ''Neighborhood Watch: Potent Weapon Against Crime.'' *Reader's Digest,* December 1981.

Rosenbaum, H. Jon, and Sederberg, Peter C., eds. *Vigilante Politics.* Philadelphia: University of Pennsylvania Press, 1976.

Rosenthal, A. M. *Thirty-eight Witnesses.* New York: McGraw-Hill, 1964.

Ross, Philip. ''Have Nightstick, Will Walk.'' *New York Magazine,* November 15, 1982.

Rossum, Ralph A. *The Politics of the Criminal Justice System: An Organizational Analysis.* New York: Marcel Dekker, Inc., 1978.

''ROTC for the Nation's Cops?'' *Newsweek,* April 4, 1983.

Rubinstein, Jonathan. *City Police*. New York: Ballantine Books, 1973.

Ryan, James E. "Auxiliary Police." *Spring 3100* 43 (July-August 1972).

Sandmel, Samuel. *The Hebrew Scriptures: An Introduction to Their Literature and Religious Ideas*. New York: Alfred A. Knopf, 1963.

Saunders, Charles B., Jr. *Upgrading the American Police: Education and Training for Better Law Enforcement*. Washington, D.C.: The Brookings Institution, 1970.

Scheuer, James H. *To Walk the Streets Safely*. New York: Doubleday, 1969.

Schofield, Daniel L. "The Fourth Amendment Exclusionary Rule and the United States Supreme Court." *FBI Law Enforcement Bulletin* 46 (March 1977).

Seedman, Albert A., and Hellman, Peter. *Chief!* New York: Avon Books, 1975.

Shelden, Randall G. *Criminal Justice in America: A Sociological Approach*. Boston: Little, Brown and Co., 1982.

Sheleff, Leon S. *The Bystander: Behavior, Law, Ethics*. Lexington, Mass.: D. C. Heath and Co., 1978.

Sloan, Irving J. *Our Violent Past: An American Chronicle*. New York: Random House, 1970.

Stern, Henry J., and Olivieri, Antonio G. "Report on New York City's Auxiliary Police Program." February 11, 1979.

Swaton, J. Norman, and Morgan, Loren. *Administration of Justice: An Introduction*. New York: D. Van Nostrand Co., 1975.

Taft, Philip, and Ross, Philip. "American Labor Violence: Its Causes, Character, and Outcome." In *Violence in America: Historical and Comparative Perspectives*, edited by Hugh D. Graham and Ted T. Gurr. Beverly Hills, Calif.: Sage Publications, Inc., 1979.

Taylor, Maria B. "Volunteerism—A Police Department's Response to Changing Times." *FBI Law Enforcement Bulletin* 51 (January 1982).

Tenney, Charles W., Jr. *Higher Education Programs in Law Enforcement and Criminal Justice*. Washington, D.C.: Government Printing Office, 1971.

Unsinger, Peter C. *Personnel Practices of Reserve/Auxiliary Law Enforcement Programs*. Springfield, Va.: National Technical Information Service, 1973.

"A Voluntary Police Force." *Outlook*, February 16, 1916.

Wales, James E. "A City's Volunteer Police Force." *American City* 16 (February 1917).

Walinsky, Adam, et al. *The New Police Corps*. August 4, 1982.

Walker, Samuel. *A Critical History of Police Reform: The Emergence of Professionalism*. Lexington, Mass.: D. C. Heath and Co., 1977.

———. *Popular Justice: A History of American Criminal Justice*. New York: Oxford University Press, 1980.

Ward, Benjamin. "The Search for Safety—A Dual Responsibility." In *Deterrence of Crime in and Around Residences*. Washington, D.C.: Government Printing Office, 1973.

Washnis, George J. *Citizen Involvement in Crime Prevention*. Lexington, Mass.: D. C. Heath and Co., 1976.

Weber, Max. *The Theory of Social and Economic Organization*. New York: Oxford University Press, 1947.

Wertlieb, Ellen C., and Greenberg, Martin A. "The Police and the Elderly (Part I)." *FBI Law Enforcement Bulletin* 52 (August 1983).

———. "The Police and the Elderly (Part II)." *FBI Law Enforcement Bulletin* 52 (September 1983).

————. "The Police and the Elderly (Conclusion)." *FBI Law Enforcement Bulletin* 52 (October 1983).

Wilkinson, Lyndol. "Gun Control Legislation Experts Think Law Limiting Ownership 'Too Difficult to Accomplish.' " *Security Systems Digest* 13 (February 24, 1982).

Wilson, George R. "Historic Guardians of Our Nation's Capital." *FBI Law Enforcement Bulletin* 45 (April 1976).

Wilson, James Q. "What Makes a Better Policeman." *Atlantic Monthly*, March 1969.

Wrobleski, Henry M., and Hess, Karen M. *Introduction to Law Enforcement and Criminal Justice*. St. Paul, Minn.: West Publishing Co., 1979.

Yin, R. K., et al. *Patrolling the Neighborhood Beat: Residents and Residential Security*. Santa Monica, Calif.: The Rand Corp., 1976.

Newspapers

Brooklyn Daily Eagle
Brooklyn Eagle
Chicago Tribune
The Chief
The Christian Science Monitor
Long Island Daily Press
Long Island Press
Long Island Star Journal
New York Daily News
New York Herald Tribune
New York Law Journal
New York Post
New York Times
Our Town
The Queens Tribune
Sacramento Union
Target
The Villager
The Wall Street Journal
World Journal Tribune
World-Telegram

•Index

About the Author

MARTIN ALAN GREENBERG possesses a rich blend of academic and practical experience. In addition to his service as an auxiliary police officer, he was a senior court officer in New York City for seven years. His experience includes teaching at the University of Hawaii at Hilo, Arkansas State University, and Washburn University of Topeka. He is the author of numerous articles on law enforcement and police administration appearing in publications such as *Journal of Police Science and Administration, The Police Chief, FBI Law Enforcement Bulletin,* and the *Campus Law Enforcement Journal.*